The estate version of the Volvo 245 DL

Volvo 240 Series 1974-79 Autobook

By Kenneth Ball
Associate Member, Guild of Motoring Writers
and the Autobooks Team of Technical Writers

Volvo 242, GL, GLE 1975-78
Volvo 244 DL, GL, GLE 1974-79
Volvo 245 DL, DLE, GLE 1974-79

Autobooks Ltd. Golden Lane Brighton BN1 2QJ England

The AUTOBOOK series of Workshop Manuals is the largest in the world and covers the majority of British and Continental motor cars, as well as the majority of Japanese and Australian models.

Whilst every care has been taken to ensure correctness of information it is obviously not possible to guarantee complete freedom from errors or omissions or to accept liability arising from such errors or omissions.

CONTENTS

ISBN 0 85147 952 9

First Edition   1978
Second Edition, fully revised   1979

908

Printed in Brighton England for Autobooks Ltd by G. Beard and Son Ltd
Bound in Hove England for Autobooks Ltd by Jilks Ltd

B

ACKNOWLEDGEMENT

My thanks are due to Volvo for their unstinted co-operation and also for supplying data and illustrations.

Considerable assistance has also been given by owners, who have discussed their cars in detail, and I would like to express my gratitude for this invaluable advice and help.

Kenneth Ball
Associate Member, Guild of Motoring Writers
Ditchling Sussex England.

INTRODUCTION

This do-it-yourself Workshop Manual has been specially written for the owner who wishes to maintain his vehicle in first class condition and to carry out the bulk of his own servicing and repairs. Considerable savings on garage charges can be made, and one can drive in safety and confidence knowing the work has been done properly.

Comprehensive step-by-step instructions and illustrations are given on most dismantling, overhauling and assembling operations. Certain assemblies require the use of expensive special tools, the purchase of which would be unjustified. In these cases information is included but the reader is recommended to hand the unit to the agent for attention.

Throughout the Manual hints and tips are included which will be found invaluable, and there is an easy to follow fault diagnosis at the end of each chapter.

Whilst every care has been taken to ensure correctness of information it is obviously not possible to guarantee complete freedom from errors or omissions or to accept liability arising from such errors or omissions.

Instructions may refer to the righthand or lefthand sides of the vehicle or the components. These are the same as the righthand or lefthand of an observer standing behind the vehicle and looking forward.

CHAPTER 1

THE ENGINE

1 : 1 Description

The engine is an in-line four cylinder water cooled unit, front mounted and driving the rear wheels through a four-speed manual transmission or optional automatic transmission unit. On models manufactured in 1975 for the USA export market, the overhead valves are operated by pushrods and rockers from the camshaft journalled in plain bearings in the crankcase. The camshaft is driven from the crankshaft through a gear train. On all other (OHC) models, the camshaft is driven from the crankshaft by a toothed belt, a spring-loaded tensioner being provided to maintain belt tension correctly. The camshaft runs in plain bearings in the cylinder head and operates the valves directly through inverted bucket tappets. Valve clearance adjustment is carried out by the selective fitting of shims to the valve tappets. Apart from the obvious differences in cylinder head, valve gear and timing gear components, the engines are similar in basic design and construction, so descriptions and servicing instructions given in this chapter will apply to both types unless otherwise stated.

The cylinder block is integral with the upper half of the crankcase, the lower half of which is formed by the pressed steel sump. The light-alloy pistons are each provided with two compression rings and one oil control ring assembly. The gudgeon pins are a sliding fit in connecting rod small-ends and piston bores, being retained in the pistons by means of circlips.

The five bearing counterbalanced crankshaft is a special steel casting. Crankshaft end float is taken by the flanged rear main bearing. The main and big-end bearings are provided with renewable shell type inserts.

The gear type oil pump draws oil from the sump beneath the engine and supplies it to the system under pressure. A relief valve is fitted to the system to limit the maximum oil pressure when the engine is cold. Pressure oil is fully filtered before being passed to the main oil gallery, from which point it is routed to the main and big-end bearings and to the auxiliary shaft and camshaft bearings in OHC engines, or to the camshaft and rocker gear on pushrod engines. The valve gear is lubricated by oil draining from the camshaft or rocker shaft bearings, the pistons and cylinders being lubricated indirectly by oil splash from the big-end bearings.

A section through an OHC (overhead camshaft) engine equipped with carburetter is shown in **FIG 1 : 1**, that for a similar engine equipped with a fuel injection (FI) system being shown in **FIG 1 : 2**.

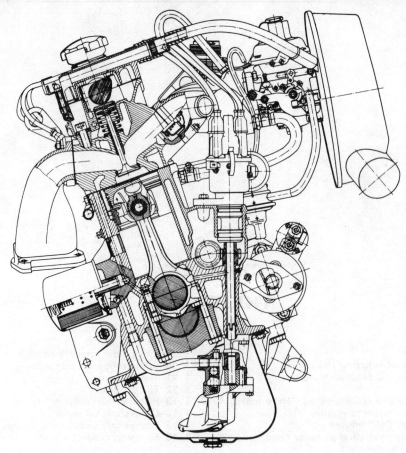

FIG 1:1   B21A engine cross-section

1:2 Removing and refitting the engine

The normal operations of decarbonising and servicing the cylinder head can be carried out without the need for engine removal, as can the majority of engine servicing procedures. However, if several different engine components are to be serviced it will be found more convenient to remove the engine and transmission from the car, and this will be essential if a major overhaul is to be carried out. For some overhaul work, certain special tools are essential and the owner is advised to check on the availability of these factory tools or suitable substitutes before tackling the items involved. Note, also, that the attachment screws and bolts for certain components must be turned by means of a special hexagon (Allen) key of the correct size.

If the operator is not a skilled automobile engineer, it is suggested that much useful information will be found in **Hints on Maintenance and Overhaul** at the end of this manual and that it be studied before starting work. It must be stressed that the lifting equipment used to remove the engine from the car should be sound, firmly based and not likely to collapse under the weight it will be supporting. The engine and transmission are removed as a unit, then the transmission separated from the engine.

Owners of vehicles fitted with air conditioning (refrigeration) systems should consult a Volvo service station before attempting engine removal procedures, or any servicing procedure which involves the disconnecting or removal of system components or hoses, so that advice can be obtained concerning the discharging of the system. For instance, in some cases it is possible to detach the system compressor unit for access to other components without disconnecting the hoses, but in other cases the hoses must be detached first. If the pressurised system is opened, liquid refrigerant will escape, immediately evaporating and instantly freezing anything it contacts. Uncontrolled release will cause severe frostbite or possibly more serious injury if refrigerant contacts any part of the body. For this reason, all work involving air conditioning system components should be entrusted only to a Volvo service station having the necessary special equipment and trained personnel.

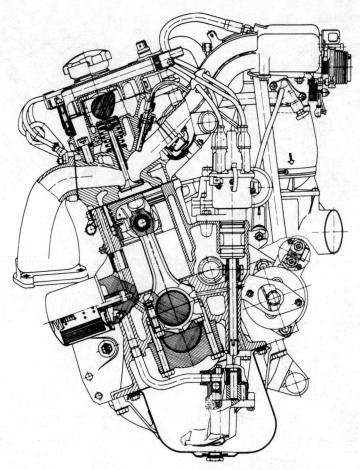

FIG 1:2 B21E engine cross-section

Removal, pushrod engine:

On manual transmission models, refer to **Chapter 6** and remove the gearlever. Drain sump oil if engine is to be dismantled (see **Section 1:10**).

Refer to **Chapter 13** and remove the bonnet, then disconnect the battery earth cable. Remove the protective cover from beneath the engine, then refer to **Chapter 4** and drain the coolant from radiator and cylinder block.

Disconnect the hose for the positive crankcase ventilation system (see **Section 1:16**), then disconnect the hoses at the inlet manifold and vacuum pump (see **Chapter 11**). Disconnect the HT leads at the ignition coil and unplug the distributor wires (see **Chapter 3**). Disconnect the cable and wire from the starter (see **Chapter 12**) then disconnect the earth cable at the cylinder block. Disconnect the air bellows connecting the fuel injection unit and the inlet manifold (see **Chapter 2**).

Disconnect the fuel hoses. These are the two hoses from the front fuel filter to engine, two hoses from fuel distributor to engine, single hose from top of fuel distributor at control pressure regulator, single hose at cold start injector on air intake and four hoses at injectors. Move the hoses aside to clear the work area, taking care not to splash fuel on body paintwork. Disconnect the fuel filter from the bulkhead and move to one side.

Disconnect the engine electrical wires. These are feed and earth wires at control pressure regulator and single wires at cold start injector, auxiliary air valve in throttle bypass, thermal time switch at rear of engine, oil pressure switch and temperature sender.

Disconnect hoses at diverter valve on bulkhead (see **Section 1:16**) and remove the air injection reactor pipe. Disconnect two vacuum hoses from charcoal canister at inlet manifold.

Disconnect throttle cable at throttle housing and from inlet manifold bracket (see **Chapter 2**). Disconnect alternator wiring connector. Remove the exhaust gas recirculation valve from inlet manifold. Remove thermal time switch complete with extension. Disconnect expansion tank hose at radiator.

On automatic transmission models, disconnect fluid cooler hoses.

FIG 1:3   Pushrod engine lifting lugs and bracket

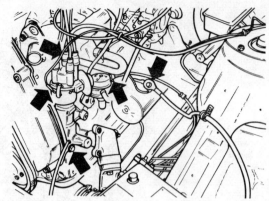

FIG 1:6   Disconnecting cables, carburetter engine

FIG 1:4   AC compressor drive pulley removal

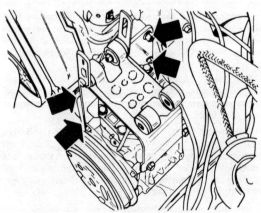

FIG 1:5   AC compressor unit removal

Remove the two fan shroud retaining screws and push shroud rearwards. Disconnect upper radiator hose at engine then remove radiator retainers. Lift out radiator and fan shroud, then disconnect water hoses at the bulkhead. Remove the windscreen washer container.

Slacken the steering pump drive belt and remove the pump pulley. Disconnect the pump from the engine bracket and support securely to avoid strain on the hoses, which remain connected. Remove the idler roller for the air pump drive belt.

On automatic transmission models, disconnect fluid filler pipe from flywheel housing. Remove the rear eye bolt from the manifold.

If available, fit front lifting lug 2869 and rear lug 2870, together with bracket 2810, as shown in **FIG 1:3**. If these tools are not available, securely attach alternative lifting equipment to the engine unit.

Raise the vehicle for access to the underside and support safely on floor stands. The correct locations for floor stands are shown in **FIGS 8:6** and **9:2**. Remove exhaust pipe flange nuts at the manifold, then remove the exhaust gas recirculation valve and pipe. Remove the retaining nuts for the front and rear engine mountings. Adjust the lifting equipment so that it acts at the rear of the engine, then raise sufficiently to relieve the weight from the transmission mounting crossmember.

Disconnect the transmission earth cable. On manual transmission models, refer to **Chapter 5** and disconnect the clutch cable from release lever and housing. On automatic transmission models, refer to **Chapter 7** and disconnect the selector linkage from transmission.

Remove the front exhaust pipe clamp and transmission support member, then disconnect the speedometer cable and electrical wires from transmission. Refer to **Chapter 8** and disconnect propeller shaft from transmission output flange. Lower the rear end of the engine by adjusting lifting equipment towards front of engine.

On automatic transmission models, remove the front heat shield then remove the fluid pipes between transmission and engine.

Raise the engine slightly at the front while pushing the rear end of the transmission downwards, then pull the engine forwards over the front axle and raise to clear the engine compartment, taking care to avoid damage.

Swing the assembly clear of the bodywork to remove completely. If necessary, remove the transmission as described in **Chapter 6** or **Chapter 7**.

Refitting:

This is a reversal of the removal procedure, using new exhaust pipe gaskets. On completion, check and if necessary top up levels of engine oil and manual transmission oil or automatic transmission fluid. If necessary, adjust ignition timing as described in **Chapter 3** and carry out slow-running adjustments as described in **Chapter 2**.

Removal, OHC engines:

On manual transmission models, remove the gearlever as described in **Chapter 6**. Disconnect the battery earth cable. Refer to **Chapter 13** and remove the bonnet. Refer to **Chapter 4** and drain the radiator and cylinder block.

Disconnect the upper radiator hose from engine and, on fuel injection engine, disconnect crankcase ventilation hose. Refer to **Chapter 4** and remove the radiator and fan shroud. Refer to **Chapter 2** and remove the air cleaner assembly.

On models fitted with power steering but not air conditioning equipment, remove the steering pump tensioning bolt, then remove the drive belt. Remove bolt securing the bracket to the engine block, then support the pump assembly away from the work area so that the hoses are not strained. On models with both power steering and air conditioning systems, remove the bolts on the tensioning bar and detach the drive belt, then remove the steering pump and support it away from the work area so that the hoses are not strained.

On models equipped with air conditioning systems, the compressor unit must now be detached from the engine block. **On some models, it will be necessary to disconnect the system hoses from the unit before it can be detached, so the warning given earlier in this section should be noted.** To remove the unit with hoses attached, first remove the drive pulley as shown in **FIG 1:4**, noting the position of any shims used. Detach the drive belt(s), then refit the pulley temporarily with two bolts. Refer to **FIG 1:5** and detach the compressor unit at the points arrowed, noting that there is a further retaining point beneath the unit. Tie the compressor to the wheel housing so that the hoses are not strained. Remove the two nuts and detach the compressor bracket from the engine.

On carburetter engines, refer to **FIG 1:6** and disconnect the earth cable, distributor cable, coil HT lead from distributor, fuel line from pump and starter motor cable. Disconnect the electric cable from the regulator and remove the clamp, as shown by the arrows in **FIG 1:7**. Refer to **FIG 1:8** and disconnect the vacuum servo hose from engine, heater hoses from bulkhead, wiring from sender units, choke and throttle cables from engine and the kick-down cable on models with automatic transmission. Remove the pre-heating plate from the exhaust manifold, which is located just beneath the exhaust pipe connection to the manifold.

On fuel injection engines, disconnect the four vacuum hoses from the engine, carefully noting the location of each hose so that it can be refitted in its original position. Refer to **FIG 1:9** and disconnect the distributor cable,

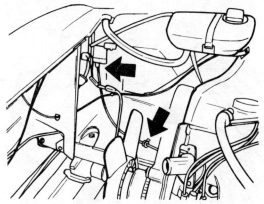

FIG 1:7   Regulator cable and clamp, carburetter engine

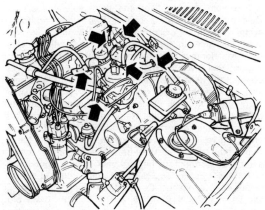

FIG 1:8   Hose and wiring connections, carburetter engine

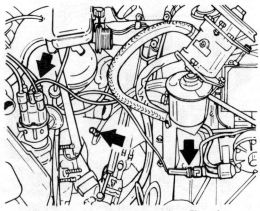

FIG 1:9   Disconnecting wiring, FI engine

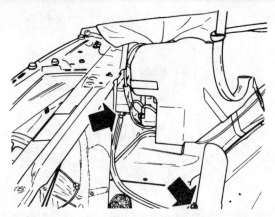

FIG 1:10   Regulator cable and clamps, FI engine

coil HT lead from distributor, starter motor wiring and, on lefthand drive models, the clutch cable from the starter motor bracket. Refer to **FIG 1:10** and disconnect the wiring from the regulator and the two cable clamps. Disconnect the throttle cable. If an air conditioning system is fitted, disconnect the electric cable from solenoid valve on shutter housing then pull the cable forwards. Remove the fuel tank cap temporarily to release any internal pressure, then refer to **FIG 1:11** and disconnect the hose from filter, return hose from return pipe and remove the protection for pre-engaging resistor. Note that, on later models, this resistor is mounted behind the radiator grille. Refer to **FIG 1:12** and disconnect wires from the points arrowed, one from pre-engaging resistor, four from cable harness and bands, two from relay and one from pre-engaging resistor switch. Disconnect the heater hoses from the bulkhead.

Raise the car for access to the underside and support safely on floor stands. Correct floor stand locations are shown in **FIGS 8:6** and **9:2**. Remove the drain plug from the engine and sump and allow the oil to drain fully into a suitable container. Refit the plug and tighten to 60Nm (45lb ft). Remove the fixing nuts, then detach the exhaust pipes at the manifold flange. Remove the flange gasket. Refer to **FIG 1:13** and remove the bolts

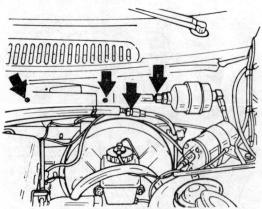

FIG 1:11   Disconnecting fuel system components, FI engine

for the front engine mountings. Remove the front exhaust pipe clamp bracket as shown in **FIG 1:14**. Disconnect the speedometer cable from the transmission.

On models with automatic transmission, refer to **Chapter 7** and disconnect the gearchange linkage at the transmission. On models with manual transmission, refer to **Chapter 5** and either detach the clutch cable from release lever and transmission or remove the clutch slave cylinder, whichever is the case. In the latter case, do not disconnect the fluid hose from the slave cylinder. Instead, support the cylinder away from the work area so that the hose is not strained. As the hose remains connected it will not be necessary to bleed the system when the cylinder is refitted.

Refer to **Chapter 8** and disconnect the propeller shaft from the transmission output flange. On models fitted with overdrive, disconnect the electric cable at the transmission.

Place a suitable jack beneath the transmission and raise sufficiently to support the weight of the assembly. Remove the transmission mounting crossmember from underbody and transmission. Attach lifting bracket 2810 in a similar manner to that shown in **FIG 1:3**, but using bracket 5035 connected to the three lift eyelets on the engine. If these tools are not available, attach suitable alternative lifting equipment to the lift eyelets. Adjust the equipment so that the lifting effort is applied to the rear of the engine, then raise the assembly a little to allow the guide pins in front engine mountings to release. Adjust the lifting equipment to act at the front of the engine, then tilt the engine and transmission assembly downwards at the rear and carefully raise to remove from the engine compartment. Swing the assembly to the side to remove completely taking care not to damage the bodywork.

If necessary, refer to **Chapter 6** or **Chapter 7** and remove the transmission from the engine.

Refitting:

This is a reversal of the removal procedure, using a new exhaust pipe flange gasket. On completion, refill with engine oil to the correct level and check manual transmission oil level as described in **Chapter 6** or automatic transmission fluid level as described in **Chapter 7**. Where necessary, set power steering pump belt tension as described in **Chapter 10** and air conditioning compressor belt tension as described in **Chapter 13**. If necessary, set ignition timing as described in **Chapter 3** and carry out slow-running adjustments as described in **Chapter 2**.

1:3 Dismantling and reassembling pushrod engine

Dismantling:

FIG 1:15 shows main components of the pushrod engine. Mount the engine on stand 2520 with fixture 2521, if available. Failing this, use wooden blocks to support the engine in the appropriate attitudes for dismantling.

Remove starter motor and the brace on the front of flywheel housing. Refer to **Chapter 5** and remove the clutch. Remove the flywheel from the rear of the crankshaft. Remove the rear flange, taking care not to damage the contact surfaces.

Remove alternator, water pump and distributor. Refer to **Section 1:7** and remove the cylinder head. Remove the oil filter as described in **Section 1:12**. Remove the tappets from the cylinder block using tool 2624 or other suitable means, as shown in **FIG 1:16**.

Remove the timing gear cover, then check camshaft end float before removing timing gears. If the upper figure given in **Technical Data** is exceeded, a new camshaft spacer ring will be required when reassembling. Refer to **Section 1:5** and remove the timing gears, then carefully remove the camshaft taking care not to damage the bearings. Examine the camshaft for wear or damage of lobes, journals and gear, renewing if faults are found. If the bearings in the cylinder block are worn or damaged, repairs must be carried out by a fully equipped service station using special in-line equipment.

Remove the sump and oil pump. Remove any carbon ridges from the tops of cylinder bores, then remove the connecting rod caps and push pistons and rods out through the tops of their bores. Note that all components, including big-end bearing shells, must be kept in the correct order for refitting in their original positions and the same way round, if they are not to be renewed.

Invert the engine and remove the main bearing caps and lower shells, then lift out the crankshaft and remove the upper shells from the block. Again, keep all parts in the correct order.

All components should be thoroughly cleaned then serviced according to the instructions given in the appropriate later sections. The oilways in the crankshaft and block should be thoroughly cleaned, using compressed air and suitable solvents and brushes. To carry out this work, all sealing plugs in the oilway openings of the block must be removed, then new plugs fitted on completion.

Reassembly:

Reassembly is a reversal of the dismantling procedure, noting the following points:

Check that all parts are clean and lubricate all bearing and sliding surfaces with engine oil. Use new gaskets, seals, splitpins and lockwashers throughout. Do not apply any sealing compound to gaskets. The 'O' ring seals on the ends of both oil pump delivery pipe and water pump pipe should be renewed, using only genuine Volvo replacement parts. Installation of 'O' rings can be facilitated by coating them with soap solution.

Make sure that main and big-end bearing caps are installed correctly in their original positions. Big-end bearing bolts and nuts should always be renewed. Lubricate threads of these and main bearing bolts, and observe torque wrench settings given in **Technical Data** when tightening the main fixings for engine components. Lubricate the pilot bearing in the rear of the flywheel with high melting point grease.

1:4 Dismantling and reassembling the OHC engine

Dismantling:

The instructions given in this section apply to both carburetter and fuel injection (FI) engines, except where otherwise indicated in specific notes or paragraphs. Mount the engine on stand 2520 with fixture 5023, if

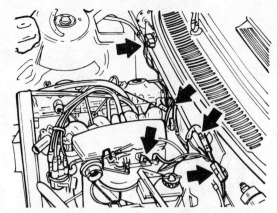

FIG 1:12   Disconnecting wiring, FI engine

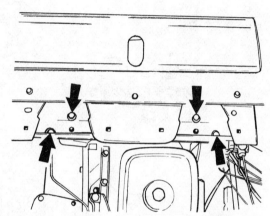

FIG 1:13   Front engine mounting bolts

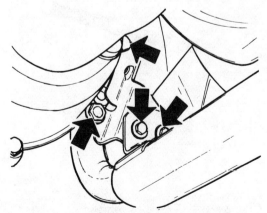

FIG 1:14   Front exhaust pipe clamp bracket

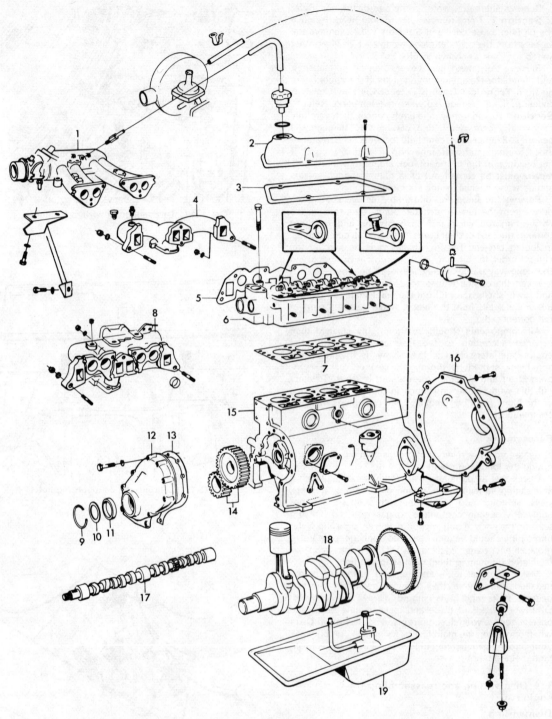

FIG 1:15 Pushrod engine main components

Key to Fig 1:15   1 Inlet manifold   2 Rocker cover   3 Gasket   4 Exhaust manifold   5 Gasket   6 Cylinder head
7 Head gasket   8 Manifolds assembled   9 Circlip   10 Washer   11 Felt ring   12 Timing gear cover   13 Gasket
14 Timing gears   15 Cylinder block   16 Bellhousing   17 Camshaft   18 Crankshaft   19 Sump

available. If not, use wooden blocks to support the engine in the appropriate attitudes for dismantling.

Remove the exhaust manifold and gaskets. Disconnect lower radiator hose from water pump. Use a suitable 17mm spanner to remove the ignition timing sender unit, if fitted (see **Chapter 3**).

On carburetter engines (see **Chapter 2**), disconnect fuel hose, coolant hose and vacuum hose from carburetter and manifold. Disconnect ventilation hose from manifold, then remove manifold and gasket, complete with carburetter. Remove the fuel pump.

On FI engines, disconnect crankcase ventilation hose from inlet manifold and valve casing, switch and fuel hose from cold start valve, then remove cold start valve with a 5mm Allen key. Remove switch and hoses from auxiliary air valve, then remove the valve. Remove stay between block and inlet manifold then disconnect vacuum hose from distributor and slacken upper hose clamp at rubber bellows to manifold connection. Remove inlet manifold and gasket. Disconnect cables from starter motor and from the sender units on the inlet side of the engine. Disconnect injector hoses from injectors at cylinder head and remove the fuel distributor and control pressure regulator.

On all models, check that wiring on all sender units is disconnected. Remove the starter motor (see **Chapter 12**) and, on FI engines, the bracket mounted above the motor. Disconnect the heater hoses then remove the engine mountings. Remove the fixing screw and detach dipstick tube, then remove the cooling fan (see **Chapter 4**). Remove the wiring plug from the alternator, then slacken mounting bolts and detach drive belt(s) and remove alternator. Remove the alternator bracket and slotted link. Remove water pump pulley.

Remove the oil filter as described in **Section 1:12**. Disconnect HT leads from sparking plugs, then remove distributor as described in **Chapter 3**.

Remove the four bolts and detach timing gear cover, then remove the two bolts to detach heater pipe from side of engine block. Refer to **Chapter 4** and remove water pump and thermostat housing with thermostat.

Slacken timing belt tensioner nut, then slacken belt by pushing roller back against spring as shown in **FIG 1:17**. Lock the plunger in this position by inserting a 3mm pin or drill shank in the hole in the plunger. Pull the belt from the tensioner roller and from camshaft gear. **Camshaft and crankshaft must not be turned while the belt is removed, otherwise pistons may contact valves and cause serious damage.** Remove nut and washer and pull off tensioner. Lock camshaft gear against rotation using tool 5034 or similar as shown in **FIG 1:18**, then remove the centre retaining bolt and detach gear. Remove the six securing bolts and detach crankshaft pulley, then remove the centre bolt and remove pulley hub. Fully remove the timing belt. Remove the crankshaft gear and guide plate, using a suitable puller if necessary, but do not remove spacer sleeve on crankshaft behind guide plate. Hold auxiliary shaft idler gear against rotation with tool 5034 or similar, remove centre bolt, then withdraw the gear.

Remove front sealing flange and seals, then remove the two fixing bolts and detach cable harness from front of engine. Slacken the two front sump bolts which secure the sealing flange, and also slacken the two

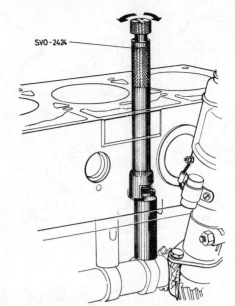

FIG 1:16   Tappet removal, pushrod engine

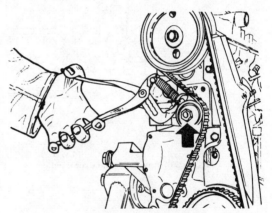

FIG 1:17   Slackening timing belt tensioner

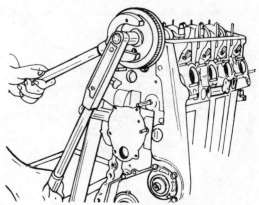

FIG 1:18   Camshaft gear removal

FIG 1:19 Oil pump pinion removal

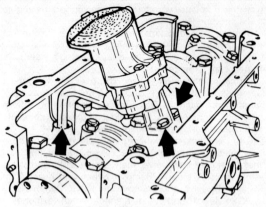

FIG 1:22 Oil pump removal

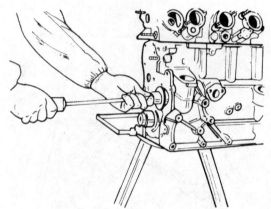

FIG 1:20 Auxiliary shaft removal

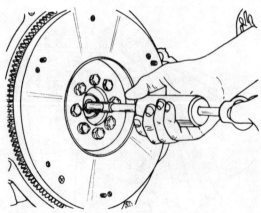

FIG 1:21 Pilot bearing removal

adjacent sump bolts on each side, six successive bolts in all. Remove the five fixing bolts and detach the rear timing belt cover, then remove the two bolts and detach the front crankshaft and auxiliary shaft sealing flange. Press the seals from the flange, using tools 5025 and 5024, or other suitable drivers.

Remove the oil pump pinion cover, then remove the pinion as shown in **FIG 1:19**. Pull the auxiliary shaft from engine block, using puller tool 4030 or similar as shown in **FIG 1:20** if necessary, taking care not to damage the bearings.

Refer to **Section 1:7** and remove the cylinder head. On manual transmission models, remove the clutch assembly as described in **Chapter 5**. Remove the circlip from the recess in the centre of the flywheel, then remove the washer and pull out the pilot bearing using tool 4090 or other suitable puller (see **FIG 1:21**). Make sure that the pin for ignition setting sender, if fitted, is not pushed in, then remove the fixing bolts and detach flywheel or flange plate. Remove the reinforcing bracket from beneath the sump at the flywheel end, remove the two bolts securing sump to rear sealing flange, then slightly slacken the adjacent two bolts on each side as for the front sealing flange. Remove the six retaining bolts and detach the rear sealing flange and seal from the engine. Press the seal out, using tool 2817 or other suitable driver.

Remove the remaining fixing bolts and detach sump and gasket from cylinder block. Refer to **FIG 1:22**. Remove the fixing bolts and lift off the oil pump, carefully detaching the pipe connection. Remove rubber ring from engine block and, from the pipe, if fitted.

Note the positions of matching numbers on connecting rods and caps. Remove the cap fixing nuts arrowed in **FIG 1:23**, then remove the caps together with bearing shells and store all parts in correct order for refitting in their original positions and the same way round, if not to be renewed. Carefully scrape any carbon ridges from the tops of the cylinder bores, taking care not to damage the surfaces, then push each piston and rod assembly out through the top of its bore. Keep the upper big-end bearing shells in the correct order.

Check numbers stamped on main bearing caps for correct refitting, then remove the bolts and lift off bearing caps complete with shell bearings. Carefully lift out the crankshaft and remove the upper shells from the block, removing the spacer sleeve arrowed in **FIG 1:24** where necessary. Keep all bearing shells in the correct order.

Thoroughly clean all internal components and carry out any necessary servicing procedures as described in the appropriate later sections. If a bearing failure has occurred, or if the engine has been fully dismantled for complete overhaul, the channels in the cylinder block and crankshaft should be cleaned. The plugs in the block should be removed in order to carry out the work. Use compressed air and suitable solvents and brushes for cleaning purposes. When the plugs are refitted, they should be tightened to the following torque figures: $\frac{1}{4}$NPFT (20Nm (15lb ft), $\frac{3}{8}$NPTF 30Nm (22lb ft), M28 120Nm (88lb ft). If the cylinder block is cracked or otherwise damaged, it may be possible for repairs to be carried out by a specialist, but if not it must be renewed.

Reassembly:

Reassembly is a reversal of the dismantling procedure, adhering to the correct component installation sequence and observing the torque wrench settings given in the text and in **Technical Data**. Lubricate all bearings and sliding surfaces with engine oil, except for the pilot bearing in the flywheel which should be packed with high melting point grease. Use new oil seals and gaskets throughout. Also renew any lockplates or splitpins which may be fitted.

Install main bearing shells in block and caps, then lubricate shells and install crankshaft. Oil the cap bolt threads and evenly tighten to 125Nm (92lb ft). If a spacer sleeve is used, refit it the other way round to present a new working surface. Crankshaft end float should be checked as shown in **FIG 1:25**, using a suitable dial gauge assembly, or alternatively checked by using feeler gauges at the rear main bearing flange. Push the crankshaft fore and aft to check end float, which should be 0.037 to 0.147mm (0.0014 to 0.0058in). Excessive end float will dictate renewal of the flanged rear main bearing shells. These should be selected by the method described in **Section 1:13** to obtain the correct journal running clearance.

Fit the big-end upper bearing shells to connecting rods, then install pistons and rods to cylinder block, making sure that notches in piston crowns face towards front (timing belt) end of engine. Use a suitable piston ring clamp when entering rings into bores. Fit bearing shells to rod caps, then lubricate shells and install caps, making sure that matching marks are correctly aligned. Oil the threads then fit nuts and tighten evenly to 63Nm (45lb ft) if the original bolts are used, or 70Nm (52lb ft) if new bolts are used. Check that the crankshaft rotates freely.

Install the oil pump. Fit a new seal to the rear flange, using tool 2817 or other suitable driver. Press the seal in sufficiently to obtain a new wearing surface on the crankshaft. Grease the seal lip and mating surface on crankshaft with mineral grease, then carefully install seal and flange taking care not to turn back the seal lips or distort the assembly.

Turn the engine until the piston in No 1 (front) cylinder is at the top of its bore. Refer to **FIG 1:26** and install

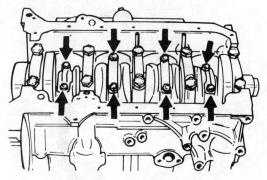

FIG 1:23   Connecting rod cap nuts

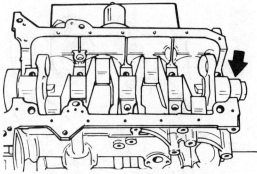

FIG 1:24   Crankshaft removal

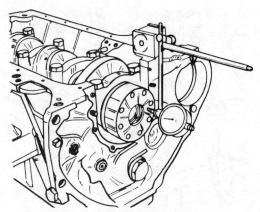

FIG 1:25   Checking crankshaft end float

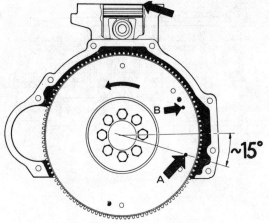

FIG 1:26   Flywheel or flange plate installation

FIG 1:29   Belt tensioner installation

Key to Fig 1:29   1 Nut   2 Pivot   3 Locking pin

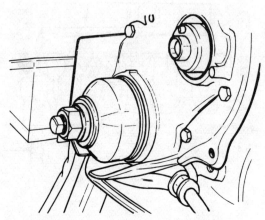

FIG 1:27   Crankshaft seal installation

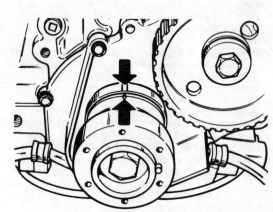

FIG 1:30   Crankshaft gear alignment

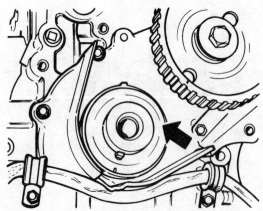

FIG 1:28   Guide plate installation

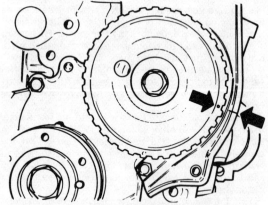

FIG 1:31   Auxiliary shaft gear alignment

flywheel or flange plate on crankshaft so that pin A is approximately 15° from horizontal and pointing away from starter motor location. Note that there are two pins, A and B. Install the fixing bolts and tighten alternately and evenly to 70Nm (52lb ft). Install input shaft pilot bearing, using tool 1426 or other suitable drift. Install the washer and retaining circlip, making sure that the circlip seats fully. On cars with manual transmission, install the clutch as described in **Chapter 5**.

Lubricate auxiliary shaft journals and install the shaft, taking care not to damage the bearings. If necessary, use tool 4030 or similar to drive shaft fully home. Install the front sealing flange with new gasket, then cut off any gasket which projects beyond the flange. The seals are installed to the flange later. Fit a new sump gasket and install the sump, tightening the bolts alternately and evenly to 11Nm (8lb ft). Install the reinforcing bracket. Fit the rear belt guard, then install cable harness below sealing flange. Use a suitable dial gauge to check auxiliary shaft end float, which should be 0.20 to 0.46mm (0.008 to 0.018in). If end float is excessive, worn components must be renewed as necessary.

Install a new crankshaft seal, using tool 5024 or similar as shown in **FIG 1:27**. Note that the seal lip and spacer sleeve, if fitted, should be smeared with mineral grease. If the spacer sleeve has not been removed, do so and refit it in the reverse direction to bring a new wearing face into position. Take care not to damage seal lip against edge of sleeve and make sure that seal is not distorted. In a similar manner, install a new auxiliary shaft seal using tool 5025 or similar.

Fit the gear to the auxiliary shaft, locating the slot in the gear on the shaft locating pin. Fit the retaining bolt, use tool 5034 or similar to hold the gear against rotation, then tighten bolt to 50Nm (37lb ft). Fit guide plate on crankshaft as shown in **FIG 1:28**. Install the crankshaft gear, making sure it is correctly keyed to the shaft. Fit crankshaft front hub and centre bolt, then tighten to 165Nm (122lb ft) using a suitable tool to hold the flange or the engine flywheel against rotation. Grease the tensioner plunger and install as shown in **FIG 1:29**. Tighten the bolt gently then remove the drill 3 used to lock the plunger. Rotate the crankshaft until the timing marks are aligned as shown in **FIG 1:30**, then rotate the auxiliary shaft until timing marks are aligned as shown in **FIG 1:31**. **It is important that the shafts are not moved from this position during the cylinder head and timing gear installation procedures, otherwise valves may contact pistons and cause serious damage.**

Refit the cylinder head and camshaft as described in **Section 1:7**, then temporarily refit camshaft cover. Install the camshaft gear, making sure that it is located correctly on shaft guide pin. Turn the gear a little as necessary to align the timing marks as shown in **FIG 1:32**. Hold the gear against rotation by suitable means, then tighten the retaining nut. Make sure that the camshaft is not turned significantly during this procedure, otherwise damage may occur.

Install a new timing belt, noting that new belts have colour markings. The two marks on the belt should be set against the crankshaft gear timing mark, then the next mark aligned against the auxiliary gear mark. The remaining mark should then align with the camshaft gear

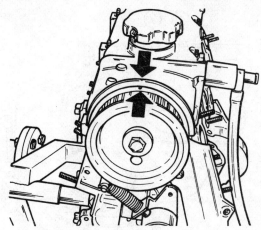

FIG 1:32 Camshaft gear alignment

mark. Wrap the belt correctly around the lower gears, taking care to avoid undue twisting and any contamination of belt from oil or grease. Pull gently on the belt to remove all slack on the side opposite the tensioner before wrapping it around the camshaft gear, then fit belt over tensioner roller. Do not use tools for this purpose otherwise belt damage may occur. Slacken the belt tensioner nut so that the spring stretches the belt as shown in **FIG 1:33**, then retighten the nut to 50Nm (37lb ft).

Check that the timing marks on all three gears are correctly aligned as described previously. If not, the belt must be removed again and gears turned slightly as necessary to reset. This done, turn the engine through one full revolution until the timing marks realign, using a spanner on the crankshaft pulley bolt. Now slacken the tensioner nut and retighten as before to finally set belt tension correctly.

Install the crankshaft pulley, fitting temporarily with two bolts only if air conditioning system is fitted. This allows for belt tensioning later. Install the oil pump pinion, noting that the crankshaft may have to be rotated a little in order to mesh the pinion correctly. Fit a new 'O' ring on

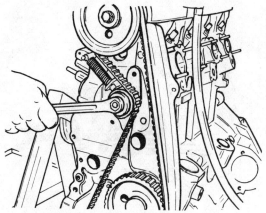

FIG 1:33 Timing belt installation

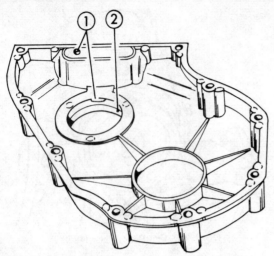

FIG 1:34   Pushrod engine timing cover

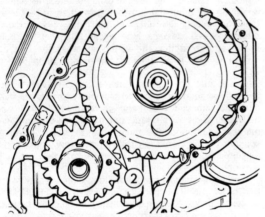

FIG 1:35   Aligning timing marks on gears

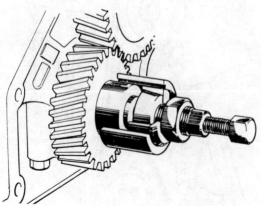

FIG 1:36   Crankshaft hub removal

oil pump drive gear cover and install the cover, making sure that the surface which contacts the pinion is not worn. If so, the cover should be renewed.

Install water pump and thermostat assembly as described in **Chapter 4**, then fit a new rubber ring to water pipe and install pipe to side of engine block. Note that engine lifting eye should be installed at thermostat cover. Install the timing belt outer cover. Check and if necessary adjust valve clearances, as described in **Section 1:9**.

Install distributor as described in **Chapter 3**. Install new oil filter as described in **Section 1:12**. Install water pump pulley. Fit alternator with bracket and slotted link, then fit and adjust drive belt(s) as described in **Chapter 4**. Install the cooling fan and fit the dipstick tube. Fit engine mountings, if removed. Fit heater hoses, starter motor and bracket and, on FI engine, additional bracket above starter.

On carburetter models, install fuel pump then fit inlet manifold with carburetter using a new gasket. Fit lifting eye at manifold. Tighten manifold nuts alternately and evenly to 20Nm (15lb ft). Reconnect ventilation, vacuum, coolant and fuel hoses to carburetter and manifold.

On FI models, fit fuel distributor and control pressure regulator then reconnect hoses, switches and sender units and starter motor cables. Install inlet manifold with new gasket and evenly tighten nuts to 20Nm (15lb ft). Fit lifting eye at manifold. Install stay between block and inlet manifold, fitting lower stay mount together with lefthand engine mounting. Connect vacuum hose from distributor to shutter housing and tighten upper hose clamp at rubber bellows. Install auxiliary air valve and connect hoses and switch. Fit or reconnect cold start valve with earth cables under one retaining screw, fuel hose to cold start valve, fuel hose and switch for cold start valve and crankcase ventilation hose.

Install ignition setting sender, if fitted. Fit lower radiator hose to water pump. Install the exhaust manifold using new gaskets, noting that the marking 'UT' must face outwards. Also be sure to centre manifold round No 1 cylinder lower stud and face washer so that marking 'UT/OUT' is facing outwards. The engine lift eyelet should be fitted under the upper manifold fixing bolt for No 3 cylinder. Evenly tighten fixing nuts to 20Nm (15lb ft).

1:5 Timing gear, pushrod engine

Timing gear cover removal:

Remove the two screws securing fan shroud and pull it to the rear, then remove the fan and shroud. Slacken the drive belt then remove water pump pulley and crankshaft pulley. Slacken the two lower front sump securing bolts, then remove the timing gear cover. Remove circlip, washer and felt ring from cover.

Refitting:

FIG 1:34 shows timing gear cover oil holes 1 and installed position of felt ring 2. Thoroughly clean the cover and make sure that the oil holes are clear. Check the gasket and renew if not in good condition. Install the cover and fit the mounting bolts finger tight, then use sleeve 2438 pushed over the end of the crankshaft to centralise the cover. Adjust the cover until the sleeve can be rotated freely with no sign of jamming, then tighten the bolts and recheck. Install a new felt washer and circlip, using sleeve 2438 to push them into place. Make sure that circlip is fully seated in groove. Tighten sump bolts, refit remaining parts and correctly tension drive belts.

Timing gear removal:

Remove the timing gear cover as described previously. If the engine is not to be fully dismantled, it will facilitate installation if the engine is first turned by means of the refitted crankshaft pulley bolt until the marks on timing gears are aligned as shown at 2 in **FIG 1 : 35**. This done, use puller 2440 or similar to remove the hub from the crankshaft (see **FIG 1 : 36**). First screw the large nut and centre bolt out so that the cone is not tensioned, then install the tool. Tighten the large nut so that the hub is held firmly, then pull off the hub by screwing in the centre bolt. Remove camshaft gear securing nut, after which both gears can be pulled from the shafts. For crankshaft gear, use puller 2405 or other suitable puller using two bolts of correct thread size screwed into the holes provided in the gear face. To remove camshaft gear, use tool 2250 or other suitable three-legged puller with legs hooked into holes provided in gear. Collect the keys which lock the gears to the shafts.

If the cylinder head is installed, neither camshaft nor crankshaft must be turned unless the rocker gear and pushrods are removed, otherwise valves may contact pistons and cause serious damage.

Refitting:

Remove the oil jet shown at 1 in **FIG 1 : 35**, clean with compressed air, then refit in position. If the crankshaft and camshaft have not been moved from their set positions, install the gears with locating keys and push as far as possible into place by hand. Check that the timing marks are correctly aligned as shown in **FIG 1 : 35**. If the settings have been lost, the shafts must be turned as necessary until the gears can be fitted correctly. If the cylinder head is fitted, do not turn either shaft unless the rocker gear and pushrods are first removed.

The gears must now be pulled into position using tool 2407 for crankshaft and 2408 for camshaft. Failing these tools, use a suitable screwed rod or bolt threaded into the end of the shaft and a suitable nut, tube and washer tightened on the threads to pull gear into place. Never attempt to drive a gear into place as this can cause damage particularly to the sealing washer at the other end of the camshaft. Fit and tighten camshaft gear nut, then refit remaining components in reverse order of removal.

1 : 6 Timing gear, OHC engine

The toothed timing belt should be renewed at the intervals recommended in the manufacturer's service schedule as routine maintenance, and additionally whenever timing gears are overhauled or if any sign of belt damage is apparent.

The belt can be renewed with the engine in situ, after removing the timing gear cover. Before slackening the belt tensioner, turn the engine by means of a spanner on the crankshaft pulley bolt until the timing marks on crankshaft, auxiliary shaft and camshaft gears are

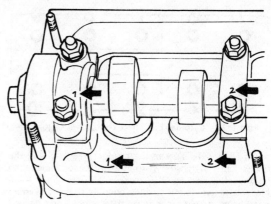

FIG 1 : 37 Camshaft bearing cap markings

correctly aligned as described in **Section 1 : 4**. Release the tensioner as described in that section then remove the belt from the gears. **Neither crankshaft nor camshaft must be rotated while the belt is removed, otherwise valves may contact pistons and cause serious damage.**

Install the new belt as described in **Section 1 : 4** then refit the timing gear cover.

1 : 7 Removing and refitting cylinder head

Disconnect the battery, drain the cooling system as described in **Chapter 4**, then turn the engine to the firing point for No. 1 cylinder as described in **Chapter 3**. Remove the air cleaner assembly as described in **Chapter 2**. Disconnect all wires, cables and hoses from cylinder head, inlet manifold and, if fitted, the carburetter. Disconnect the exhaust pipe at the manifold flange. On some automatic transmission models, it will also be necessary to disconnect the fluid filler pipe from the flywheel housing. Disconnect the inlet manifold to engine block stay, if fitted.

On pushrod engines, remove the rocker cover then evenly loosen the mounting bolts and remove the rocker assembly. Lift out the eight pushrods, keeping them in the correct order for refitting in their original positions.

On OHC models, remove the camshaft cover, noting that the ignition setting indicator, if fitted, will be attached to the cover by one of the nuts. Remove the semicircular rubber seal from its location at the top rear of the cylinder head. Slacken and remove the timing belt as described in **Section 1 : 4**. If the camshaft is to be removed, proceed as follows:

Remove camshaft gear as described in **Section 1 : 4**. Check marks on camshaft bearing caps and cylinder head for correct refitting in their original positions and the same way round (see **FIG 1 : 37**). If tool 5021 is available, the centre bearing cap should first be removed then the tool installed using the two cap nuts. The tool is then tightened to hold the camshaft down while the remaining caps are removed. If the tool is not available, slacken all cap nuts alternately and evenly until valve spring pressure is released from the camshaft, making sure that the camshaft does not turn during the procedure. If a cap sticks in position, release by carefully tapping against the sealing lug. Lift out the camshaft.

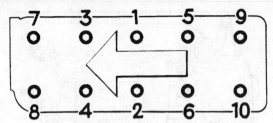

FIG 1:38 Cylinder head bolt tightening sequence

On all models, slacken the cylinder head bolts in the reverse order of that shown in **FIG 1:38**, then remove the bolts completely. On OHC models, a 10mm ($\frac{3}{8}$in) Allen key will be required to turn the bolts. Lift off the cylinder head complete with manifolds, then remove and discard the head gasket. Servicing procedures are given in **Section 1:8**.

Refitting:

Carefully clean the mating surfaces of cylinder head and block. Fit a new gasket to the block, making sure that it is the correct way up by checking that each hole in the gasket matches the appropriate bore in the block surface. Renew the rubber seal for water pump and the flange gasket, where applicable.

Install the cylinder head, then oil the cylinder head bolt threads and washers and install the bolts finger tight. If the camshaft is installed on OHC engine cylinder head, it is essential that the marks on the timing gears are in correct alignment before head is installed, as described in **Section 1:4**. The bolts must now be tightened in two stages, in the order shown in **FIG 1:38**. On pushrod engine, tighten first to 40Nm (30lb ft) then to 80Nm (60lb ft). On OHC engine tighten first to 60Nm (44lb ft) then to 110Nm (81lb ft). In both cases, final tightening is carried out after running the engine, as described later.

FIG 1:39 Removing fuel injectors

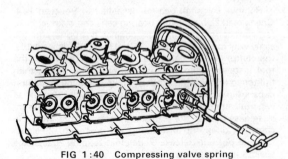

FIG 1:40 Compressing valve spring

On pushrod engine, install the pushrods in their original positions then refit rocker gear and tighten bolts alternately and evenly. On OHC engine, make sure that camshaft and crankshaft pulleys are correctly aligned, then install the camshaft, making certain that the guide pin for the belt gear is upwards. Lubricate camshaft bearings and lobes, then install bearing caps and tighten alternately and evenly to avoid distortion, to a final torque of 20Nm (15lb ft). During this procedure, make certain that the camshaft does not turn from the set position otherwise damage may occur. Install camshaft gear then fit and tension belt as described in **Section 1:4**.

Check and adjust all valve clearances as described in **Section 1:9**. Refit the remaining components in the reverse order of removal, using a new gasket for camshaft cover or rocker cover. Refill the cooling system as described in **Chapter 4** and reconnect the battery. Start the engine and allow it to run until it reaches normal operating temperature, then switch off and allow it to cool for 30 minutes. The rocker cover or camshaft cover must now be removed and the cylinder head bolts finally tightened. To do this, slacken each bolt slightly before tightening to the final torque figure, working in the order shown in **FIG 1:38**. It is important to slacken each bolt first otherwise static friction of the bolt will give a false reading. Final torque for bolts on pushrod engine is 90Nm (65lb ft), for OHC engine it is 110Nm (81lb ft). For pushrod engines, spanner 2898 is available for use in conjunction with a torque wrench when tightening head bolts. On completion, recheck and if necessary readjust valve clearances as described in **Section 1:9**. If necessary, check ignition timing as described in **Chapter 3** and carry out slow running adjustments as described in **Chapter 2**.

1:8 Servicing the cylinder head

Remove the cylinder head as described in **Section 1:7** and transfer it to the bench, taking care not to damage the joint surfaces. Remove the inlet and exhaust manifolds and gaskets. On OHC engines, remove camshaft as described in **Section 1:7** if not done previously.

Dismantling:

Note that all valve gear components, including tappets and shims on OHC engines and rocker gear components on pushrod engines must be kept in the correct order for refitting in their original positions if not to be renewed.

Remove the sparking plugs. On FI engines, pull injectors from holders and remove them (see **FIG 1:39**). On OHC engines, remove the tappet with adjustment shim from each valve position and keep in the correct order.

Use a suitable valve spring compressor to remove the valve gear from the cylinder head, as shown in **FIG 1:40**. On OHC models, refer to **FIG 1:41** and remove rubber ring 1 and split taper collets 3. Release the compressor then remove spring 4 with upper and lower retainers 2 and 6 and remove valve from guide. Proceed in a similar manner for pushrod engine, but note that upper rubber ring and lower valve spring retainer are not included. In all cases, remove stem seal 5 from inlet valve guides.

Servicing:

Servicing instructions are the same for both pushrod and OHC engine, except where otherwise stated.

Valves:

When valves are being cleaned of carbon deposits, they must be inspected for serviceability. Valves with bent stems or badly burned heads must be renewed. Valves that have pitted seating surfaces can be re-cut at a service station, but if they are too far gone for this remedial treatment, new valves will be required. Valves that are in a serviceable condition can be ground to their seats as described later.

Valve guides:

Valve guides that are worn or scored must be renewed. As the guides must be pressed into or out of place, then the valve seat re-cut to ensure concentricity, this work should be carried out by a service station having the necessary special equipment. Valve seats in the cylinder head that are pitted or burned must be re-cut or renewed at a service station. If the seats are in reasonable condition, they should be ground to the valves as described later.

Valve springs:

Valve spring free length should be 45mm (1.77in). The springs can be tested under pressure using a special gauge, or their efficiency can be compared with that of a new spring. To compare with a new spring, insert both old and new springs end to end with a metal plate between them in the jaws of a vice. If the old spring is weakened, it will close up first when pressure is applied. Take care that the springs do not fly out of the vice under pressure. Any spring which is distorted, or which is weaker or shorter than standard should be renewed, but note that, if any spring is defective it is recommended that all springs should be renewed as a set.

Tappets, OHC engine:

Check that each tappet moves freely in its original bore in the head. Clearance in the bore should be checked and tappets renewed if this is excessive. Check radial clearance of adjusting shim in the top of each tappet, the correct clearance with new parts being 0.009 to 0.068mm (0.0004 to 0.0027in). Renew the shim if clearance is excessive, or if the top surface is worn. Renew with one of the same thickness unless valve clearance is incorrect (see **Section 1:9**).

Camshaft, OHC engine:

Check the camshaft lobes and bearing journals and the bearing surfaces in cylinder head and bearing caps for wear or scoring, renewing parts as necessary.

Pushrods and rockers, pushrod engine:

Pushrods should be perfectly straight and the bearing surfaces at top and bottom should have a smooth, polished appearance. Check for bending by rolling pushrods gently down a flat surface while viewing from a point near the surface. Renew if any fault is found.

Examine the rockers for wear or damage, particularly at the tip which contacts the valve stem, and check for wear between bearing bush and rocker shaft. Worn bushes can be renewed, but as they must be pressed in and out of position and reamed after installation, the work should be carried out by a fully equipped service station. If necessary,

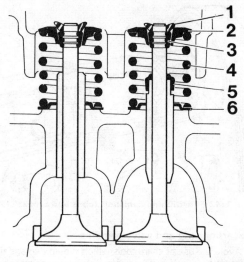

FIG 1:41 Valve gear installation, OHC engine shown

the shaft assembly can be dismantled by removing the retaining circlips and sliding off the parts. Reassemble in the reverse order after renewing faulty components, lubricating rocker bearing surfaces.

Cylinder head:

Check the cylinder head for cracks or other damage which would dictate renewal. Use a steel straightedge to check the joint face for flatness. Working lengthwise, it should not be possible to insert a 0.5mm (0.020in) feeler gauge between straightedge and head surface at any point. Across the head, it should not be possible to insert a 0.25mm (0.010in) gauge. If head distortion is excessive, the surface can be machined at a service station, but if this would require the removal of too much metal to correct distortion, the head must be renewed instead.

On pushrod engine, the cylinder head is provided with an oil hole to supply lubricant to the rocker gear (see **FIG 1:42**). Make sure that this hole is completely clear, cleaning with a suitable solvent and compressed air if necessary.

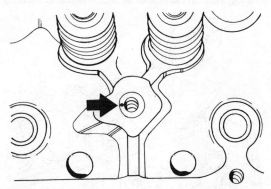

FIG 1:42 Lubrication hole in cylinder head, pushrod engine

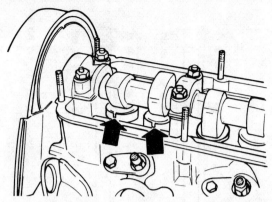

FIG 1:43 Positioning camshaft lobes and tappet slots

Decarbonising and valve grinding:

Avoid the use of sharp tools which would damage the cylinder head and piston surfaces. Remove all traces of carbon deposits from the combustion chambers, inlet and exhaust ports and joint faces. If the pistons have not been removed and cleaned during previous engine dismantling, plug the waterways and oilways in the top surface of the cylinder block with pieces of rag to prevent the entry of dirt, then carefully clean the carbon from piston crowns. If the OHC engine crankshaft is turned to bring the pistons into position for cleaning, make sure that the timing marks are correctly realigned on completion, as described in **Section 1:4**.

To grind in valves, use medium grade carborundum paste unless the seats are in very good condition when fine grade paste can be used at once. Smear a small amount of paste around the valve seating surface, then grind-in using a suction cup tool. Use a semi-rotary movement, turning the tool handle back and forth between the palms, lifting the valve off its seat occasionally and turning to a new position before continuing. When seats in head and on valve have a smooth, matt-grey finish, clean away every trace of grinding paste from port and valve.

Reassembly:

Install new valve stem seals to inlet valve guides, then refit valve gear in the reverse order of removal, lubricating

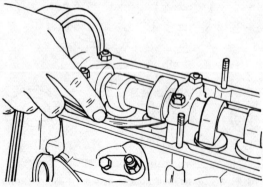

FIG 1:44 Checking valve clearances, OHC engine

valve stems and guides with engine oil. On OHC engines, lubricate tappets and install together with adjustment shims to their original positions. Use new seals when installing injectors on FI engines.

Refit the cylinder head as described in **Section 1:7**.

1:9 Valve clearance adjustment

The correct adjustment of valve clearances is important as it affects engine timing and performance considerably. Excessive clearance will reduce valve lift and opening duration and reduce engine performance, causing excessive wear on valve gear components and noisy operation. Insufficient or zero clearance will again affect valve timing and, in some circumstances, can hold the valve clear of its seat. This will result in much reduced performance due to lost compression and the possibility of burned valves and seats. Valve clearances should be checked and adjusted at the intervals recommended in the manufacturer's service schedule as routine maintenance and additionally, whenever the cylinder head has been serviced. Retightening of cylinder head bolts on pushrod engines can alter valve clearances, so they should always be checked afterwards. In all cases, valve clearances can be checked with the engine either hot or cold.

The engine must be turned in order to bring each pair of valves in turn to the correct position for adjustment. On manual transmission models, this can be done by first making sure that the car is on level ground so that it will not move when the brake is released, then selecting top gear and pushing the car backwards or forwards to turn the engine. Alternatively rotate the engine by using a spanner on the crankshaft pulley securing bolt. Do not attempt to turn the engine by means of any other pulley or gear retaining bolt, as this will overload and damage internal components. On automatic transmission models, the latter method must be used to rotate the engine as it cannot be turned by pushing the car in gear. In all cases, the engine will be easier to turn if the sparking plugs are first removed to avoid resistance from compression in engine cylinders.

OHC engine:

Adjustment should be carried out when the engine is either hot or cold. If the engine is merely warm, either run it up to normal operating temperature or allow extra time for it to cool down fully.

Remove the camshaft cover and then turn the engine until the cams for No 1 cylinder point obliquely upwards at equal angles as shown in **FIG 1:43**. This will be when the mark on the crankshaft pulley aligns with the zero mark on the scale. Use feeler gauges to check clearance between base of cam lobe and top surface of tappet shim as shown in **FIG 1:44**. Clearance for both inlet and exhaust valves should be 0.30 to 0.45mm (0.012 to 0.018in) when the engine is cold, or 0.35 to 0.50mm (0.014 to 0.020in) when hot. If clearance is within limits, no adjustment is necessary. However, if outside limits adjustment should be carried out to bring the clearance to within 0.35 to 0.40mm (0.014 to 0.016in) for a cold engine, or 0.40 to 0.45mm (0.016 to 0.018in) if hot.

If adjustment is necessary, rotate the tappet until the slots arrowed in **FIG 1:43** are at right angles to the line of the camshaft, then install compressor tool 5022 or similar as shown in **FIG 1:45**. Screw down tool spindle to depress the tappet by its edges against spring pressure with slots accessible, then remove adjusting shim using pliers 5026 or similar.

Thickness of removed shim should be found marked on the underside, but thickness should be checked with a micrometer to be certain. The required thickness of new shim to be installed should be calculated from the measured clearance, required clearance and thickness of shim removed. For instance, if the measured clearance was 0.30mm (0.012in) and correct clearance 0.40mm (0.016in), then clearance difference is 0.10mm (0.004in). If the measured thickness of existing shim is 3.80mm (0.150in), correct thickness for new shim is 3.70mm (0.146in). Shims are available in thicknesses from 3.30 to 4.50mm (0.13 to 0.18in) in increments of 0.5mm (0.002in). Lubricate new shim with engine oil, locate in position with the thickness marking downwards, then remove the special tool. Recheck the clearance, then repeat the entire operation at the second valve position for No 1 cylinder. This done, turn the engine to bring each pair of cams for the remaining cylinders to the correct positions in turn, and check and adjust all valve clearances as before. On completion, refit camshaft cover using a new gasket if the original is not in good condition.

If the special tools mentioned are not available it is possible to adjust valve clearances by first checking the clearances at all valve positions and noting them carefully, then removing the camshaft as described previously and replacing shims where necessary with new ones of correctly calculated thickness. The camshaft must then be refitted and clearances rechecked. If this method is used, make sure that the timing marks are correctly aligned as described in **Section 1:4** before camshaft removal, and that neither camshaft nor crankshaft is turned while the belt is detached.

Pushrod engine:

The valve clearances for inlet and exhaust valves at No 1 (front) cylinder must be adjusted when the valves for No 4 cylinder are on the overlap. Remove the rocker cover and turn the engine until both valves for No 4 (rear) cylinder are open, then turn a little more as necessary until these valves are equally depressed by the rockers. Now check the clearances between the valves and rocker tips at No 1 cylinder, as shown in **FIG 1:46**, using feeler gauges. The correct clearance is 0.40mm (0.016in) for both inlet and exhaust, at all engine temperatures. However, if the clearances are being set after engine overhaul so that the engine can be started and run, set to 0.45 to 0.50mm (0.018 to 0.020in), then reset to correct final clearances when cylinder head bolts have been finally tightened.

The clearance must be measured between rocker tip and valve stem. Slacken the locknut on the adjuster with a suitable spanner, then turn the adjuster with a screwdriver to increase the clearance until the feeler will slide into place. Now tighten the adjuster until the feeler slides in the gap with a slight drag, being neither tight nor loose.

Without turning the adjuster, tighten the locknut and recheck. Repeat the checking and adjustment procedure at the second valve for No 1 cylinder, then proceed to the next cylinder. Check the clearances at No 3 cylinder with the valves for No 2 cylinder on overlap as

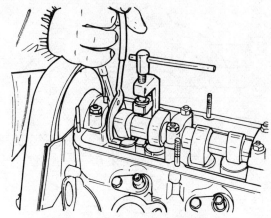

FIG 1:45 Adjusting shim removal

described, No 4 with No 1 on overlap and No 2 with No 3 on overlap. On completion, refit the rocker cover using a new gasket if the original is not in good condition. Refit the sparking plugs, if removed.

1:10 Sump removal and refitting

The sump can be removed and refitted without the need for engine removal.

Pushrod engine:

Raise the car and support safely on floor stands. Remove the protective cover from beneath the engine. Remove the drain plug and allow engine oil to drain into a suitable container, then refit and tighten drain plug. On models with automatic transmission, remove the clamp for fluid pipes at the brace then remove the brace. Remove the fixing bolts then detach the sump and gasket.

Clean all traces of gasket material from sump and cylinder block, then clean the inside of the sump with a

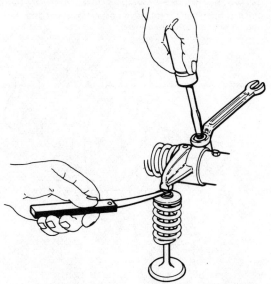

FIG 1:46 Checking valve clearances, pushrod engine

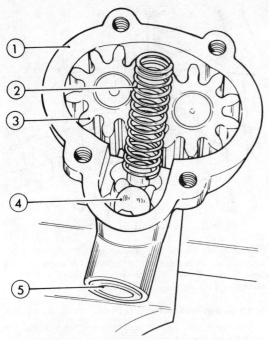

FIG 1:47 Oil pump internal components

Key to Fig 1:47 1 Pump body 2 Relief valve spring
3 Gear 4 Valve ball 5 Oil pipe connection

suitable solvent. Install the sump using a new gasket. Gaskets are either marked to indicate the side that should face the block, or are provided with an extrusion which should point towards the starter motor flange when installed. Alternately and evenly tighten the sump bolts to avoid distortion. Position the brace and install bolts finger tight, then tighten first the bolts to flywheel housing followed by bolts to cylinder block. Install clamp for fluid pipes, if fitted. Refit protective cover, lower car and refill engine with oil to correct level.

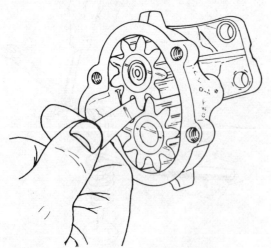

FIG 1:48 Checking gear backlash

OHC models:

Fit suitable lifting equipment to the engine and raise slightly to take the weight of the assembly. On cars equipped with air conditioning, observe the warning given in **Section 1:2**.

Remove the three bolts securing the lefthand engine mounting, then raise the engine slightly. Remove the drain plug and allow engine oil to drain into a suitable container, then refit the plug and tighten to 60Nm (45lb ft). Remove the protective cover from beneath the engine, then remove the lower two bolts and detach lefthand engine mounting. Remove reinforcing bracket from rear of sump, then remove all sump fixing bolts. Release the sump from engine block, then turn and lower it to remove. Remove and discard the gasket.

Clean all old gasket material from sump and block, then clean the inside of the sump with a suitable solvent. Install the sump using a new gasket, then tighten the retaining bolts alternately and evenly to 11Nm (8.0lb ft). Refit the remaining components in the reverse order of removal, then fill the engine with oil to the correct level.

1:11 The oil pump

The oil pump can be removed with the engine in situ, after removing the sump as described in **Section 1:10**. Refer to the appropriate removal instructions given in **Section 1:3** or **1:4**.

Oil pump servicing:

Carefully pull the pressure pipe from pump housing. Remove the lock wire and detach strainer. Remove the four fixing bolts and detach pump cover, then remove spring and ball as shown in **FIG 1:47**. Remove driven gear with shaft and idler gear from body. Thoroughly clean all parts in a suitable solvent and inspect for wear or damage which would dictate renewal.

Refit gears to body and check backlash between teeth using feeler gauges as shown in **FIG 1:48**. This should be 0.15 to 0.35mm (0.006 to 0.014in). Use a straightedge and feeler gauge to check end float as shown in **FIG 1:49**. This should be 0.02 to 0.12mm (0.0008 to 0.0047in). Excessive clearance in either case will dictate renewal of pump gears. Renew the pump cover if its inner surface is worn or scored. Check the relief valve spring for a free length of 39.2mm (1.54in). Under pressure of 50N (11.0lb), spring length should be 26.25mm (1.03in) and should be 21.0mm (0.83in) under a load of 70N (16lb). If spring is weak or distorted it should be renewed.

Reassemble the pump in the reverse order of dismantling, lubricating internal parts with engine oil. Always use new rubber seals for the pressure pipe. These seals are of a special rubber compound and should be replaced only with genuine Volvo spare parts. Refit the pump and install the sump in the reverse order of removal. Make sure that the pump drive shaft correctly engages with the drive gear in the engine.

1:12 The oil filter

The oil filter is of the cartridge type and should be renewed at the intervals recommended in the manufacturer's service schedule. The unit is located on the front righthandside of the engine beneath the exhaust manifold.

To remove, first disconnect the battery then unscrew the filter unit and discard it.

Clean the filter mounting face on the engine, then lightly coat the seal on the new filter with engine oil (see **FIG 1:50**). Make sure that the seal is correctly fitted, then screw the filter into place until it just contacts its seating. From this point, tighten a further half turn by hand only. Do not overtighten or oil leaks may result. A strap type tool may be used to remove the filter if it is too stiff to be turned by hand, but never use anything but hand pressure to tighten. On completion, run the engine and check for oil leaks around the filter unit. Switch off and allow time for oil to drain down into the sump, then top up engine oil to the correct level to compensate for that used to fill the new filter.

1:13 Pistons and connecting rods

Pistons and connecting rods can be removed with the engine in situ, after removing the cylinder head as described in **Section 1:7** and the sump as described in **Section 1:10**, then following the appropriate removal instructions given in **Section 1:3** or **1:4**.

Pistons and rings:

Note that all components should be kept in the correct order for refitting in their original positions and the same way round if they are not to be renewed. Clean carbon from the piston crowns, then gently ease the rings from the grooves and remove them over the tops of the pistons. Clean carbon from the grooves, for which job a piece broken from an old piston ring and ground to a chisel point will prove an ideal tool. Inspect pistons for score marks or any signs of seizure, which would dictate renewal. If the pistons are to be removed from the connecting rods, carefully remove the retaining circlips and push out the gudgeon pin. The gudgeon pin should move through the bores with light hand pressure. If not, a 0.05mm (0.002in) oversize gudgeon pin can be installed, after suitably reaming piston and small-end bores. If suitable reaming tools are not available, have the work carried out by a service station. If only the small-end bush is worn, this should be renewed at a service station, using special press equipment.

Fit the piston rings one at a time into the bore from which they were removed, pushing them down with the inverted piston to ensure squareness. If the bores are worn, the rings should be pushed down to the bottom dead centre position as this is the point of minimum wear. Measure the gap between the ends of the ring while in the bore, using feeler gauges as shown in **FIG 1:51**. The clearance should be 0.35 to 0.55mm (0.014 to 0.022in) for compression rings, 0.25 to 0.40mm (0.010 to 0.016in) for oil control rings. Hold each ring in the piston groove from which it was removed as shown in **FIG 1:52**, then measure side clearance with feeler gauges. Make checks at several points around the piston. Clearance should be 0.040 to 0.072mm (0.0014 to 0.0028in) for compression rings, 0.030 to 0.062mm (0.0012 to 0.0024in) for oil control rings. If the clearance measurement in either test is at or near the wear limit, new rings should be fitted. Excessive ring clearance can be responsible for high oil consumption and poor engine performance.

Check the cylinder bores for score marks and remove glaze and carbon deposits. Badly scored or worn surfaces

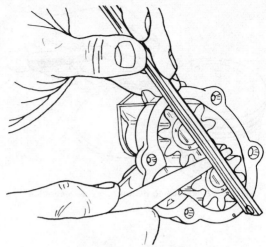

FIG 1:49   Checking gear end float

FIG 1:50   Oil filter seal

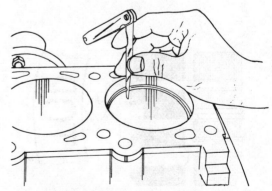

FIG 1:51   Checking piston ring end gap

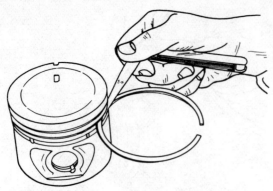

FIG 1:52 Checking piston ring side clearance

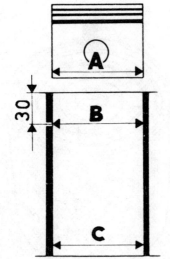

FIG 1:53 Checking piston to bore clearance

FIG 1:54 Piston ring locations

will dictate a rebore to accept new pistons, this being a specialist job.

Check the clearance of each piston in its bore, measuring the outside diameter of the piston at right angles to gudgeon pin bore (A) (see **FIG 1:53**) and the inside diameter of the bore at two points B and C. From the figures obtained, calculate piston clearance in bore. This should be 0.01 to 0.03mm (0.0004 to 0.0012in). Excessive clearance will dictate the fitting of new pistons and, possibly, reboring the cylinders, the latter being a specialist job.

When installing piston rings to pistons, make sure that they are correctly located as shown in **FIG 1:54**. Note that the second compression ring is marked 'TOP' to ensure that it is fitted the right way up. Arrange the rings so that their gaps are spaced at 120° intervals around the piston diameter. When installing pistons and connecting rods, note that the notch mark on the piston crown must face towards the front of the engine and number on connecting rod must face righthand side of block (oil filter side), as shown in **FIG 1:55**. Use a suitable piston ring clamp to prevent damage to the rings when they are entered into cylinder bores. Lubricate piston and rings with engine oil before installing.

Connecting rods:

If there has been a big-end bearing failure, the crankpin must be examined for damage and for transfer of metal to its surface. The oilway in the crankshaft should be checked to ensure that there is no obstruction. Big-end bearing clearance can be checked by the use of Plastigage, which is the trade name for a precisely calibrated plastic filament. The filament is laid along the bearing to be measured for working clearance, the cap fitted and the bolts or nuts tightened. The bearing is then dismantled and the width of the flattened filament measured with the scale supplied. The figure thus obtained is the actual bearing clearance. Both main and big-end bearings are measured in the same manner.

Note that each main bearing must be measured separately and that none of the remaining bearing caps must be fitted during the operation. The bearing surfaces must be clean and free from oil and the crankshaft must not be turned during the measurement procedure. The point at which the measurement is taken must be close to the respective dead centre position and no hammer blows must be applied to the bearing or cap.

Place a length of plastic filament identical to the width of the bearing on the crankshaft journal, then fit the bearing cap with shell bearings and tighten to the specified torque. Remove the cap and measure the width of the flattened filament to obtain the bearing running clearance. Check the figure with those given in **Technical Data**. If the bearing clearance is too high, new bearing shells must be selected by the measurement procedure to bring the clearance to within limits.

1:14 Crankshaft oil seals

Rear oil seal renewal:

For access to the rear oil seal either the automatic transmission must be removed as described in **Chapter 7** or the clutch removed as described in **Chapter 5**, which ever is the case. Remove the flywheel and rear oil seal carrier, then renew the seal and refit the components, referring to the appropriate instructions given in **Section 1:3** or **1:4**.

Front oil seal renewal:

Pushrod engine:

The oil seal renewal procedure is given in the instructions for timing gear cover removal and refitting in **Section 1:5**.

OHC engine:

For access to the front oil seal, the timing gear and sealing flange must be removed from the front of the engine, the old seal removed, then a new seal pressed into place and the components refitted. The work should be carried out following the appropriate instructions given in **Section 1:4** and **1:6**.

1:15 Crankshaft and main bearings

In order to service the crankshaft the engine must first be removed as described in **Section 1:2** then dismantled as described in **Section 1:3** or **1:4**.

If there has been a main bearing failure, the crankshaft journal must be checked for damage and for transfer of metal to its surface. The oilways in the crankshaft must be checked to ensure that there is no obstruction. Main bearing clearance can be checked by the use of Plastigage, in the manner described in **Section 1:13** for big-end bearings, the procedure being the same. If there is any doubt about the condition of the crankshaft it should be taken to a specialist for more detailed checks.

1:16 Emission control systems

All engines are equipped with a positive crankcase ventilation (PCV) system, the layout of which is shown typically in **FIG 1:56**. The system operates to prevent harmful crankcase vapours from venting into the atmosphere. Crankcase vapours are drawn in through the inlet manifold to be burnt harmlessly in the combustion chambers, the vapours being mixed with fresh air from the air cleaner. During idling and under light load fresh air passes through the hose between air cleaner and flame guard. The air and crankcase vapours then flow through hose between flame guard and calibrated nipple on inlet manifold. Function of this nipple is to ensure that volume of air and gas does not become so great as to affect carburetter operation. At higher speeds and under full load conditions, when vacuum in crankcase reduces and vacuum in air cleaner increases, the direction of flow in the hose between flame guard and air cleaner changes to allow gases to flow two ways, partly through hose between flame guard and air cleaner and partly through calibrated nipple. The nipple is calibrated to balance the vacuum in the crankcase so that it does not become excessive. Loss of oil is prevented by an oil trap built into the valve casing. The hoses and calibrated nipple in the system should be cleaned, and the flame guard should be renewed, at the intervals specified in the manufacturer's service schedule.

If an exhaust gas recirculation (EGR) system is fitted, the valve in the system should be periodically renewed and the valve, pipes and connection nipple in the exhaust manifold cleaned at interim periods, at the

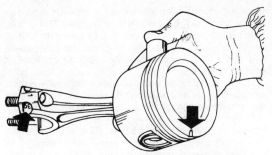

FIG 1:55   Piston and connecting rod markings

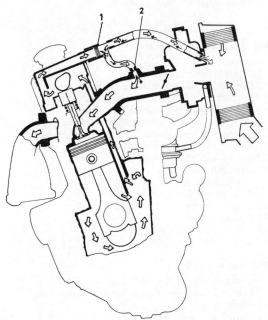

FIG 1:56   Typical layout of PCV system

Key to Fig 1:56   1 Flame guard   2 Calibrated nipple

FIG 1:57   Typical EGR valve

specified intervals. The valve can be removed after disconnecting from the pipes in the system (see **FIG 1 : 57**). After cleaning, check valve operation by racing the engine momentarily and visually checking that the valve opens and closes. If the valve does not operate correctly, it should be renewed.

USA export models are fitted with additional emission control equipment to ensure that harmful emissions from engine exhaust and the fuel system are maintained at the very low levels required by legislation. Due to the complexity of the systems and the need for special analytical equipment to properly test their operation, checking and servicing at the appropriate intervals and any necessary repairs to the system components should be carried out by a fully equipped service station.

1 : 17 Fault diagnosis

(a) Engine will not start

1 Defective coil
2 Faulty distributor capacitor
3 Dirty, pitted or incorrectly set contact points
4 Ignition wires loose or insulation faulty
5 Water on sparking plug leads
6 Battery discharged, corrosion of terminals
7 Faulty or jammed starter
8 Sparking plug leads wrongly connected
9 Vapour lock in fuel pipes
10 Defective fuel pump
11 Overchoking or underchoking
12 Blocked fuel filter or carburetter jet
13 Leaking valves
14 Sticking valves
15 Valve timing incorrect
16 Ignition timing incorrect

(b) Engine stalls

1 Check 1, 2, 3, 4, 5, 10, 11, 12, 13, and 14 in (a)
2 Sparking plugs defective or gaps incorrect
3 Retarded ignition
4 Mixture too weak
5 Water in fuel system
6 Petrol tank vent blocked
7 Incorrect valve clearances

(c) Engine idles badly

1 Check 2 and 7 in (b)
2 Air leak at manifold joints
3 Carburetter adjustment wrong
4 Air leak in carburetter
5 Over-rich mixture
6 Worn piston rings
7 Worn valve stems or guides
8 Weak exhaust valve springs

(d) Engine misfires

1 Check 1, 2, 3, 4, 5, 8, 10, 12, 13, 14, 15 and 16 in (a)
2 Weak or broken valve springs

(e) Engine overheats (see **Chapter 4**)

(f) Compression low

1 Check 13 and 14 in (a) ; 6 and 7 in (c) ; and 2 in (d)
2 Worn piston ring grooves
3 Scored or worn cylinder bores

(g) Engine lacks power

1 Check 3, 10, 11, 12, 13, 14, 15 and 16 in (a) ; 2, 3, 4 and 7 in (b) ; 6 and 7 in (c) ; and 2 in (d). Also check (e) and (f)
2 Leaking joint washers or gaskets
3 Fouled sparking plugs
4 Automatic advance not working

(h) Burned valves or seats

1 Check 13 and 14 in (a) ; 7 in (b) ; and 2 in (d). Also check (e)
2 Excessive carbon around valve seats and head

(j) Sticking valves

1 Check 2 in (d)
2 Bent valve stem
3 Scored valve stem or guide
4 Incorrect valve clearances

(k) Excessive cylinder wear

1 Check 11 in (a)
2 Lack of oil
3 Dirty oil
4 Piston rings gummed up or broken
5 Badly fitting piston rings
6 Connecting rod bent

(l) Excessive oil consumption

1 Check 6 and 7 in (c) and check (k)
2 Ring gaps too wide
3 Oil return holes in piston choked with carbon
4 Scored cylinders
5 Oil level in sump too high
6 External oil leaks

(m) Crankshaft and connecting rod bearing failure

1 Check 2 in (k)
2 Restricted oilways
3 Worn journals and crankpins
4 Loose bearing caps
5 Extremely low oil pressure
6 Bent connecting rod

(n) Engine vibration

1 Loose alternator or other belt driven component
2 Engine mountings loose or defective
3 Mounting stresses in exhaust system
4 Misfiring due to mixture, ignition or mechanical faults

CHAPTER 2

THE FUEL SYSTEM

2:1 Description

On models fitted with carburetter fuel system, the fuel pump delivers fuel from the storage tank to the carburetter through a series of pipes and flexible hoses. The pump is mechanical, being operated by means of a rocker arm acting against a special eccentric on the pushrod engine camshaft, or OHC engine auxiliary shaft.

Either a 175 CD-2SE, SU-HIF 6 or DVG 175 CDSU carburetter may be fitted, according to model type, year of manufacture and market territory.

On all carburetters only one jet is fitted, the fuel flow being regulated by a moving tapered needle. The position of the needle is determined by the amount of vacuum in the carburetter housing, which acts upon a piston in which the needle is mounted. All carburetters are very accurately calibrated by the manufacturers to provide a finely balanced fuel/air mixture throughout the engine operating range, ensuring that toxic exhaust emissions are maintained at very low levels required by current legislation.

All models are provided with a renewable paper cartridge type filter unit which is attached to the carburetter air intake.

High performance variants are fitted with a system of direct fuel injection in place of the carburetter system. A description of the fuel injection system and details of the necessary routine maintenance procedures are given in **Section 2:7**.

2:2 Routine maintenance

The items of routine maintenance described in this section should be carried out at the intervals recommended in the manufacturer's service schedule.

Checking carburetter damper:

Refer to **FIG 2:1**. Unscrew and remove the damper assembly from the top of the carburetter and look inside the hollow piston rod and check fluid oil level. The level should be 6mm ($\frac{1}{4}$in) below the top of the rod. If not, top up as necessary, using Automatic Transmission Fluid type F. **Never use anything except the correct grade of fluid to top up the carburetter damper.**

Refer to **FIG 2:2** and check damper piston axial clearance as shown at **A**. This clearance should be 1.1 to 1.7mm (0.043 to 0.067in) for SU-HIF 6 carburetters, 1.0 to 1.8mm (0.040 to 0.070in) for 175 CD-2 SE carburetters or 0.5 to 1.5mm (0.020 to 0.060in) for DVG 175 CDSU carburetters. If this clearance is outside the limits stated, the damper piston assembly should be renewed complete. Note that incorrect piston axial

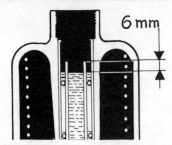

FIG 2:1   Carburetter damper fluid level

FIG 2:2   Checking damper piston axial clearance

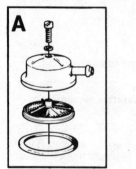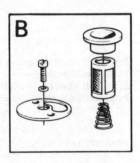

FIG 2:3   Typical fuel pump filter units

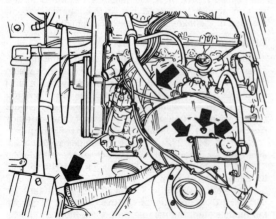

FIG 2:4   Air cleaner installation

clearance or incorrect damper fluid level can be a cause of hesitation during acceleration.

On completion, carefully refit the damper assembly to carburetter and screw the cap firmly into place.

Clean fuel pump filter:

Refer to **FIG 2:3** and remove the pump cover, filter and seal. Clean all dirt and sediment from cover, filter and pump body. If the filter is damaged or will not clean up properly, it should be renewed. Check the seal and renew if defective in any way. Refit the components in the reverse order of removal, but do not overtighten when installing the cover. On type B the pin in the cover must fit in the spring. Start the engine and check for fuel leaks around the pump cover seal.

Remove air cleaner element:

See **Section 2:3**.

Additional maintenance:

Additional items of maintenance include the checking of engine idling speed and exhaust CO content and carrying out any necessary adjustments as described in **Section 2:5**, check on condition and operation of carburetter controls and the lubrication of control linkages.

2:3 Air cleaner

Air cleaner installation is shown in **FIG 2:4**. To remove the assembly complete, disconnect air intake hose at shutter and crankcase ventilation hose then remove the fixing screws and detach the assembly from the carburetter.

To renew the filter element, separate the air cleaner casing and cover, then remove and discard the old filter element. Wipe clean the inside of case and cover, then reassemble using a new element.

2:4 Fuel pump

Testing:

Before testing the pump, ensure that the fuel tank vent system is not blocked. A blockage is indicated if removal of the fuel filler cap results in a sound of air being drawn into the tank. If so, the fuel tank vent system must be checked and cleaned.

If the vent system is clear and it is still suspected that fuel is not reaching the carburetter, disconnect the carburetter feed pipe and hold a suitable container under the end of the pipe. Turn the engine over a few times with the starter and watch for fuel squirting from the end of the pipe, which indicates that the pump is working.

Reduced fuel flow can be caused by blocked fuel pipes or a clogged filter. Check the filter element as described in **Section 2:2**.

If an obstructed pipeline appears to be the cause of the trouble, it may be cleared with compressed air. Disconnect the pipeline at both ends. **Do not pass compressed air through the pump or the valves will be damaged.** If there is an obstruction between the pump and the tank, remove the tank filler cap before blowing the pipe through from the pump end.

If the pump delivers insufficient fuel, suspect an air leak, between the pump and the tank, dirt under the pump valves or faulty valve seatings. Also check for leaks at the cover seal and fixing screw washer(s) (see **FIG 2:3**). If no fuel is delivered, suspect a sticking valve or a faulty pump diaphragm.

Test the action of the pump valves by blowing and sucking at the inlet and outlet points. Do this with the pump in situ, using a suitable piece of hose connected to the pump inlet and outlet in turn. It should be possible to blow air through the pump inlet but not to suck air out, and it should be possible to suck air out of the pump outlet but not to blow air in. If the valves do not work properly according to this test, or if the pump is defective in any other way, a new unit must be fitted as the pump is serviced as a complete assembly.

Removal:

Remove the fuel hoses from the pump fittings, plugging the ends of the hoses to prevent leakage and ingress of dirt. Remove the fixing bolts or nuts and detach fuel pump and gaskets from engine.

Refit in the reverse order of removal, using a new gasket. Make sure that the mating faces of pump and engine are clean. Ensure that pump operating arm rides correctly on top of the eccentric on camshaft or auxiliary shaft. Tighten the retaining bolts or nuts alternately and evenly to avoid distortion of the mounting flange. Reconnect the fuel pipes, then run the engine and check for fuel leaks.

2:5 Carburetter tuning and adjustment

Control linkages:

First remove the air cleaner assembly as described in **Section 2:3**. Disconnect the link rod from the lever on carburetter, as shown in **FIG 2:5**. Bend out the lock tab and carefully lever off the ball socket, then position the end of the link rod away from the throttle cable drum. Refer to **FIG 2:6**. When the throttle is released, the tag must contact the stop shown by the arrow and there must be no slack in the throttle cable. If incorrect, turn the cable adjuster as shown until the tag firmly contacts the stop, then adjust in the opposite direction until cable slack is just eliminated.

The choke control should be set so that there is a small amount of slack in the cable when the control is fully off, to avoid any possibility of choke control being held partially on in the closed position. Check for smooth operation over the full range of movement and ensure that the mixture control on the carburetter is fully applied when the choke control in the car is fully extended. There must be a small amount of clearance between the fast-idle screw and the cam on the choke control at the carburetter which contacts this screw, when the choke control is fully off. If no clearance exists, the screw must be adjusted to provide a small clearance, then the fast-idle setting checked and adjusted as described later.

When throttle and choke linkages are correctly adjusted, reconnect the link rod arrowed (see **FIG 2:7**) to carburetter lever, unless the carburetter slow-running adjustments are to be carried out as described later. When the link rod is finally connected, check that a clearance of 0.5mm (0.02in) exists between the lever and the spindle

FIG 2:5 Disconnecting link rod

FIG 2:6 Throttle cable adjustment

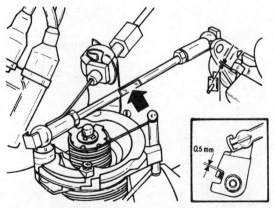

FIG 2:7 Adjusting throttle clearance for SU-HIF 6 and DVG 175 CDSU carburetters. The method is similar for 175 CD-2SE carburetters, with clearance checked as shown inset

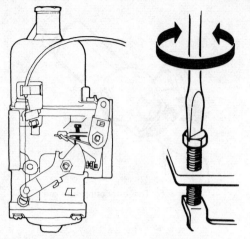

FIG 2:8 Idle speed adjustment, SU-HIF 6 carburetter

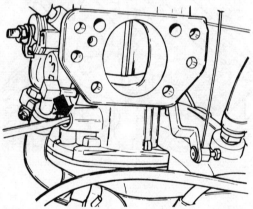

FIG 2:9 CO adjustment screw, SU-HIF 6 carburetter

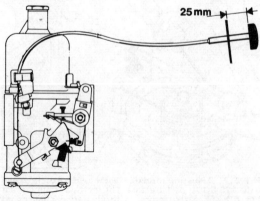

FIG 2:10 Fast-idle adjustment, SU-HIF 6 carburetter

flange, as shown in **FIG 2:7**. If not, slacken both lock-nuts on the link rod, then rotate the rod until clearance is correct. On completion, tighten the locknuts and recheck the clearance. Refit the air cleaner assembly.

Slow-running adjustments:

Note that slow-running adjustments will only be effective if the sparking plugs and ignition system are in good order and the valve clearances are correctly set. The engine must be run at approximately 1500rev/min until the radiator top hose feels warm, this indicating that the cooling system thermostat has opened and the engine is at the correct temperature for adjustments to be carried out.

Note that accurate tachometer equipment will be needed to set engine idle speed correctly and that suitable analytical equipment must be used during final adjustment procedures to ensure that the CO (carbon monoxide) content of the exhaust gas is within the specified limits. If suitable equipment is not available, the work should be carried out by a fully equipped service station.

Carburetter faults which cannot be cured by the adjustment procedures given in this section should be referred to a fully equipped service station, so that further checks can be made using special analytical equipment. It is not recommended that owners attempt carburetter servicing or overhaul procedures, as special equipment is essential in order to precisely check and set carburetter ancillary components and to carry out the necessary internal adjustments.

Idle speed adjustment:
SU-HIF 6 carburetter:

Run the engine until it reaches the correct operating temperature as described previously, then switch it off and check damper fluid level as described in **Section 2:2**. Check, and if necessary, adjust throttle and choke linkages as described previously. Note that the carburetter link rod must not be reconnected until slow-running adjustments have been completed.

Connect the tachometer equipment according to the manufacturer's instructions, then start the engine and allow it to idle. Refer to **FIG 2:8** and turn the adjustment screw as necessary to obtain an engine idle speed of 700rev/min for B20A engine or 850rev/min for B21A engine.

CO content of the exhaust gas must now be checked using the appropriate analytical equipment. Before a reading is taken on the CO meter, engine speed must first be raised to 1500rev/min then returned to idle and the vacuum chamber on the top of the carburetter gently tapped with a screwdriver handle to ensure that the vacuum piston is properly settled. This procedure ensures an accurate reading. CO content should be 2.5% for B20A 1975 and all B21A engines, or 1.5% for B20A 1976 models.

If adjustment is necessary, this is carried out at the screw shown in **FIG 2:9**. Turning the screw inwards increases CO, turning it outwards reduces CO.

When CO content is correct, reset engine idle speed to the correct level by adjusting the idle speed screw.

On completion, reconnect and if necessary, adjust the carburetter link rod, then check fast-idle adjustment as described next.

To check fast-idle setting, first make sure that the engine is at the correct operating temperature as described previously, then allow it to idle. Pull out the choke control in the car be approximately 25mm (1in), so that the mark on the cam is aligned with the head of the fast-idle screw, as shown in **FIG 2:10**. In this position, the engine should run at a fast-idle speed of 1100 to 1500rev/min for B20 engines or 1200 to 1600rev/min for B21 engines. If engine speed is outside these limits, slacken the locknut and turn the fast-idle adjustment screw as necessary, then tighten the locknut to secure. On completion, push in the choke control and check that a small gap exists between the end of the screw and the cam. If not, adjust slightly to achieve this condition.

175 CD-2SE carburetter, 1977 and earlier models:

Warm up the engine to the correct temperature as described previously, then check and if necessary adjust throttle and choke linkages as described previously. Note that the throttle link rod must remain disconnected until carburetter slow-running adjustments have been completed. Check and if necessary top up damper fluid level as described in **Section 2:2**.

Connect the tachometer equipment according to the manufacturer's instructions, then start the engine and allow it to idle. Refer to **FIG 2:11** and turn the idle speed adjustment screw as necessary to obtain an engine speed of 700rev/min for B20A engine or 850rev/min for B21A engine.

The CO content of the exhaust gas must now be checked using suitable analytical equipment. Before a reading is taken on the CO meter, engine speed must first be raised to 1500rev/min then returned to idle and the vacuum chamber on the top of the carburetter gently tapped with a screwdriver handle to ensure that the vacuum piston is properly settled. This procedure ensures an accurate reading. CO content should be 2.5% for B20A 1975 engines and all B21A engines, 1.5% for B20A 1976–77 engines.

If CO content is outside limits, fine adjustments can be carried out at the screw shown at **A** in **FIG 2:12**. Turning the screw clockwise increases CO content, turning anticlockwise reduces CO. If this method is successful in bringing CO content to within limits, proceed with the fast-idle adjustments given later. If not, the car should be taken to a fully equipped service station for adjustments to the basic setting of fuel jet to be carried out, using special tools and equipment.

When CO content has been correctly set, readjust the idle speed screw if necessary to reset the engine idle speed correctly, as described previously. Reconnect and if necessary adjust the link rod as described previously.

The fast-idle speed must now be checked and adjusted if necessary, noting that the engine must be at the correct operating temperature as described previously. Start the engine and allow it to idle, then refer to **FIG 2:13**. Pull out the choke control in the car by approximately 25mm (1in), so that the mark on the cam aligns with the head of the fast-idle screw indicated by the

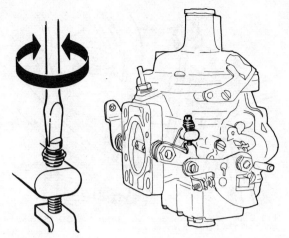
FIG 2:11 Idle speed adjustment, 175 CD-2SE carburetter

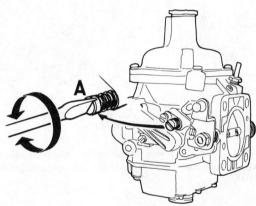
FIG 2:12 CO adjustment screw, 175 CD-2SE carburetter

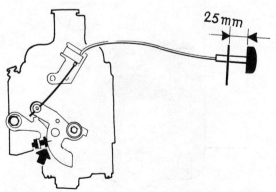
FIG 2:13 Fast-idle adjustment, 175 CD-2SE carburetter

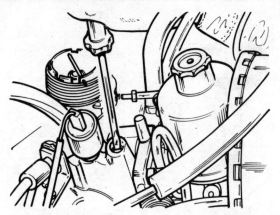

FIG 2:14 Idle trimming screw, later 175 CD-2SE and all DVG 175 CDSU carburetters

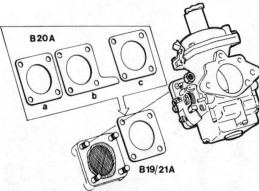

FIG 2:15 Carburetter gasket installation, earlier models

Key to Fig 2:15 a Gasket b Protective plate c Insulation flange

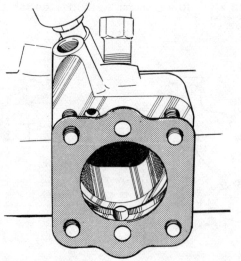

FIG 2:16 Carburetter gasket installation, later models

arrow. In this position, the engine should run at a fast-idle speed of 1100 to 1500rev/min for B20 engines, or 1200 to 1600rev/min for B21 engines. If outside limits, slacken the locknut, turn the adjustment screw as necessary, then tighten the locknut to secure. Now push the choke control fully home and check that small gap exists between the head of the screw and the cam. If not, carry out further slight adjustments to obtain this condition.

175 CD-2E carburetters from 1978 on and all DVG 175 CDSU carburetters:

On these carburetters, the throttle stop is preset at the factory and its position must not be altered unless carburetter overhaul procedures have been carried out, these being specialist operations. Service adjustments to idle speed are carried out at the idle trimming screw shown in **FIG 2:14**.

Warm the engine up to the correct operating temperature as described previously, then switch it off. Check and if necessary top up damper fluid level as described in **Section 2:2**. Check and if necessary adjust throttle and choke linkages as described previously. Note that the link rod must not be reconnected until carburetter slow-running adjustments have been completed.

Connect the tachometer equipment according to the manufacturer's instructions, then start the engine and adjust the idle trimming screw to obtain an engine idle speed of 900rev/min.

The CO content of the exhaust gas must now be checked using suitable analytical equipment. With the engine idling, CO content should be between 1.5 and 3.0%. If outside these limits, the car should be taken to a fully equipped service station so that the appropriate adjustment procedures can be carried out. Reconnect and if necessary adjust link rod as described previously.

Fast-idle adjustment should now be carried out, to obtain an engine speed of 1400 to 1600rev/min, in a similar manner to that described previously for earlier model 175CD-2SE carburetters.

2:6 Carburetter removal

Remove the air cleaner assembly as described in **Section 2:3**. Disconnect the throttle link rod from lever on carburetter as described in **Section 2:5**, then disconnect the choke cable. Disconnect hoses and vacuum pipes as necessary to allow for carburetter removal, then remove the four fixing nuts securing the carburetter to inlet manifold flange. Remove the carburetter, then remove and discard the flange gasket.

Refitting:

This is a reversal of the removal procedure, using a new gasket. Installation of gasket for earlier models is shown in **FIG 2:15**, that for later models in **FIG 2:16**. In the latter case, make sure that the gasket is installed the correct way up, as shown in the illustration. Tighten the carburetter fixing nuts alternately and evenly to avoid distortion of the flange. On completion, check and if necessary top up damper fluid level as described in **Section 2:2**, then carry out throttle and choke cable adjustments as described in **Section 2:5**.

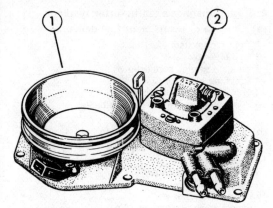

FIG 2:17   The CI system air/fuel control unit

2:7 Fuel injection system

In place of the carburetter on some engines, a system of direct fuel injection is used in which a quantity of fuel, carefully metered according to engine operating conditions, is injected straight into each cylinder inlet port where it is mixed with its air supply entering through an inlet duct and regulated by a conventional type throttle valve.

The principle of the CI (continuous injection) system is to measure continuously the airflow into the engine and allow this flow to control the amount of fuel fed to the engine. Measurement and control is by means of the air/fuel control unit shown in **FIG 2:17**, this consisting of the air flow sensor 1 and the fuel distributor 2. The valves in the CI system are always open while the engine is operating, the amount of fuel being controlled by variation of the fuel flow through the injectors. Intake air is filtered through an air cleaner unit fitted with a renewable paper cartridge type filter element.

Those items of maintenance and adjustment which can be carried out by an owner/driver are given in this section, but it must be stressed that fault finding and rectification requires many highly specialised tools and special equipment. Even when faults have been traced, the remedy is usually by substitution rather than by adjustment or repair. For these reasons, the car should be taken to a fully equipped service station for any necessary work to be carried out, should operational faults develop in the CI system.

Air filter element renewal:

Release the spring clips securing the rubber bellows to air cleaner assembly, then disconnect the plug at fuel distributor. Refer to **FIG 2:18**. Release the spring clips and lift off the air cleaner upper part complete with fuel distributor, then remove and discard the air filter cartridge. Clean the inside of the air cleaner casing, then reassemble in the reverse order using a new filter cartridge.

Fuel filter element renewal:

Refer to **FIG 2:19**. Clean the hose connections, then disconnect the hoses and remove and discard the filter unit. Fit the new unit in the reverse order, making sure that it is properly positioned for correct direction of fuel flow.

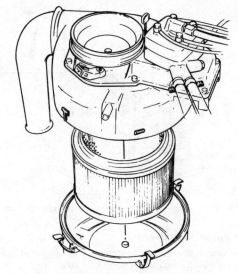

FIG 2:18   Air filter cartridge renewal

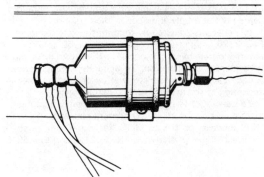

FIG 2:19   Typical fuel filter installation

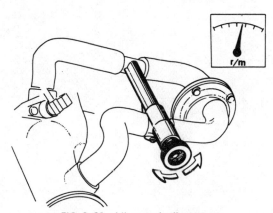

FIG 2:20   Idle speed adjustment

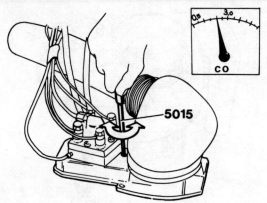

FIG 2:21   Adjusting CO content with special tool

Idle speed adjustment:

Note that idle speed adjustments will only be effective if the sparking plugs and ignition system are in good order and the valve clearances are correctly set. The engine must be at normal operating temperature. After the idle speed has been adjusted, the CO (carbon monoxide) content of the exhaust gas should be checked and adjusted if necessary. If the analytical equipment needed for this work is not available. final adjustments should be carried out at a fully equipped service station.

Idle speed is adjusted by rotating the screw shown in **FIG 2:20**. Adjust until engine idles at 800rev/min for automatic transmission models, or 900rev/min for those with manual transmission. To accurately gauge engine speed, a suitable tachometer will be needed, connected according to the manufacturer's instructions.

To check CO level, connect suitable analytical equipment and take a reading. CO content should be 1.5% for USA models, or 0.5 to 3.0% for other territories. If incorrect, adjust as shown in **FIG 2:21**, using tool 5015.

2:8 Fault diagnosis (carburetter systems)

(a) Leakage or insufficient fuel delivered

1 Tank vent system blocked
2 Fuel pipes blocked
3 Air leaks at pipe connections
4 Fuel filter blocked
5 Pump diaphragm defective
6 Pump valve sticking or seating badly

(b) Excessive fuel consumption

1 Carburetter incorrectly adjusted
2 Fuel leakage
3 Sticking mixture control
4 Dirty air cleaner
5 Worn carburetter jet
6 Excessive engine temperature

(c) Idling speed too high

1 Idle speed adjustment required
2 Throttle control sticking
3 Mixture control sticking
4 Worn throttle valve

(d) Noisy fuel pump

1 Loose pump mountings
2 Air leaks on suction side of pump
3 Obstruction in fuel pipeline
4 Clogged fuel filter

(e) No fuel delivery

1 Float needle valve stuck
2 Tank vent system blocked
3 Defective fuel pump
4 Pipeline obstructed
5 Bad air leak on suction side of pump

CHAPTER 3

THE IGNITION SYSTEM

3:1 Description

Either an ignition system incorporating a contact breaker assembly, or a breakerless electronic ignition system may be incorporated, according to models' specification and year of manufacture.

The conventional system comprises an ignition coil, distributor and contact breaker assembly (see FIG 3:1). The distributor incorporates automatic timing control by centrifugal mechanism and a vacuum operated unit. As engine speed increases, the centrifugal action of rotating weights pivoting against the tension of small springs moves the contact breaker cam relative to the drive shaft and progressively advances the ignition. The vacuum control unit is connected by small bore pipe to a fitting on the carburetter. At high degrees of vacuum the unit advances the ignition, but under load, at reduced vacuum, the unit progressively retards the ignition.

The electronic ignition system is similar to the contact breaker type just described, with the exception of the distributor unit. In this unit, the centrifugal and vacuum control mechanisms are retained, but the contact breaker assembly is replaced by an electronic system (see FIG 3:2). The electronic timing system has a stator and rotor, each with a number of tags. A permanent magnet which is incorporated generates a magnetic field which is conducted into the stator. When stator and rotor tags are aligned, the magnetic circuit is closed, but when they are separated the circuit is broken. These timed pulses are passed to the control unit, which switches LT current to the primary circuit on and off. The coil secondary circuit is therefore triggered in the normal manner to provide HT current pulses which are directed to the sparking plugs by the distributor rotor.

Additionally, the coil used with the electronic system is provided with a ballast resistor in the LT circuit. During normal running the resistor reduces nominal battery voltage to approximately 6 volts at the coil terminal. The resistor is bypassed when the starter is being operated, so that full battery voltage is supplied to the coil. The coil then provides increased voltage to the HT system for maximum sparking plug efficiency when the engine is being started.

3:2 Routine maintenance

Standard ignition system:

Pull off the two spring clips and remove the distributor cap. Pull the rotor from the top of the distributor shaft to gain access to the contact breaker points. Distributor upper components are shown in FIG 3:3.

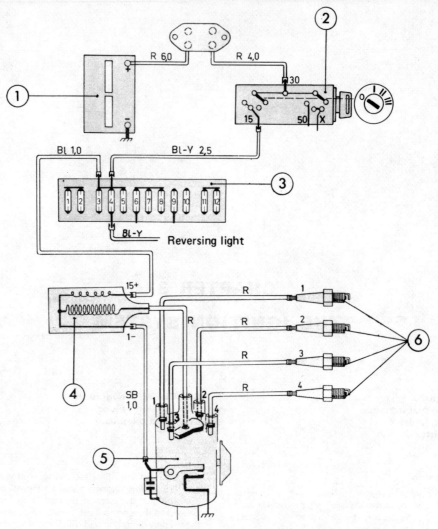

FIG 3:1   Layout of contact breaker type ignition system

Key to Fig 3:1   1 Battery   2 Ignition switch   3 Fuse box   4 Coil   5 Distributor   6 Sparking plugs

Lubrication:

Apply just sufficient engine oil to soak the felt pad in the top of the distributor shaft. Wipe clean the cam which opens the contact points and apply a thin smear of approved grease to the cam. Take care to avoid contaminating the contact points with grease or oil, lubricating sparingly for this reason.

Adjusting the contact breaker points:

Turn the engine till one of the cams has opened the contact points to their fullest extent, then check the gap between the points with a clean feeler gauge. The correct gap is 0.35mm (0.014in) for B20A, 0.40mm (0.016in) for B21A. To adjust, slacken the fixed contact point retaining screw, move the point on the base plate as necessary, then tighten the screw and recheck the gap. If dwell meter equipment is available, adjusting the points to give the dwell angle (see **Technical Data**) will provide the most accurate setting.

Cleaning the contact breaker points:

Use a fine carborundum stone or special contact point file to polish the points if they are dirty or pitted, taking care to keep the faces flat and square. If the points are too worn to clean up in this manner, they should be renewed. On completion, wipe away all dust with a cloth moistened in petrol then set the points gap as described previously.

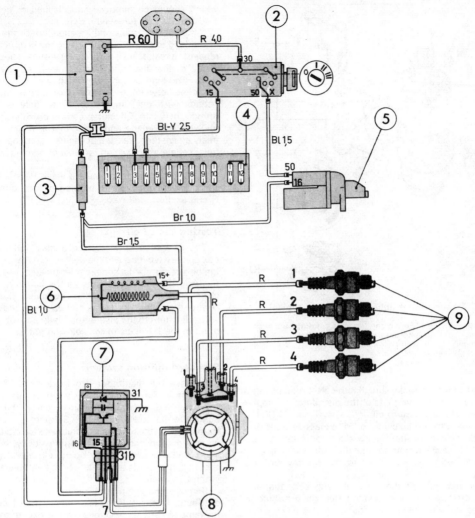

FIG 3:2 Layout of electronic ignition system

Key to Fig 3:2   1 Battery   2 Ignition switch   3 Ballast resistor   4 Fuse box   5 Starter motor   6 Coil   7 Control unit
8 Distributor   9 Sparking plugs

Renewing the contact breaker points:

Remove the retaining screw to free the contact points set from the base plate, then disconnect the wire from the terminal. Lift out the contact points set.

Wash the mating faces of the new contact points with methylated spirit to remove the protective coating. Fit the contact points set to the base plate and secure with the screw. Reconnect the wire to the terminal. Set the points to the correct gap, then lubricate the felt pad and cam, all as described previously.

Checking rotor arm:

To check rotor arm insulation, fit the rotor into place and remove the central HT lead from the distributor cap.

Hold the end of the HT lead approximately 12mm (0.5in) from the rotor centre contact. To avoid shocks, hold the lead well away from the end. Turn the engine until the contact points are closed then, with the ignition switched on, flick open the contact points. If a spark jumps the gap the rotor is faulty and must be renewed. Always fit a new rotor if the original is cracked or the brass parts are badly eroded.

Electronic ignition system:

Release the spring clips and lift off the distributor cap, then carefully pull the rotor from the distributor shaft. Apply one or two drops of engine oil to the felt pad provided in the top of the distributor shaft, taking care

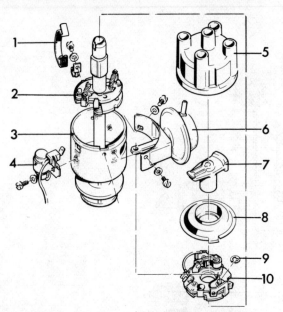

FIG 3:3 Distributor upper components, typical

Key to Fig 3:3 1 Spring clip 2 Centrifugal advance mechanism 3 Distributor housing 4 Capacitor 5 Cap 6 Vacuum unit 7 Rotor 8 Dust cover 9 Circlip 10 Contact breaker assembly

not to over-lubricate. Make sure that the electronic timing components in the upper parts of the distributor are kept completely free of grease or oil.

Check the rotor for cracking, or for excessive wear or burning of the brass parts. Renew the rotor if any faults are found. Use a clean cloth to wipe the distributor cap on both inside and outside surfaces to remove any dirt or moisture.

On completion, refit the rotor, making sure that it engages correctly in the slot provided. Refit the distributor cap and retain with the spring clips.

3:3 Ignition faults

If the engine runs unevenly, set it to idle at about 1000rev/min and, taking care not to touch any conducting part of the sparking plug leads, remove and replace the lead at each plug in turn. To avoid shocks during this operation it is necessary to wear a pair of thick gloves or use insulated pliers. Doing this to a plug which is firing correctly will accentuate the uneven running but will make no difference if the plug is not firing.

Having by this means located the faulty cylinder, stop the engine and remove the plug lead. Pull back the insulation or remove the connector so that the end of the lead is exposed. Alternatively, use an extension piece, such as a small bar or drill, pushed into the plug connector. Hold the lead carefully to avoid shocks, so that the end is about 3mm ($\frac{1}{8}$in) away from the cylinder head. Crank the engine with the starter or, on models with standard ignition systems, flick open the contact points. The ignition must be switched on. A strong, regular spark confirms that the fault lies with the sparking plug

which should be removed and cleaned as described in **Section 3:6**. or renewed if defective.

If the spark is weak and irregular, check the condition of the lead and, if it is perished or cracked, renew it and repeat the test. If no improvement results, check that the inside of the distributor cap is clean and dry and that there is no sign of tracking, which can be seen as a thin black line between the electrodes or to some metal part in contact with the cap. Tracking can only be cured by fitting a new cap. Check the carbon brush inside the cap for wear or damage and check that it moves in and out freely against the pressure of its internal spring. Check the brass segments in the cap for wear or burning. Renew the cap if any fault is found.

If these checks do not cure a weak HT spark, or if no spark can be obtained at the plug or lead, check the LT circuit as described next.

Testing the LT circuit:

The LT circuit connects the battery, ignition switch, coil primary winding and the contact breaker or electronic ignition components, and provides timed pulses of current to the coil primary windings as the contacts open and close or the electronic system operates. These pulses control the secondary coil windings which provides high voltage current to the distributor, where the rotor directs it through the HT leads to the sparking plugs.

Standard ignition system:

Remove the distributor cap as described previously. Check that the contact breaker points are clean and correctly set. Disconnect the thin wire from the coil at the connection at the distributor. Connect a 12-volt test lamp between the terminals to complete the circuit. switch on the ignition and turn the engine slowly. If the lamp lights and goes out as the points close and open, the circuit is in order. If the lamp fails to light, there is a fault in the LT circuit.

Remove the lamp and reconnect the wire to the distributor terminal. If the fault lies in the LT circuit, use the lamp to carry out the following tests with the ignition switched on. Remove the wire from the ignition switch side of the coil and connect the lamp between the end of the wire and earth. If the lamp fails to light, it indicates a fault in the wiring between the battery and coil, or in the ignition switch. Reconnect the wire if the lamp lights.

Disconnect the wire from the coil that connects to the distributor. Connect the lamp between the coil terminal and earth. If the lamp fails to light it indicates a fault in the coil primary windings and a new coil must be fitted. Reconnect the wire if the lamp lights and disconnect its other end from the distributor. If the lamp does not light when connected between the end of this wire and earth, it indicates a fault in the section of wire.

Capacitor:

The best method of testing a capacitor (condenser) is by substitution. Disconnect the original capacitor and connect a new one between the LT terminal at the distributor and earth for test purposes. If a new capacitor is proved to be required, it can then be properly fitted.

An alternative check for the capacitor is to charge it from a DC source, such as the car battery, then leave it for about five minutes. The terminal and case of the capacitor should then be shorted with a piece of wire and, if it is in good condition, a noticeable spark should result. The capacitor is mounted on the outside of the distributor body and can be removed after taking out the single fixing screw and disconnecting the wire.

Electronic ignition system:

Remove the distributor cap as described previously. Disconnect the thin wire from the coil that connects to the distributor. Connect a 12-volt test lamp between the two terminals to complete the circuit, switch on the ignition and crank the engine with the starter. If the lamp lights and goes out as the distributor operates, the circuit is in order. If the lamp fails to light, there is a fault in the LT circuit.

Remove the lamp and reconnect the wire to the distributor. Disconnect the other end of this wire from the coil, then connect the test lamp between the coil terminal and earth and switch on the ignition. If the lamp now lights it indicates a fault in the wiring between coil and distributor. Note that a 12-volt test lamp bulb will not glow with full brightness unless the engine is being cranked with the starter, due to the ballast resistor fitted in the circuit. This resistor is cut out of the circuit when the starter is operated, so that extra current is supplied to the coil to ensure a quick start.

If the test lamp does not light, disconnect the wire from the coil positive terminal and connect the test lamp between the end of this wire and earth. If the lamp lights with the ignition switched on, it indicates a fault in the coil primary windings and a new coil must be fitted. If the lamp does not light, it indicates a fault in the wiring between the battery and coil, or in the ignition switch. If tests show continuity through the remainder of the circuit, a fault in the distributor electronic components is indicated. If so, the car should be taken to a service station for more detailed checks to be carried out with special analytical equipment.

If tests indicate that the impulse sender unit in the distributor is faulty, it can be renewed as described in the next section.

3:4 Distributor

Removal:

Refer to **FIG 3:4**. On OHC engine, remove the oil filler cap from the camshaft cover, then turn the engine until the cams for No 1 cylinder are pointing upwards by equal amounts as shown in the inset. On pushrod engine, set engine so that valves at No 4 cylinder are on the overlap as described in **Chapter 1, Section 1:9**. Turn the engine a little further as necessary to align the notch in the crankshaft pulley with the 0° mark on the timing scale. Refer to **FIG 3:5** and disconnect LT wire 1 and the pipe from vacuum unit 3. Pull off the two spring clips and remove the distributor cap, then place to one side. Remove clamp bolt 2, then pull the distributor from the cylinder block.

Refitting:

If the engine has been turned, reset to the TDC point for No 1 cylinder as described previously. Offer the

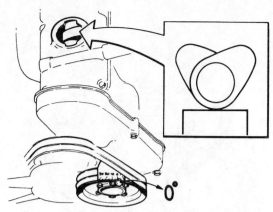

FIG 3:4 Aligning engine at TDC for No 1 cylinder

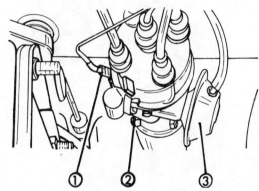

FIG 3:5 Distributor removal

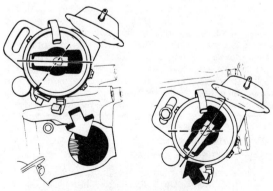

FIG 3:6 Distributor installation

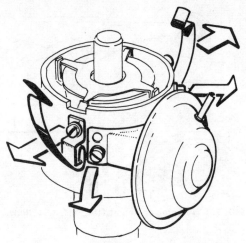

FIG 3:7　Removing spring clips and vacuum unit

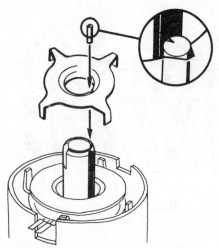

FIG 3:8　Removing armature and lockpin

distributor to the cylinder block as shown on the left in **FIG 3:6**, with the rotor turned approximately 60° away from the notch in the distributor housing. Install the distributor, making sure that it seats fully. As the drive gears mesh, the distributor shaft will rotate slightly and bring the rotor to the position shown at the right, with the rotor tip aligned with the notch. Slight adjustment to ensure correct alignment can be made by rotating the distributor housing, but if it is out by a large amount repeat the installation procedure, turning the rotor a little more or less as necessary. Install the clamp bolt loosely, then check ignition timing as described in **Section 3:5**.

Distributor dismantling:

Standard ignition system:

Servicing of the upper distributor components is described in **Section 3:2**. The distributor can be dismantled for checking of remaining internal components

but, as special equipment is needed to correctly reset centrifugal and vacuum advance mechanism, this work should be carried out by a service station. However, if general wear of the distributor is evident after a long service life, it is recommended that a new or exchange unit be fitted.

Electronic ignition system:

If tests have indicated that the impulse sender unit in the distributor is faulty, it can be renewed as described in this section, but if general wear of the distributor is evident it is recommended that new or exchange unit be fitted. If faults in the centrifical or vacuum advance mechanisms are suspected, the unit should be checked on special equipment at a service station.

Impulse sender removal:

Remove the distributor from the engine as described previously. Remove the rotor and dust cover. Remove the two screws and detach the vacuum control unit, as shown in **FIG 3:7**. Remove the single screw at the opposite side of the distributor body, then remove the LT contact by pulling it straight out.

Use suitable circlip pliers to remove the circlip from the top of the distributor shaft, then remove the armature and lockpin as shown in **FIG 3:8**. Removal should be carried out by placing a screwdriver beneath the armature on each side and carefully levering the unit from the shaft.

Remove the three screws securing the impulse sender assembly and remove the second circlip from the shaft. Lift the assembly from the distributor body (see **FIG 3:9**), then remove the three screws as shown in **FIG 3:10** to detach the impulse sender from the base plate.

Refitting:

Attach the impulse sender to the plate so that the connector pins are opposite and above the lug for the sender plate. Install the assemblies so that the connector pins are opposite the lug in the distributor housing for the contact, then install the three screws. Refit the circlip.

Install the armature so that the slot is opposite the ridge on the distributor shaft and fit the lockpin as shown in **FIG 3:8**, with the slot in the pin towards the distributor shaft. If the pin is not fitted correctly, it may shear off in service.

Install the expander washer and circlip, then reconnect the LT connector and tighten the single fixing screw. Refit the vacuum unit and install the dust cover and rotor. Check that the distributor shaft rotates freely by turning the drive gear to and fro. There should only be slight resistance to turning caused by the magnets in the impulse sender. If stiffness is evident, check for faulty or incorrectly installed components. On completion, refit the distributor to the engine as described previously.

3:5 Timing the ignition

On models with standard ignition systems, it can be sufficient to set the timing by the static method only, provided that reasonable care is taken, but it is recommended that a final check be made with stroboscopic equipment.

On models with electronic ignition systems, the ignition timing should always be checked with stroboscopic equipment, providing that the engine can be started and run. If not, it will be necessary to check the static timing first.

Later models are provided with means for checking the ignition timing accurately without the need for stroboscopic equipment, in the form of a sensor in the engine which is wired to a special plug. This system is intended to be used with a special electronic instrument. If this instrument is not available, the work should be carried out by a service station or the timing set by means of the normal stroboscopic method described in this section.

Static timing:

Standard ignition system:

Turn the engine until it is at the firing point for No 1 cylinder as described in **Section 3:4** and shown in **FIG 3:4**. The correct ignition setting according to engine specification will be found in **Technical Data** in the **Appendix**. Turn the engine slightly away from the TDC position until the notch in the crankshaft pulley aligns with the correct timing point on the scale at the front of the engine. Always turn the engine back past the required setting, then turn it forwards again until correct, to take up backlash in the distributor drive train. Slacken the distributor mounting bolt shown at 2 in **FIG 3:5** so that the distributor body can just be turned by hand.

Connect a 12-volt test lamp in parallel with the contact points. One lead will go to the terminal on the side of the distributor and one to earth. Turn the distributor body clockwise as far as possible to ensure that the contacts are fully closed. Now switch on the ignition and turn the distributor body very slowly in an anticlockwise direction until the lamp just lights. Without moving the distributor at all, firmly tighten the mounting bolt.

Electronic ignition system:

Remove the distributor cap as described in **Section 3:2**. On OHC engine, remove the filler cap from the camshaft cover so that the cam lobes for No 1 cylinder can be seen (see **FIG 3:4**). Turn the engine in the normal direction of forward rotation until the cam lobes point upwards by equal amounts and the notch in the crankshaft pulley aligns with the TDC mark on the scale at the front of the engine. On pushrod engine, set valves at No 1 cylinder in the correct positions for clearance adjustment as described in **Chapter 1, Section 1:9**, then align pulley notch with TDC mark. In this position, the distributor rotor should point towards the notch in the distributor housing as shown on the right in **FIG 3:6**. If not, the distributor must be removed and correctly refitted so that these conditions are met, as described in **Section 3:4**. This will allow the engine to be started and run so that stroboscopic timing checks can be carried out.

Stroboscopic timing, all models:

Connect the stroboscopic equipment to the ignition circuit for No 1 (front) cylinder sparking plug according to the manufacturer's instructions. Slacken the distributor mounting bolt just sufficiently to allow the distributor body to be turned. An accurate service tachometer will be required in order to set the engine idle speed to

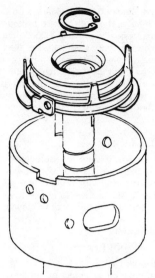

FIG 3:9 Removing impulse sender and plate

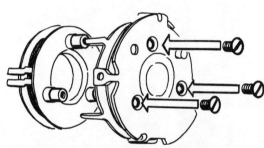

FIG 3:10 Separating impulse sender and plate

within the prescribed limits, but if such equipment is not available satisfactory results can usually be obtained by setting the engine to run at a slow, reliable idle speed.

The correct ignition timing setting and the engine idle speed at which they should be made will be found in **Technical Data** in the **Appendix**.

Disconnect the pipe from the vacuum unit shown at 3 in **FIG 3:5**, then start the engine and allow it to idle. Direct the timing lamp to shine on the crankshaft pulley and timing scale (see **FIG 3:4**). Set the engine to run at the specified speed and turn the distributor body as necessary until the notch in the pulley appears to align with the correct point on the timing scale. Without moving the distributor body, firmly tighten the mounting bolt. On completion, disconnect the test equipment and restore the circuit to normal. Refit the vacuum pipe.

3:6 Sparking plugs

Inspect and clean sparking plugs regularly. When removing sparking plugs, ensure first that their recesses are clean and dry so that nothing can fall into the cylinders. Have sparking plugs cleaned on an abrasive-blasting machine and tested under pressure, with the electrode gaps correctly set at 0.7 to 0.8mm (0.028 to 0.032 in). The electrodes should be filed until they are bright and parallel. The gaps must always be set by adjusting the earth electrode. Never attempt to bend the centre electrode. As a general rule, plugs should be cleaned and tested at about 6000 mile intervals and renewed at about 12,000 mile intervals or before if badly worn.

Sparking plug leads:

Renew HT leads if they are defective in any way. Inspect for broken, swollen or deteriorated insulation which can be the cause of current leakage, especially in wet weather conditions. Also check the condition of the plug connectors at the ends of the leads.

3:7 Fault diagnosis

(a) Engine will not fire

1 Battery discharged
2 Contact points dirty, pitted or incorrectly adjusted (standard ignition)
3 Faulty impulse sender (electronic ignition)
4 Distributor cap dirty, cracked or tracking
5 Carbon brush worn or stuck in mounting
6 Faulty cable or loose connection in LT circuit
7 Distributor rotor arm cracked
8 Faulty coil
9 Broken contact breaker spring (standard ignition)
10 Contact points stuck open (standard ignition)

(b) Engine misfires

1 Check 2, 3, 4, 6 and 8 in (a) as appropriate
2 Weak contact breaker spring (standard ignition)
3 HT plug or coil lead cracked or perished
4 Loose sparking plug
5 Sparking plug insulation cracked
6 Sparking plug gaps incorrect
7 Ignition timing too far advanced

(c) Poor acceleration

1 Ignition retarded
2 Centrifugal advance weights seized
3 Centrifugal advance springs weak, broken or disconnected
4 Distributor mounting bolt loose
5 Excessive contact points gap (standard ignition)
6 Worn sparking plugs
7 Faulty vacuum unit or leaking pipe

CHAPTER 4

THE COOLING SYSTEM

4:1 Description

The cooling system is pressurised and thermostatically controlled. Water circulation is assisted by a centrifugal pump which is mounted at the front of the cylinder block and the cooling fan, which draws air through the radiator, is fitted to the same shaft as the pump impeller. The pump and fan and the alternator are belt-driven from a pulley on the crankshaft, either a single or twin belts being fitted according to engine specification. Belt tension is adjustable at the alternator mountings. On some models, the fan is driven through a viscous coupling which allows direct drive through the coupling to the fan up to a predetermined speed. As engine speed increases above this limit, drive through the coupling to the fan is progressively decreased to reduce fan noise and power absorption without impairing cooling efficiency.

The pump takes coolant from the bottom of the radiator and delivers it to the cylinder block from which it rises to the cylinder head. At normal operating temperatures the thermostat is open and the coolant returns from the head to the top of the radiator. At lower temperatures, the thermostat valve is closed and the coolant flow bypasses the radiator and returns to the pump inlet to provide a rapid warm up.

An expansion tank containing a quantity of coolant is connected to the radiator by means of two hoses. At high operating temperatures, when the coolant in the sealed system expands, excess coolant passes into the expansion tank. When the system cools, coolant from the tank flows back into the radiator. With this system, the main coolant circuit is always completely filled and no coolant loss should occur during normal operation.

4:2 Routine maintenance

Apart from an occasional check on the condition of the hoses and hose clips and a visual check on coolant level in the expansion tank, very little maintenance should be necessary. There should also be no need for regular topping up of the coolant. If topping up is required frequently, the system should be examined for leaks before adding coolant.

Check the level of coolant in the expansion tank and top up as required. The level should be between the two marks provided on the translucent tank. If the level is at or near the lower mark, remove the cap and top up until the level is at the upper mark. Note that the level will rise when the system is hot, so topping up should only be carried out when cool. If it is essential to remove the

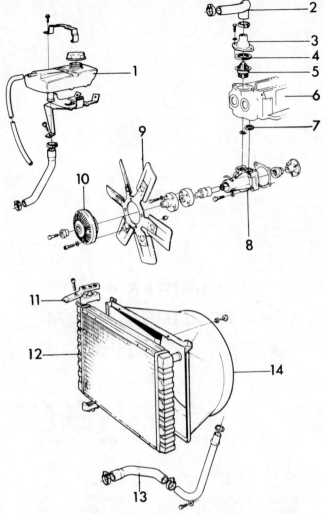

FIG 4:1   Cooling system components

Key to Fig 4:1   1 Expansion tank   2 Top radiator hose   3 Thermostat cover   4 Gasket   5 Thermostat   6 Cylinder head   7 Sealing rings   8 Water pump assembly   9 Cooling fan   10 Viscous coupling   11 Mounting clamp   12 Radiator   13 Lower radiator hose   14 Fan shroud

expansion tank cap when the system is hot, hold the cap with a large piece of rag. Turn the cap anticlockwise to the safety stop and wait for pressure to be released before lifting off the cap.

It is recommended that a solution consisting of half plain clean water and half antifreeze of an approved grade be maintained in the system all year round. This will provide protection against overheating in summer as well as against freezing in winter, and will help to prevent corrosion. Topping up should therefore be carried out with the correct mixture of antifreeze and water to avoid weakening the solution in use.

Every two years the cooling system should be drained, flushed to remove sediment, then refilled with fresh antifreeze solution. Check that the clips are tight on all hoses and that the expansion tank cap is in good condition and sealing effectively. Loss of system pressure due to a leaking filler cap can be a cause of overheating.

Regular checks should be made on drive belt condition and tension, as described in **Section 4:3**.

Draining the system:

Place the heater temperature control in the car to the maximum heat position. Make sure that the system is cool, then remove the expansion tank cap. Refer to **FIG 4:1**. Slacken the clip and remove the lower hose 13 from radiator 12 and allow the coolant to drain out, collecting it in a clean container if it is to be re-used.

Refer to **FIG 4:2** and slacken the drain tap (arrowed) on the cylinder block. A hose can be fitted to the tap to lead the coolant into a clean container if it is to be re-used.

Flushing:

When all coolant has drained, reconnect the lower hose and tighten the drain tap. Fill the system with clean water and run the engine until the top radiator hose feels warm, which indicates that the thermostat has opened for complete circulation. Now completely drain the system again before the sediment has time to settle.

Filling:

Check that the drain tap and all hose clips are tight. Leave the heater control in the maximum heat position. Prepare the new antifreeze mixture according to the manufacturer's instructions. If the system is still warm, allow it to cool down as adding the cold liquid when the system is warm may crack the engine cylinder block. Fill the system through the expansion tank until the level is at the upper mark on the tank. Refit and securely tighten the tank cap.

4:3 Drive belt adjustment

This section concerns the belt or belts which drive the water pump, fan and alternator. Belt tensioning procedures for power steering pump and air conditioning system compressor, if fitted, are given in **Chapters 10** and **13** respectively.

A tight drive belt will cause undue wear on the pulleys and component bearings, a slack belt will slip, and, possibly, result in lower output from the driven components. If a drive belt is worn, damaged or oil contaminated, it must be renewed.

Belt tension is correct when the belt(s) can be deflected 5 to 10mm ($\frac{3}{16}$ to $\frac{3}{8}$in) by firm hand pressure at the centre of the run shown in **FIG 4:3**. If adjustment is necessary, slacken the nut at the alternator slotted mounting shown in **FIG 4:4** and the two lower alternator mounting bolts. Pivot the alternator away from the engine until belt tension is correct, then tighten all mounting bolts and nuts and recheck tension. If a lever is used to move the alternator, it must be applied to the upper mounting bracket only, never to the alternator body. The belt or belts can be removed by slackening the alternator mountings, swinging the unit towards the engine, then removing the belt(s) over the pulleys and fan blades. Fit the new belt(s) then set to the correct tension. The tension of a new belt should be checked after the engine has been run for approximately 10 minutes, to take up the initial stretch.

4:4 Removing radiator

Drain the radiator as described in **Section 4:2**. Refer to **FIG 4:1** and disconnect top hose 2 from the radiator. On models with automatic transmission, disconnect the fluid cooler pipes from the radiator as shown by the arrows in **FIG 4:5**. When loosening or tightening pipe connections, hold the fittings which are screwed into the radiator with one spanner to prevent them from being loosened, then turn the connectors with a second spanner. If the connectors are accidentally loosened, they should be retightened to 6Nm (4.5lb ft).

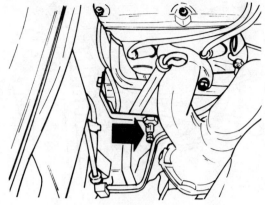

FIG 4:2 Cylinder block drain tap

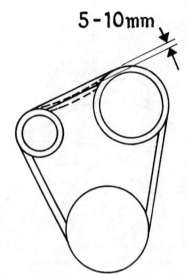

5-10mm

FIG 4:3 Checking drive belt tension

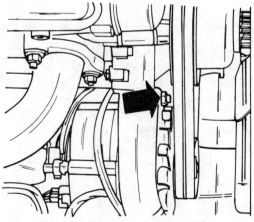

FIG 4:4 Alternator upper mounting

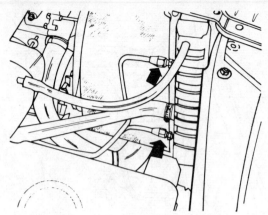

FIG 4:5 Automatic transmission fluid cooler pipe connections

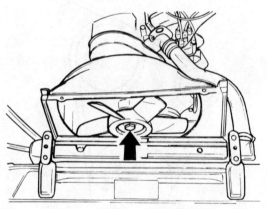

FIG 4:6 Cooling fan removal

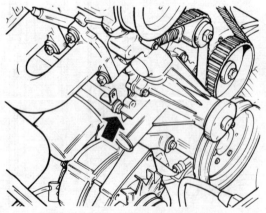

FIG 4:7 Water return pipe connection

Plug the open ends of pipes and connectors to prevent fluid loss and the entry of dirt. If air conditioning is fitted, **do not** disconnect any of the refrigeration system pipes.

Remove the fixing screws and detach fan shroud 14 (see **FIG 4:1**). Move the shroud rearwards to clear the radiator. Remove the upper mountings 11, then carefully lift radiator 12 from the lower mountings and remove from the car.

Refit the radiator in the reverse order of removal, refilling the system with coolant as described in **Section 4:2**. On automatic transmission models, check transmission fluid level as described in **Chapter 7**.

4:5 Cooling fan and water pump

Fan removal:

Remove the bolts securing the fan shroud to the radiator, then push back the shroud. Remove the central fixing bolt arrowed in **FIG 4:6** and detach the cooling fan. If a viscous coupling is installed, the central bolt must be slackened with a suitable Allen key.

To detach a viscous coupling from the fan, use a suitable Allen key to remove the four fixing bolts (see **FIG 4:1**).

Fan installation, including viscous coupling if fitted, is a reversal of the removal procedure.

Viscous coupling:

A faulty coupling unit must be renewed complete, as no repairs are possible. In order to test for correct coupling operation, special stroboscopic equipment is necessary, so checks should be carried out by a service station.

Water pump removal:

Drain the cooling system as described in **Section 4:2**, then remove the cooling fan as described previously and lift off the fan shroud. Remove the alternator drive belt(s) as described in **Section 4:3**. Remove the central fixing bolt and detach the water pump pulley. Remove the four fixing screws and detach the front cover from the engine timing gear. Disconnect the lower radiator hose from the water pump.

Refer to **FIG 4:7** and remove the fixing bolts for the water return pipe arrowed, then pull the pipe rearwards to disconnect. Remove the six fixing bolts arrowed in **FIG 4:8**, then remove the water pump from the cylinder block. If the pump is faulty or damaged, a new unit should be fitted.

Installation:

Carefully clean the mating surfaces on pump and block to remove all traces of old gasket material. Fit a new rubber ring to the pump, as shown by the arrow in **FIG 4:9**. Fit the water pump, with new gasket, and install the mounting bolts loosely. Press the pump upwards to ensure a good seal against the cylinder head, then hold in this position while tightening the bolts alternately and evenly. Fit a new rubber sealing ring to the water return pipe arrowed in **FIG 4:7**, then press the pipe into position and fit and tighten the retaining bolts.

Refit the remaining components in the reverse order of removal, setting belt tension and refilling cooling system as described previously.

4:6 The thermostat

Removal:

Refer to **Section 4:2** and drain sufficient coolant to bring the level below the thermostat housing. Refer to **FIG 4:1** and remove the bolts securing thermostat cover 3, then pull off the cover leaving it connected to top hose 2. Remove thermostat 5, then remove and discard gasket 4.

Testing:

Clean the thermostat and note the temperature marking stamped on the unit. Place the thermostat in a container of cold water together with a zero to 100°C thermometer. Heat the water, keeping it stirred and check that the valve opens at the rated temperature. The valve should be fully open when the water boils. If the thermostat operates satisfactorily it may be refitted, if not it must be renewed.

Refitting:

This is a reversal of the removal procedure, using a new thermostat gasket. Make sure that the mating surfaces of thermostat cover and housing are clean. Refill the cooling system as described in **Section 4:2**.

4:7 Frost precautions

With the correct coolant solution in use as described **Section 4:2**, no additional frost precautions should be necessary. However, it is advisable to have the solution tested before winter to make certain that it is not weakened. An hydrometer calibrated to read both specific gravity and temperature for the type of coolant in the system must be used, most garages having such equipment. Always ensure that the antifreeze mixture used for filling the system is of the correct strength, to avoid weakening the solution in use.

4:8 Fault diagnosis

(a) Internal coolant leakage

1 Cracked cylinder wall
2 Loose cylinder head bolts
3 Cracked cylinder head
4 Faulty head gasket

(b) Poor circulation

1 Radiator core blocked
2 Engine coolant passages restricted
3 Low coolant level
4 Defective thermostat
5 Perished or collapsed radiator hose

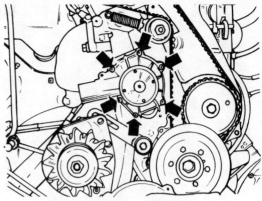

FIG 4:8   Water pump mounting screws

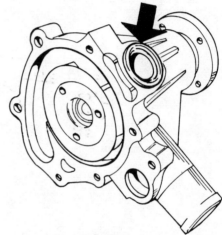

FIG 4:9   Pump sealing ring installation

(c) Corrosion

1 Impurities in the coolant
2 Infrequent draining and flushing

(d) Overheating

1 Check (b)
2 Sludge in crankcase
3 Faulty ignition timing
4 Low oil level in sump
5 Tight engine
6 Choked exhaust system
7 Binding brakes
8 Slipping clutch
9 Incorrect valve timing
10 Weak fuel mixture

NOTES

CHAPTER 5

THE CLUTCH

5:1 Description

The clutch is a single dry plate unit of diaphragm spring type. The main components are the driven plate, pressure plate assembly and release bearing.

The driven plate consists of a resilient steel disc attached to a hub which slides on the splined gearbox input shaft. Friction linings are riveted to both sides of the disc. The pressure plate assembly consists of the pressure plate, diaphragm spring and housing, the assembly being bolted to the engine flywheel. The release bearing is a ballbearing of special construction with an elongated outer ring which presses directly against the diaphragm spring when the clutch pedal is operated. The bearing is mounted on the clutch release lever which is journalled in the clutch housing.

On lefthand drive models, clutch pedal movement is transmitted to the release bearing by a sheathed steel cable attached to the clutch release lever. On righthand drive models, the clutch operating mechanism is hydraulic, the clutch pedal actuating a master cylinder where pressure on the fluid is generated, this pressure being transmitted through a hose to the clutch slave cylinder mounted on the clutch housing. Slave cylinder action is transmitted to the release lever by a short pushrod.

When the clutch is fully engaged, the driven plate is nipped between the pressure plate and the flywheel and transmits torque to the gearbox by turning the splined input shaft. When the clutch pedal is depressed the pressure plate is withdrawn from the driven plate by cable tension or by hydraulic pressure, the driven plate then ceases to transmit torque.

5:2 Adjusting the clutch

Clutch adjustment should be checked regularly as normal wear of the driven plate linings will alter the adjustment in service. If clutch adjustment is too tight, the clutch may be prevented from engaging properly, causing slip and rapid clutch plate wear. If adjustment is too slack, the clutch will not release properly, causing drag and consequent poor gearchange quality and difficulty in engaging gears from rest.

Cable operated clutch:

The clutch adjustment point at the end of the operating cable is shown in **FIG 5:1**. Clutch cable free play should be 3 to 4mm (0.12 to 0.16in) at the end of the clutch release lever. Pull the exposed end of the cable rearwards and move the end of the release lever by hand to

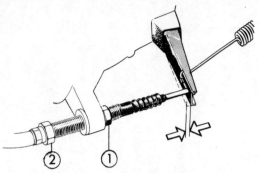

FIG 5:1   Clutch cable adjustment

check free play. If incorrect, slacken locking nut 1 and turn hexagon 2 to modify length of outer cable sleeve. When correct, firmly tighten the locknut and recheck.

Hydraulically operated clutch:

Operate the clutch pedal several times and check that the pedal is fully returned to its stop. Locate the adjustment nuts at the end of the slave cylinder pushrod where it engages the clutch release lever beneath the car (see **Section 5:6**). Free play at the end of the release lever should be zero. Move the lever forwards and backwards gently by hand to check. If free play exists, slacken the locknut and turn the adjusting nut until play is just eliminated, then firmly tighten the locknut against the adjusting nut.

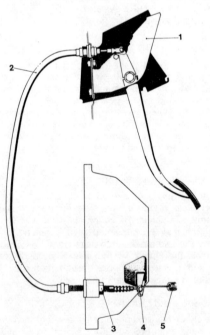

FIG 5:2   Layout of cable operated clutch mechanism

Key to Fig 5:2   1 Pedal bracket   2 Clutch cable
3 Locknut   4 Release lever   5 Return spring

5:3 Clutch cable renewal

If the car is raised for access to the underside, support safely on floor stands. Note, that, on some models, it will be necessary to remove the panel from beneath the facia for access to the cable connection at the foot pedal.

Refer to **FIG 5:2**. Disconnect return spring 5 and slacken locknut 3. Screw the outer cable sleeve towards the release lever by means of the hexagon provided until the end of the cable can be disconnected from the release lever. Remove the locknut then remove the cable assembly from the mounting on the clutch housing.

From inside the passenger compartment, remove the clevis pin to release the cable from the foot pedal, then pull the cable from the rubber grommet and into the engine compartment to remove.

Install the cable in the reverse order of removal, carrying out the adjustment procedure described in **Section 5:2** on completion.

5:4 Removing and dismantling clutch

Remove the gearbox as described in **Chapter 6**. Where the gearbox is removed without the clutch housing, disconnect the lower end of the clutch cable as described in **Section 5:3** or remove the slave cylinder as described in **Section 5:6**, then remove the fixing bolts and detach the clutch housing from the engine. Remove the release bearing from the release lever.

On models where the gearbox and clutch housing are removed together, remove the bolts securing the housing to the gearbox then pull off the housing and detach the release bearing.

Refer to **FIG 5:3**. Loosen the clutch mounting bolts alternately and evenly until all spring pressure has been released, then remove the bolts completely. Lift off the pressure plate and driven plate, taking care not to contaminate the driven plate friction linings with grease or oil. Note, that correct clutch alignment to preserve original balance is ensured by means of locating pins provided on the flywheel. **FIG 5:4** shows the pressure plate and driven plate components.

Servicing:

The clutch cover, pressure plate and diaphragm spring assembly must not be dismantled. If any part is faulty the assembly must be renewed complete.

Inspect the surfaces of the flywheel where the driven plate makes contact. Small scratches on the surface are unimportant, but if there are deep scratches the flywheel must be machined smooth or renewed. Check the pressure plate for scoring or damage and check that the working surface is flat and true, using a metal straightedge. Make the check at several points. Check the diaphragm spring for cracks or other damage and the release bearing for roughness when it is pressed and turned by hand. Clean the release bearing by wiping with a cloth only. Do not use a solvent as this would wash the internal lubricant from the bearing. Any parts which are worn or damaged must be renewed.

Check the driven plate for loose rivets and broken or very loose torsional springs. Check the plate for distortion. Slight distortion can often be cured by installing the plate on the gearbox input shaft splines and twisting the plate by hand. If not, the plate should be renewed as distortion can cause rapid wear and operational faults. Friction linings should be well proud of the rivets and have a polished glaze through which the grain of the material is clearly visible. A dark, glazed deposit indicates oil on the linings and, as this condition cannot be rectified, a new or relined plate will be required. Any sign of oil in the clutch indicates leakage from the engine or gearbox and the cause should be traced and rectified before refitting the clutch.

It is not recommended that owners attempt to reline the clutch driven plate themselves, as the linings must be fitted and trued on the disc and the whole checked under a press. For this reason, the driven plate should be relined at a service station or an exchange unit obtained and fitted.

Note that the splines are different on later models and that a new clutch driven plate **must** match the existing gearbox input shaft splines.

5:5 Assembling and refitting clutch

When the clutch assembly is refitted to the engine flywheel it must be centralised before tightening down, using special tool 2489 or a spare gearbox input shaft, or other suitable tool, as shown in **FIG 5:5**.

Fit the alignment tool through the pressure plate and driven plate and offer the assembly to the engine flywheel. Engage the end of the tool in the pilot bearing in the flywheel and engage the clutch cover assembly on the flywheel dowels. Fit the securing bolts and tighten alternately and evenly to avoid distortion. Remove the tool from the clutch unit.

Refit the release bearing in the reverse order of removal, and refit the clutch housing to the gearbox where applicable. Refit the gearbox as described in **Chapter 6**, then reconnect the clutch cable or refit the slave cylinder and carry out adjustment procedures as described in **Section 5:2**.

5:6 Clutch hydraulic system

The layout of the clutch hydraulic system is shown in **FIG 5:6**. At regular intervals the level of fluid in the clutch master cylinder reservoir should be checked and, if necessary, fluid added to bring the level up to the mark on the side of the reservoir. Wipe dirt from around the cap before removing it and make sure that the vent hole is clear before refitting. The same fluid should be used as recommended for the braking system in **Chapter 11**.

Master cylinder:

Removal:

Note, that, on some models, it will be necessary to first remove the panel beneath the facia for access to the pushrod connection at the foot pedal. From beneath the facia, disconnect the clevis to release the pushrod from the clutch pedal (see **FIG 5:6**). From inside the engine compartment, disconnect the fluid pipe from the master cylinder, holding a suitable container beneath to collect fluid leakage. Note that brake fluid is poisonous and that it can damage paintwork. Remove the screws securing the master cylinder to the bulkhead, then remove the assembly and empty the contents of the reservoir into a waste container. All used fluid should be discarded and new fluid used to fill the system when the unit is refitted.

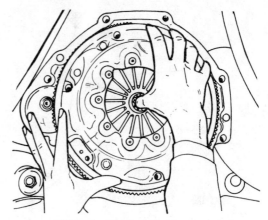

FIG 5:3   Clutch assembly removal

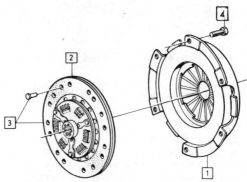

FIG 5:4   Pressure plate and driven plate

Key to Fig 5:4   1 Pressure plate assembly   2 Driven plate   3 Lining rivet   4 Retaining bolt

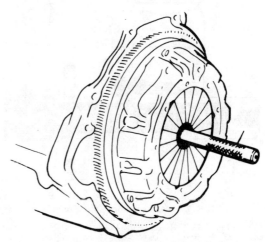

FIG 5:5   Clutch assembly alignment

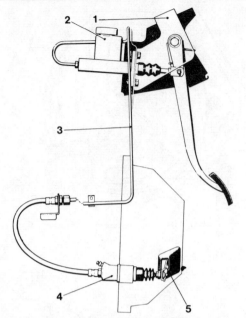

FIG 5:6 Layout of hydraulically operated clutch mechanism

Key to Fig 5:6   1 Pedal bracket   2 Master cylinder
3 Fluid pipe   4 Slave cylinder   5 Release lever

Dismantling:

Refer to **FIG 5:7**. Remove dust cover 4, circlip 3 and washer 2. Remove pushrod 5, then withdraw piston 7 and spring 9. If these components are difficult to remove, use gentle air pressure at the fluid pipe connection to force them out. Remove seals 6 and 8 from the piston.

Discard the seals and wash all remaining metal parts in methylated spirits or approved brake fluid. Use no other

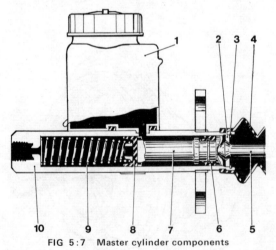

FIG 5:7   Master cylinder components

Key to Fig 5:7   1 Reservoir   2 Washer   3 Circlip   4 Dust cover   5 Pushrod   6 Outer seal   7 Piston   8 Inner seal 9 Spring   10 Master cylinder

solvent on hydraulic system components. Examine the parts and renew any found worn or damaged. Check the piston and cylinder bore for scoring, damage or corrosion and renew if any fault is found. Ensure that the inlet port from the reservoir and the outlet port to the pipe connection are clear.

Reassembly:

Observe absolute cleanliness during assembly to prevent oil or dirt from contacting the parts. Dip the piston seals in clean brake fluid before installing, making sure that the seal lips are towards the front of the cylinder. Dip all internal components in clean brake fluid and assemble them wet. Only use the fingers to enter the seals into the bore to prevent damage. Press the piston down the bore against spring pressure, then fit the pushrod washer and circlip. Refit the dust cover 4.

Installation:

Refit the master cylinder and tighten the mounting screws alternately and evenly. Refit the fluid pipe and reconnect the pushrod to the foot pedal. Operate the pedal by hand and check that there is a clearance of 1mm (0.04in) between the pushrod and master cylinder piston. If not slacken the locknut and rotate the pushrod until correct, then tighten the locknut and recheck. On completion, fill the master cylinder with fresh approved brake fluid and bleed the system as described later.

Slave cylinder:
Removal:

Raise the front of the car for access to the underside and support safely on floor stands. If the slave cylinder is to be removed only as part of a separate servicing procedure, remove the lock ring and pull the cylinder from the clutch housing, leaving the hose connected to the cylinder. Support the assembly away from the work area so that the hose is not strained. Do not touch the clutch pedal while the cylinder is detached.

If the slave cylinder is to be removed for renewal or servicing, pull apart the joint between the fluid hose and pipe, collecting fluid spillage in a suitable waste container. Disconnect the hose from the bracket. Remove the lock ring and pull the cylinder from the clutch housing.

Servicing:

This is carried out in a similar manner to that described previously for the clutch master cylinder, referring to **FIG 5:8** for component identification. On completion, check that the position of the adjusting nuts is as shown in the illustration, with a distance of 5mm (0.197in) between outer nut and end of threaded pushrod.

Installation:

Refit the slave cylinder in the reverse order of removal, reconnecting the fluid pipe if disconnected during removal. Fill the master cylinder reservoir to the correct level with fresh approved brake fluid and, if the hose was disconnected, bleed the system as described next.

Bleeding the system:

This operation is necessary to remove any air which may have entered the system due to the removal of components, or if the fluid level in the reservoir has been allowed to drop too low and air has entered through the fluid supply passage.

A need for bleeding can be indicated if the clutch drags and cannot be fully released with the pedal pushed to the floor, even though adjustment is correct as described in **Section 5:2**.

Remove the dust cap from bleed screw 1, if fitted (see **FIG 5:8**). Attach a length of rubber or plastic tubing to the bleed screw and lead the free end of the tube into a clean glass jar, into which sufficient fluid of the correct type has been added to cover the end of the tube.

Unscrew the bleed screw by about three-quarters of a turn. Have an assistant depress the clutch pedal fully to the floor, then tighten the bleed screw. Allow the pedal to return gently and wait a few seconds for the master cylinder to refill with fluid before repeating the operation. Continue this action and watch the fluid flowing into the jar. When no air bubbles can be seen, hold the pedal at the end of a downstroke and tighten the bleed screw. Replenish the fluid in the reservoir frequently during the procedure. If the level falls too low, air may be drawn into the system and the operation will have to be restarted.

On completion, top up the fluid to the correct level. It is not advisable to re-use fluid drained from the system, unless it is new and perfectly clean. If so, allow it to stand for at least 24 hours before re-use, to ensure that it is free from air bubbles. Always store the fluid in sealed containers to prevent dirt or moisture contamination.

5:7 Fault diagnosis

(a) Drag or spin

1 Oil or grease on driven plate linings
2 Misalignment between engine and splined shaft
3 Driven plate hub binding on splined shaft
4 Distorted driven plate
5 Warped or damaged pressure plate or clutch cover
6 Broken driven plate linings
7 Dirt or foreign matter in clutch
8 Air in hydraulic system
9 Clutch cable binding
10 Excessive clutch free play

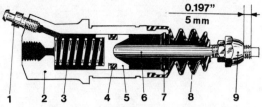

FIG 5:8   Slave cylinder components

Key to Fig 5:8   1 Bleed screw   2 Slave cylinder   3 Spring
4 Seal   5 Piston   6 Pushrod   7 Circlip   8 Dust cover
9 Adjusting nuts

(b) Fierceness or snatch

1 Check 1, 2 and 3 in (a)
2 Worn driven plate linings

(c) Slip

1 Check 1, 2, 9 and 10 in (a)
2 Worn driven plate linings
3 Weak diaphragm spring
4 Seized piston in master or slave cylinder

(d) Judder

1 Check 1 and 2 in (a)
2 Pressure plate not parallel with flywheel face
3 Contact area of driven plate linings unevenly worn
4 Bent or worn splined shaft
5 Badly worn splines in driven plate hub
6 Distorted driven plate
7 Faulty engine or gearbox mountings

(e) Rattles

1 Weak diaphragm spring
2 Check 4 and 5 in (d)
3 Broken or loose spring in driven plate
4 Worn release mechanism
5 Excessive backlash in transmission
6 Wear in transmission bearings
7 Release bearing loose on mounting

(f) Tick or knock

1 Check 4 and 5 in (d)
2 Release bearing worn or damaged
3 Loose flywheel

NOTES

CHAPTER 6
MANUAL TRANSMISSION

6:1 Description

The four-speed gearbox has synchromesh on all forward speeds and is operated by a centrally mounted remote control gearlever. On early models, either a standard M40 gearbox or M41 gearbox with overdrive is fitted. Later models are fitted with a standard M45 gearbox or M46 gearbox and overdrive. Details of the overdrive unit are given in **Section 6:6**.

Those items of maintenance and overhaul which can be carried out by a reasonably competent owner/mechanic are given in this chapter, but it is not recommended that major overhaul work be attempted. Apart from the specialised knowledge required, special tools and press equipment are needed to dismantle and reassemble gear assemblies, and special measuring equipment is required to check and set the necessary bearing preloads. For these reasons, it is recommended that any necessary gearbox overhaul procedures be carried out only by a fully equipped Volvo service station.

6:2 Routine maintenance

Regular checks on gearbox oil level and periodic changing of the gearbox oil should be carried out at the intervals specified in the manufacturer's service schedule.

The overdrive unit, where fitted, shares a common oil supply with the gearbox, so no additional procedures to those described in this section are needed to ensure correct lubrication.

Checking oil or fluid level:

For standard gearboxes, the specified lubricant is SAE 80/90 transmission oil. For early model gearboxes with overdrive, the specified lubricant is SAE 30 or SAE 20W/40 oil, but for later gearboxes with overdrive Automatic Transmission Fluid type F must be used. In the latter case, a tag marked 'ATF-oil' will be found beside the filler plug on the gearbox. **Make sure that the correct lubricant is used, according to the type of transmission fitted.**

With the car standing on level ground, remove the square-headed or socket-headed plug from the side of the gearbox, using a suitable spanner or key, as appropriate. The level of lubricant should be at the bottom of the threaded hole. If not, top up with an approved grade of oil or fluid, as specified. Allow excess lubricant to drain away fully, then refit the filler plug. No additional checking is required if overdrive is fitted, as the unit shares a common lubricant supply with the gearbox.

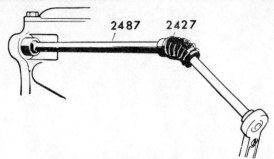

FIG 6:1 Removing transmission mounting bolts

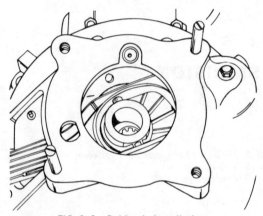

FIG 6:2 Guide pin installation

FIG 6:3 Disconnecting battery and cable connector

Changing transmission oil or fluid:

Place a suitable container beneath the gearbox, then remove the square-headed drain plug from the bottom of the case and the similar filler plug from the side of the case. Allow the old oil or fluid to drain fully, then refit the drain plug and add an approved grade of oil or fluid to the correct level as described previously. On models fitted with overdrive, recheck the level after driving the car for 8 to 16 kilometres (5 to 10 miles) and top up as necessary to compensate for the lubricant which will flow into the overdrive unit under normal operating conditions.

6:3 M40 and M41 gearbox removal and refitting

The M41 gearbox and overdrive is removed as a complete assembly, but if the overdrive is to be subsequently separated from the gearbox the car should first be driven with the overdrive engaged, then the overdrive disengaged with the clutch pedal depressed. This is important in order to avoid torsional stresses in the shaft between the overdrive planet gear carrier and one-way clutch.

If the overdrive unit alone is to be removed, this can be carried out without the need to remove the gearbox completely as described in **Section 6:6**.

Removal:

From the inside of the car, pull up the gearlever rubber gaiter then remove the securing circlip. Lift out the gearlever complete with washer and spring. Raise the vehicle for access to the underside and support safely on floor stands. Correct floor stand location is shown in **FIG 9:2** for the front of the car and in **FIG 8:6** for the rear. Drain the transmission oil as described in **Section 6:2**.

Raise a suitable jack beneath the transmission, then remove the supporting member beneath the transmission. Refer to **Chapter 8** and disconnect the propeller shaft from the transmission output flange. Disconnect the speedometer cable from the transmission, then disconnect the rear mounting exhaust pipe bracket. Fit a suitable block of wood between the rear of the engine and the engine compartment bulkhead, then lower the jack until the engine rests against the block. Disconnect the wires from the transmission and, if fitted, from the overdrive unit.

Use a suitable socket spanner with a universally jointed extension to unscrew the transmission attachment bolts, such as tools 2487 and 2427 (see **FIG 6:1**). Remove firstly the upper righthand and lower lefthand bolts, then install two guide pins 2743 or similar in the vacant holes as shown in **FIG 6:2**. Remove the remaining two fixing bolts, then support the transmission while pulling it rearwards until the imput shaft is clear of the clutch unit. Remove the transmission from beneath the car. If necessary, remove the overdrive from M41 gearbox described in **Section 6:6**.

Refitting:

This is a reversal of the removal procedure, making sure that the guide pins are correctly located as shown in **FIG 6:2**. The pins are necessary to ensure that the input shaft is correctly aligned to prevent damage to the clutch components. On completion, refill the transmission with oil as described in **Section 6:2**.

FIG 6:4 Disconnecting selector rod

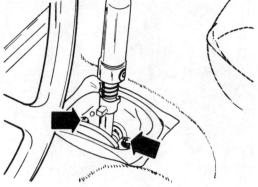

FIG 6:5 Reverse inhibitor removal

6:4 M45 and M46 gearbox removal and refitting

The M46 gearbox and overdrive is removed as a complete assembly, but if the overdrive is to be subsequently separated from the gearbox the car should first be driven with the overdrive engaged, then the overdrive disengaged with the clutch pedal depressed. This is important in order to avoid torsional stresses in the shaft between the overdrive planet gear carrier and one-way clutch. If the overdrive unit alone is to be removed, this can be carried out without the need to remove the gearbox completely, as described in **Section 6:6**.

Removal:

From inside the engine compartment, disconnect the battery earth cable and the connector for the reversing light cable (see **FIG 6:3**). Raise the vehicle for access to the underside and support safely on floor stands. Correct floor stand location is shown in **FIG 9:2** for the front of the car and in **FIG 8:6** for the rear. From beneath the car, disconnect the gearlever from the selector rod by unscrewing the lock bolt and pushing out the pivot pin (see **FIG 6:4**).

From inside the car, remove the gearlever rubber gaiter from the transmission tunnel. Refer to **FIG 6:5** and use a 4mm Allen key to remove the screws arrowed, then remove the bracket from the reverse inhibitor. Remove the circlip from the gearlever mounting, then remove the gearlever assembly.

Refer to **Chapter 5** and either disconnect the clutch cable or remove the clutch slave cylinder, according to the type of release mechanism fitted. In the latter case, leave the fluid hose connected to the cylinder and support the assembly by suitable means so that the hose is not strained. As the hydraulic circuit is not disconnected, there will be no need to bleed the clutch system when the cylinder is refitted.

Refer to **FIG 6:6** and remove the bolts arrowed to detach the front exhaust pipe attachment. Raise a suitable jack beneath the rear of the engine sump, interposing a block of wood between jack head and sump to prevent damage. Refer to **FIG 6:7** and remove the gearbox mounting crossmember. Refer to **Chapter 8** and disconnect the propeller shaft from the transmission output flange. Disconnect the speedometer cable from the transmission.

FIG 6:6 Front exhaust pipe attachment

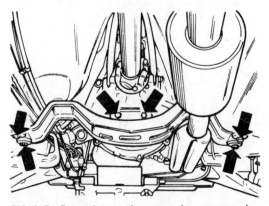

FIG 6:7 Removing gearbox mounting crossmember

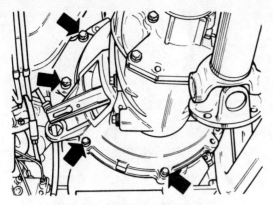

FIG 6:8 Gearbox mounting bolts

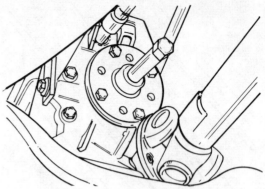

FIG 6:11 Removing flange from shaft

Refer to **FIG 6:8**. Lower the rear end of the engine for access to the gearbox mounting bolts, then remove all bolts except the upper righthand one. Remove the two bolts to release the starter motor from the bracket, then pull out the starter motor until it is free from the clutch housing.

Support the weight of the transmission with a suitable jack, in conjunction with a suitable support fixture, if available. Remove the upper righthand gearbox mounting bolt remaining, then pull the transmission rearwards until the input shaft is clear of the clutch unit, turning the gearbox as necessary to clear the transmission tunnel. Do not allow the weight of the transmission to rest on the input shaft while it is in the clutch unit, otherwise serious damage to clutch components may occur.

If necessary, remove the overdrive from M46 gearbox as described in **Section 6:6**.

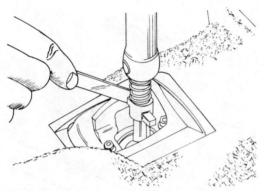

FIG 6:9 Checking reverse inhibitor bracket location

Refitting:

This is the reversal of the removal procedure. When fitting the bracket for the reverse inhibitor, engage first gear and adjust the clearance between the bracket and the gearlever as shown in **FIG 6:9**. The correct clearance, measured with a feeler gauge, is 0.5 to 1.5mm (0.020 to 0.059in). On completion, check transmission oil level as described in **Section 6:2** and clutch adjustment as described in **Chapter 5**.

6:5 M40 and M45 rear seal renewal

The gearbox rear oil seal can be renewed without the need for transmission removal.

Refer to **Chapter 8** and disconnect the propeller shaft from the transmission output flange. Counterhold the flange with tool 5149 or other suitable means, then unscrew the flange retaining nut with a 27mm socket spanner (see **FIG 6:10**). Use tool 2261 or other suitable puller to remove the flange from the shaft, as shown in **FIG 6:11**. Use extractor 5069 or other suitable means to remove the seal from the housing, as shown in **FIG 6:12**.

Make sure that the seal housing is clean, then drive a new seal squarely into position until it bottoms in the housing, using tool 5064 or other suitable driver. Fit the output flange and counterhold as before, then fit the nut and tighten to 93 to 122Nm (67 to 88lb ft). Reconnect the propeller shaft as described in **Chapter 8**, then check transmission oil level as described in **Section 7:2**.

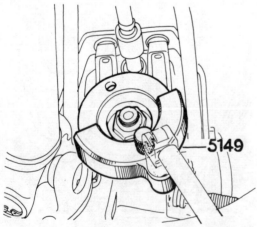

FIG 6:10 Counter holding output shaft flange

6:6 The overdrive

The overdrive unit fitted in conjunction with M41 or M46 gearboxes is mounted between the rear of the gearbox and the propeller shaft. It is bolted to an intermediate flange which is in turn bolted to the rear of the gearbox case. The unit, controlled by an electrical switch operated by the driver, provides a higher gear ratio than the normal direct-drive top gear for improved fuel economy and relaxed high speed cruising. The main internal components are the planetary gear set, one-way clutch, oil pump, hydraulic operating pistons and electrical solenoid.

When the overdrive control is switched off, the internal clutch is disengaged and the gearbox and overdrive output shafts rotate at the same speed. When the switch is turned on, the hydraulic circuit operates the clutch to engage the planetary gear set. This results in the overdrive output shaft rotating at a higher speed than the gearbox output shaft. A switch on the gearbox closes the electrical circuit to the overdrive unit only when top gear is engaged, this preventing overdrive operation in any other gear.

Due to the need for special tools and equipment to overhaul the overdrive unit and to check hydraulic system operating pressures, it is recommended that all servicing and repair work be entrusted to a fully equipped service station. If operational faults are evident, overdrive should not be engaged until checks and any necessary repairs have been carried out. **Note that, if overdrive cannot be disengaged, the car must on no account be driven in reverse or serious damage to overdrive internal components will occur.**

The overdrive unit uses a common oil supply with the gearbox, checking and topping up of the lubricant supply for the assembly being described in **Section 6:2**.

Overdrive removal and refitting:

Before overdrive removal, the car should be driven with the overdrive engaged, then the overdrive disengaged with the clutch pedal depressed. This is important in order to avoid torsional stresses in the shaft between the overdrive planetary gear carrier and one-way clutch.

Removal and refitting:

M41 transmission:

Carry out the gearbox removal instructions given in **Section 6:3**, but do not disconnect the gearbox from the clutch housing. Remove the nuts securing the overdrive unit to the intermediate flange, as shown in **FIG 6:13**. Pull the overdrive unit straight out rearwards until it is free of the gearbox output shaft. Discard the flange gasket.

Refit the overdrive in the reverse order of removal, using a new flange gasket.

M46 transmission:

Carry out the gearbox removal procedures described in **Section 6:4**, except for removal of clutch slave cylinder or cable, speedometer cable and gearbox and starter mounting bolts, so that the rear of the assembly can be lowered sufficiently to provide access for overdrive removal. When lowering the assembly, take care to

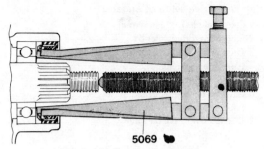

FIG 6:12   Rear seal removal

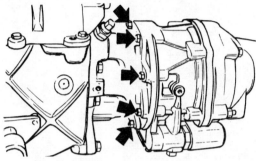

FIG 6:13   Typical overdrive installation

avoid strain on the clutch cable or hose and the speedometer cable. Remove the mounting nuts securing the overdrive unit to the intermediate flange, as shown in **FIG 6:13**. Pull the overdrive straight out rearwards until it is free of the gearbox output shaft. Discard the flange gasket.

Refit the overdrive in the reverse order of removal, using a bew flange gasket.

6:7 Fault diagnosis

(a) Jumping out of gear

1 Weak or broken detent spring
2 Worn synchromesh assemblies
3 Loose or worn selector fork
4 Excessively worn selector shafts

(b) Noisy gearbox

1 Insufficient or dirty oil
2 Laygear or bearings worn or damaged
3 Worn mainshaft bearings
4 Worn gear or synchromesh teeth
5 Excessive internal component clearances

(c) Difficulty in engaging gear

1 Clutch not releasing properly
2 Worn synchromesh assemblies
3 Worn selector shafts or forks
4 Worn gearlever mechanism

(d) Oil leaks

1 Faulty gaskets
2 Leaking oil filter or drain plug
3 Worn or damaged oil seals
4 Faulty joint faces on gearbox case components

(e) Overdrive will not engage

1 Electrical circuit fuse blown
2 Faulty overdrive solenoid
3 Fault in wiring connections
4 Faulty gearbox switch
5 Faulty overdrive selector switch
6 Low oil level in gearbox
7 Faulty non-return valve in overdrive oil pump
8 Choked overdrive oil filter

(f) Overdrive will not release

1 Fault in electrical circuit
2 Solenoid valve sticking
3 Overdrive internal components damaged
4 Sticking one-way clutch

(g) Overdrive clutch slip

1 Low oil level in gearbox
2 Solenoid valve out of adjustment
3 Worn linings on overdrive clutch

CHAPTER 7

AUTOMATIC TRANSMISSION

7:1 Description

Automatic transmission is supplied as an optional extra to take the place of the usual clutch and gearbox. The automatic transmission consists of a torque converter and hydraulically controlled automatic epicyclic gearbox with three forward speeds and one reverse. **FIG 7:1** shows a cutaway view of the automatic transmission, **FIG 7:2** shows torque converter components and fluid flow. In all gears the drive is through the torque converter which results in maximum flexibility, especially in top gear. The gears are selected automatically as the hydraulic control system engages clutches and brakes in various combinations. The hydraulic control system and the torque converter assembly are supplied with pressure fluid from a pump mounted within the transmission case. A manually controlled parking pawl is incorporated so that the transmission output shaft can be locked when the vehicle is stationary.

The torque converter consists of an impeller connected through a drive plate to the engine crankshaft, a turbine which is splined to the transmission input shaft and a stator connected to the unit by a one-way clutch. The impeller, driven by the engine, transmits torque by means of the transmission fluid to the turbine which drives the automatic gearbox. The stator redirects the flow of fluid as it leaves the turbine so that it re-enters the impeller at the most effective angle.

When the engine is idling, the converter impeller is being driven slowly and the energy of the fluid leaving it is low, so little torque is imparted to the turbine. For this reason, with the engine idling and drive engaged, the vehicle will have little or no tendency to move from rest. As the throttle is opened impeller speed increases and the process of torque multiplication begins. As the turbine picks up speed and the slip between it and the impeller reduces, torque multiplication reduces progressively until, when their speeds become substantially equal, the unit acts as a fluid coupling. In this condition, the stator is no longer required to redirect the fluid flow and the one-way clutch permits it to rotate with the impeller and turbine.

The maintenance and adjustment procedures which can be carried out by a reasonably competent owner are given in this chapter. More serious performance faults which require pressure take-off points to be opened and pressure measurements taken to diagnose faults, adjustment of the governor, partial or complete dismantling to replace worn or failed internal components dictate that the services of a fully equipped specialist should be

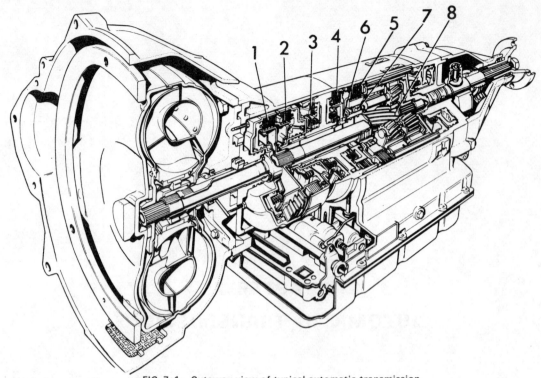

FIG 7:1   Cutaway view of typical automatic transmission

Key to Fig 7:1   1, 2 Friction clutches   3, 4, 5 Brakes   6, 7 One-way clutches   8 Planetary gear set

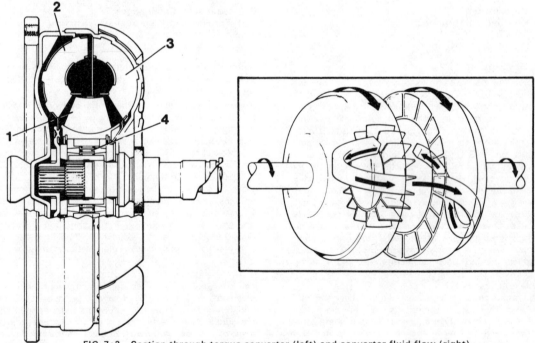

FIG 7:2   Section through torque converter (left) and converter fluid flow (right)

Key to Fig 7:2   1 Stator   2 Turbine   3 Impeller   4 One-way clutch

enlisted. Quite apart from the specialised knowledge which is required, test equipment and a large number of special tools are essential.

7:2 Routine maintenance

Routine checking of the transmission fluid level should be carried out at the intervals specified in the manufacturer's service schedule.

Checking fluid level:

The automatic transmission is designed to operate with the fluid level at the upper mark on the dipstick at normal operating temperature. This temperature will only be reached after approximately 8 to 10km (5 to 7 miles) of driving. With the transmission at operating temperature, clean the area around the dipstick and filler pipe then start the engine with the selector lever in the **P** (Park) position. Do not race the engine. Move the selector lever through all gear ranges, pausing for 5 seconds in each position, then return the lever to the **P** position. Leave the engine idling and, after a 2 minute pause, remove the transmission dipstick, wipe it clean on a lint-free cloth and refit it fully. Remove the dipstick again and check the level of fluid against the marks (see **FIG 7:3**). Top up through the dipstick pipe if necessary to bring the fluid level to mark 3 on the dipstick. Note that only approximately 0.5 litre ($\frac{7}{8}$ pints) of fluid is necessary to bring the level from the low mark 4 to the full mark 3. Add fluid slowly, checking with the dipstick after each addition. Do not overfill. Use an approved grade of Automatic Transmission Fluid, type F or Dexron. **Never use anything but the recommended fluid in the automatic transmission.**

If the vehicle cannot be driven a sufficient distance to bring the fluid up to normal operating temperature, the fluid level may be checked with the transmission cold. In this case, checking is carried out as described previously, but the engine must be allowed to idle for 2 minutes before taking a reading. The full and low marks on the dipstick for checking when the transmission is cold are shown at 1 and 2 respectively in **FIG 7:3**. Normal thermal expansion of the fluid will then bring the level to the full mark 3 when the transmission is warm.

Make sure that all containers, funnels and pipes used for adding automatic transmission fluid are perfectly clean and dry, as dirt or oil in the fluid can cause failure of transmission internal components.

Checking fluid condition:

Whenever the transmission fluid level is checked, examine the condition of the fluid adhering to the dipstick. Under normal conditions, the fluid should flow freely and the colour should not vary significantly from that of new fluid of similar type.

A grey appearance of the fluid can be caused by metallic particles, which indicates worn or damaged internal components. Black colouration of the fluid, perhaps accompanied by particles of friction material and a burnt smell, indicates a failure of internal clutch discs. Brownish fluid colouring indicates that the fluid has decomposed as a result of overheating.

If any yellow or white colouring is discernible in the fluid, it indicates that cooling water from the radiator has

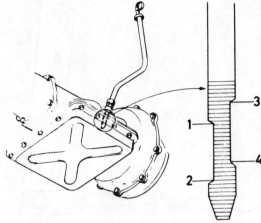

FIG 7:3 Transmission fluid dipstick markings

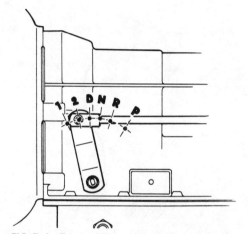

FIG 7:4 Transmission selector lever positions

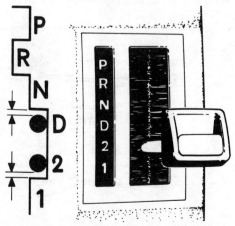

FIG 7:5 Checking linkage adjustment

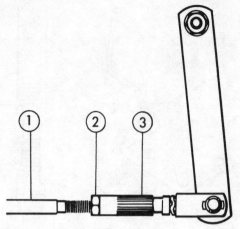

FIG 7:6   Selector linkage adjustment mechanism

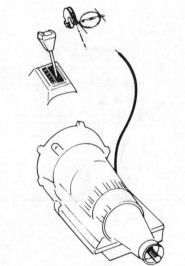

FIG 7:7   Control cable adjustment, early models

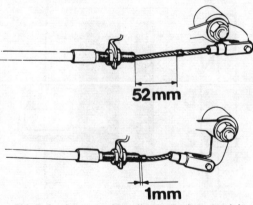

52mm

1mm

FIG 7:8   Control cable adjustment, later models

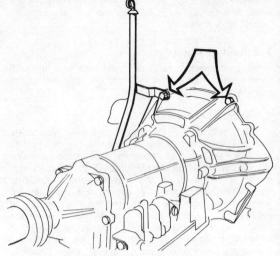

FIG 7:9   Transmission upper mounting bolts

entered the transmission fluid cooler and formed an emulsion with the fluid.

If any of the conditions described are evident, the vehicle should be taken to a fully equipped service station so that checks and any necessary remedial action can be carried out before the fault becomes more serious.

7:3 Gear selector linkages

Selector linkage adjustment:

If the selector linkage has been disconnected, first make sure that the selector lever on the transmission is in position 2 as shown in **FIG 7:4**, then place the selector lever in the car into position 2. Fit the selector rod between the two selector levers.

To check selector linkage adjustment, refer to **FIG 7:5**. Move the selector lever to position **2** and position **D** alternately, checking that the clearance between each position and the stop is approximately the same as shown by the arrows. If not, or if either position cannot be properly engaged, adjustment will be necessary. To do this, slacken the locknut shown at 2 in **FIG 7:6**. Fine adjustment should then be carried out by rotating serrated sleeve 3 as necessary. When correct, tighten locknut 2 firmly and recheck.

If a considerable amount of adjustment is required, the front or rear of the selector rod must be disconnected so that the rod can be screwed into the serrated sleeve and clevis rather than rotating the sleeve independently. When the adjustment is approximately correct, reconnect the rod and carry out fine adjustments with the sleeve only. Note that there must not be more than 28mm $(1\frac{1}{8}in)$ length of thread visible between the end of rod 1 and locknut 2.

Control cable adjustment:

Control cable adjustment procedures differ slightly between early models fitted with type BW35 transmission and later models fitted with BW55 transmission.

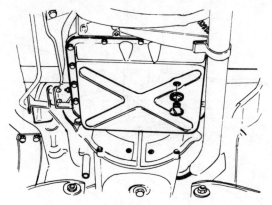

FIG 7:10   Fluid drain plug, BW35

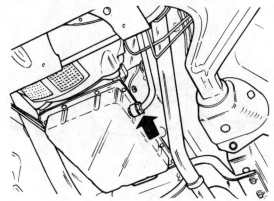

FIG 7:11   Filler pipe connection, BW55

Early models:

Refer to **FIG 7:7**. Operate the throttle control slowly until the linkage just starts to open the throttle valve, then check that the transmission control cable starts to move at the same time. If not, act on the adjustment nuts at the end of the cable outer sleeve until the correct conditions are achieved.

Later models:

Refer to **FIG 7:8**. When the throttle linkage is released, there should be a clearance of 1mm (0.039in) between the cable stop and the end of the outer sleeve. When the accelerator pedal is pressed to the floor, the clearance between cable stop and outer sleeve should be 52mm (2.05in). With the linkage held in this position, it should also be possible to pull the cable further out of the sleeve by approximately 2mm (0.08in). If any adjustment is necessary, slacken the locknuts securing the threaded outer sleeve to the bracket and turn the appropriate nut until the settings are correct. Firmly tighten the opposite nut to secure that adjustment and recheck.

If adjustments cannot be correctly carried out, or if transmission operational faults persist after adjustment, the car should be taken to a service station so that detailed checks can be made on transmission internal components.

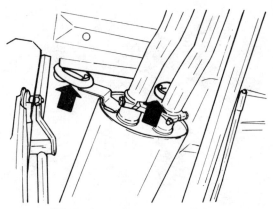

FIG 7:12   Front silencer mountings

7:4 Transmission removal and refitting

Removal:

Remove the air cleaner assembly for access, then disconnect the transmission control cable from the accelerator linkage. Disconnect the outer sleeve from the bracket so that the cable assembly can be withdrawn with the transmission. Refer to **FIG 7:9**. Remove the two upper fixing bolts arrowed, one of which retains the dipstick pipe bracket. Withdraw the dipstick from the pipe.

Raise the car for access to the underside and support safely on floor stands. On BW35 transmission, drain the fluid by removing the plug and washer shown in **FIG 7:10**. On BW55 transmission, drain the fluid by disconnecting the lower end of the filler pipe arrowed in **FIG 7:11**. In either case, the fluid should be drained into

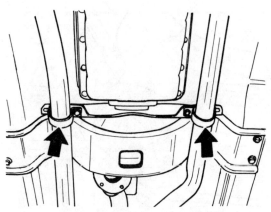

FIG 7:13   Exhaust pipe clamps

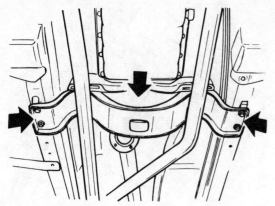

FIG 7:14 Transmission mounting crossmember

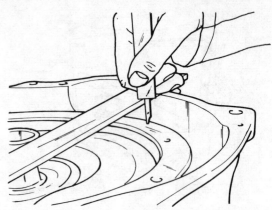

FIG 7:17 Checking torque converter installation

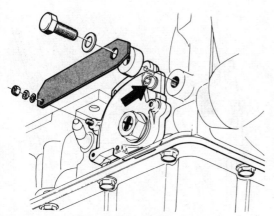

FIG 7:15 Support plate and inhibitor contact

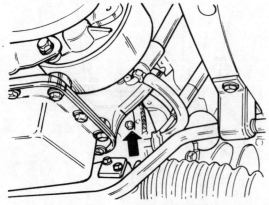

FIG 7:16 Torque converter to drive plate bolt

a suitable container, taking care to avoid scalding if the fluid is hot. It is recommended that the old fluid be discarded and new fluid used for refilling later.

Remove the filler pipe after the lower connection has been released (BW55) or remove the filler pipe after disconnecting the lower end (BW35).

Remove the eight screws and detach the guard plate from beneath the engine, if fitted. Carefully lever the rubber suspension rings from the front silencer as shown in FIG 7:12. Refer to Chapter 8 and disconnect the front end of the propeller shaft from the transmission output flange.

Remove the exhaust pipe clamps as shown in FIG 7:13, then raise a suitable jack beneath the transmission to just support its weight. Remove the rear mounting crossmember as shown in FIG 7:14. Remove the rear engine mounting and exhaust pipe bracket, then disconnect the speedometer cable from the transmission. Disconnect the two fluid cooler pipes from the transmission, plugging the ends of the pipes and the openings in the transmission for the pipes and also for the fluid filler pipe, to prevent the entry of dirt.

On early models, refer to FIG 7:15 and remove the support plate and the starter inhibitor contact which is arrowed. Detach the selector rod by disconnecting front and rear ends shown in FIGS 7:4 and 7:6. Remove the two fixing screws and detach the lower cover plate mounted between engine and transmission.

Refer to Chapter 12 and remove the starter motor. Remove the cover plate for access to the torque converter to drive plate fixing bolts, one of which is arrowed in FIG 7:16. Remove the four fixing bolts, rotating the engine with a spanner on the crankshaft pulley bolt for access to each fixing bolt in turn. Place a suitable wooden block between the rear of the engine cylinder block and the engine compartment bulkhead. This will prevent possible damage as the engine moves slightly when the transmission is lowered. Carefully lower the jack beneath the transmission until the jack head is just free, checking and if necessary disconnecting the battery lead if any strain is evident. Raise the jack again until the weight of the transmission is just supported, then remove the lower transmission to engine fixing bolts. Move the transmission rearwards to separate from the engine, carefully separating the drive plate from torque converter by levering with a suitable screwdriver. Lower the transmission and remove from beneath the car. During removal, hold the torque converter in the transmission to prevent it falling from the mounting splines.

Refitting:

This is a reversal of the removal procedure, noting the following points:

Check that the torque converter is correctly installed, by measuring between the outer rim of the converter and a straightedge placed across the mounting face as shown in **FIG 7:17**. The measurement should be between 16.20 and 19.60mm (0.64 and 0.77in). The measurement should be correct if the torque converter position has not been changed while transmission removed. If the position has been disturbed, the converter must be realigned on the splines so that it engages properly in the oil pump drive groove.

On BW55 transmission, connect the lower end of fluid filler pipe loosely to the transmission at first, tightening fully after the upper retaining bolts shown in **FIG 7:9** have been fully tightened.

On completion, check selector linkage and control cable adjustments as described in **Section 7:3**. Refill the transmission to the correct level for cold fluid as described in **Section 7:2**. The car should then be taken for a test drive and the fluid level rechecked and topped up to the correct hot setting, after the transmission cooling system and internal passages have been filled and the level of fluid properly stabilised in operation.

NOTES

CHAPTER 8

PROPELLER SHAFT, REAR AXLE
AND REAR SUSPENSION

8:1 Description

The layout of rear axle and suspension components is shown in **FIG 8:1**. Power is transmitted from the transmission output shaft to the differential unit pinion shaft by a two-piece propeller shaft, which incorporates three universal joints to accommodate suspension movement. An intermediate ballbearing is attached to the underbody by a flexible rubber mounting. Power is transmitted from the differential assembly to the rear wheels by drive shafts splined into the differential side gears.

Rear suspension is by means of coil springs and telescopic hydraulic dampers. The rear axle is positively located by means of trailing arms, reaction rods and a Panhard rod. All but 245 models are fitted with an anti-roll bar which is connected between the trailing arms on each side of the car.

The items of maintenance and overhaul which can be carried out by a reasonably competent owner/mechanic are given in this chapter, but it is not advised that any further operations be attempted. Special tools and equipment are essential to overhaul differential components and set the necessary preloads so, for this reason, the components mentioned should be dismantled and serviced only by a service station having the necessary equipment and trained fitters.

8:2 Routine maintenance

At the intervals specified in the manufacturer's service schedule, the lubricant level in the differential unit should be checked. With the car standing on level ground and the axle cold, wipe dirt from around the filler plug at the rear of the differential unit and remove the plug (see **FIG 8:2**). The correct oil level is at the lower edge of the filler hole. If necessary, top up with an approved grade of oil. Allow surplus oil to drain out before refitting the filler plug. Periodic changing of the oil in the differential unit is not required.

8:3 Propeller shaft

To overhaul universal joint assemblies it is necessary to remove the complete propeller shaft, but the centre bearing assembly can be removed after detaching the rear propeller shaft only. The front and rear propeller shafts are assembled as a matched and balanced pair, so if any part of the assembly is damaged or distorted the propeller shaft must be renewed complete. An unbalanced shaft can cause severe vibration, so care must be taken to retain the original balance of the assembly during servicing procedures. Note that an out of true shaft can also cause vibration, the maximum allowable runout at any point along the shaft being 0.25mm (0.010in). To check

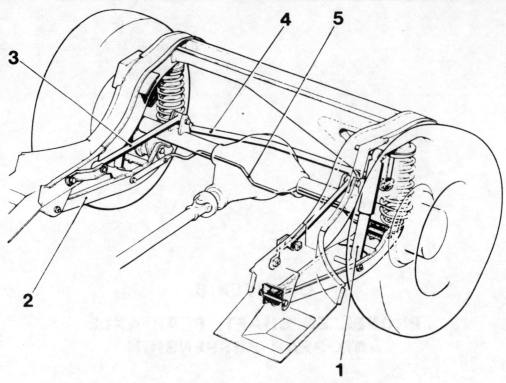

FIG 8:1 Layout of rear axle and suspension components

Key to Fig 8:1   1 Damper   2 Trailing arm   3 Reaction rod   4 Panhard rod   5 Anti-roll bar

runout, the shaft must be accurately rotated between centres and measurements taken along its entire length using a suitable dial gauge.

Removal:

Raise the car for access to the underside and support safely on floor stands. Mark the relationship of propeller shaft flanges to transmission output flange and differential pinion shaft flange, so that the components can be refitted in their original relative positions to preserve the balance of the assembly. Remove the nuts and bolts and

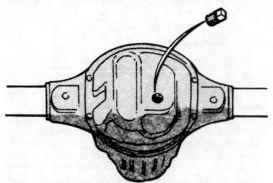

FIG 8:2 Differential oil filler and level plug

disconnect the shaft at the flanges. Lower the front and rear ends of the shaft carefully to avoid damage, then remove the centre bearing mounting, collecting the spring and washer fitted between bracket and mounting. Remove the assembly from beneath the car.

Dismantling:

FIG 8:3 shows propeller shaft components. Pull back the dust cover and release the lockwasher, then remove the nut at the centre bearing. Remove the rear propeller shaft and pull off the bearing. Remove the bearing from the housing. The centre bearing should be renewed if any roughness can be felt when it is turned by hand. Renew the rubber dust cover if damaged or deteriorated. If the propeller shaft universal joints are worn, they should be serviced as described next.

Servicing universal joints:

Repair kits for servicing universal joints are available and if a joint is worn or defective all of the parts supplied in the kit should be used. Do not renew individual parts of the joint.

Remove the four circlips that secure the bearing cups in place, using suitable circlip pliers. If difficulty is found in removing the circlips, clean the area and bore thoroughly to remove dirt and corrosion, then lightly tap the bearing cup inwards to relieve pressure from the circlip.

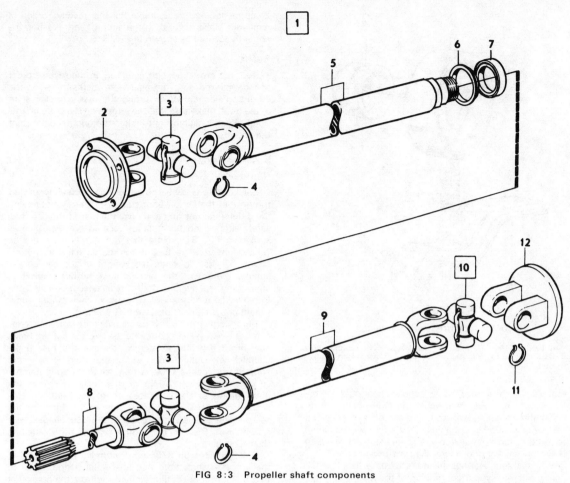

FIG 8:3 Propeller shaft components

Key to Fig 8:3   1 Front propeller shaft assembly   2 Flange and yoke   3 Universal joint   4 Circlip   5 Propeller shaft
6 Dust cover   7 Ballbearing   8 Splined shaft   9 Rear propeller shaft   10 Universal joint   11 Circlip   12 Flange and yoke

Clamp the shaft between the padded jaws of a vice, then tap the spider as far as it will go in one direction as shown in **FIG 8:4**. Now tap the spider as far as possible in the opposite direction. This will push the bearing cups out of the yokes far enough for them to be gripped with the fingers or pliers and pulled completely out. Alternatively, the cups can be driven out using a thin drift. Turn the shaft over and remove the remaining cups in a similar manner. Manoeuvre the spider out of the yoke.

If the bores in the yokes are worn, then the shaft must be renewed. Check that the bearing cups are a light drive fit through the bores.

Each bearing cup must be filled with needle rollers held in place by grease. The correct number of rollers precisely fills the cup, leaving no gaps or surplus rollers. New bearings should be half filled with grease.

Check that the seals on the spider arms are securely in place and undamaged. Fit the spider into position and push it in one direction so that the first bearing assembly can be installed in the yoke. Press this bearing into place until the circlip can be fitted, making sure that the circlip

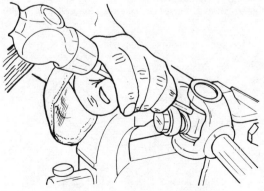

FIG 8:4 Bearing cup removal

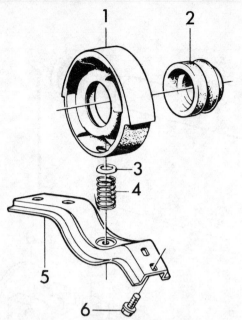

FIG 8:5 Centre bearing assembly

Key to Fig 8:5 1 Bearing rubber mounting assembly
2 Dust cover 3 Washer 4 Spring 5 Mounting bracket
6 Bolt

seats fully in the groove. Fit the opposite bearing assembly in a similar manner, then repeat the entire operation to install the remaining two bearing assemblies. If a bearing cannot be pushed into the yoke far enough for the circlip to be fitted, tap it gently down the bore using a drift which is slightly smaller in diameter than the bearing cup.

When all four bearings are in place, make sure that the joint moves freely without binding. If the joint is stiff, tap on the arms of the yokes so that the bearing cups are driven back against the circlips.

Centre bearing assembly:

The centre bearing assembly can be removed after detaching the rear propeller shaft, in the manner described previously. Check that the mounting rubber for the bearing is in good condition and that the bearing itself rotates freely without noise or binding. Renew any faulty

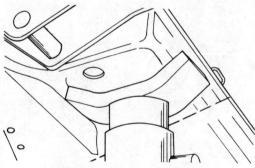

FIG 8:6 Floor stand location

components and reassemble in the reverse order of removal. Make sure that the spring and washer are correctly located as shown in **FIG 8:5**.

Refitting:

Refit the propeller shaft assembly in the reverse order of removal, indexing the alignment marks made on the mounting flanges. When fitting the rear propeller shaft to the front, make sure that the arrows on the components point towards each other to retain the original balance of the assembly.

8:4 Rear axle

Removal:

Slacken the rear wheel nuts, then raise and safely support the front of the car on floor stands. Place a jack beneath the differential housing and raise the rear of the car, then safely support on floor stands located on each side as shown in **FIG 8:6**. Note that the stands must not be placed forward of the broken line shown in the illustration. Lower the jack to settle the weight of the car on the stands, the lower the jack a little further until it is supporting the weight of the rear axle assembly only. Remove the road wheels. Disconnect the damper upper mountings on each side (see **FIG 8:7**).

Refer to **Chapter 11** for detailed instructions concerning brake system components. Disconnect the brake lines from the rear axle, then remove the rear brake calipers without disconnecting the fluid hoses and support the calipers by wiring to the upper damper supports to prevent strain on the hoses. Remove the brake drums and brake shoes, then press out the pins securing the brake cables to the levers. Remove the screws and pull out the cable and plastic hoses with rubber seals. Remove the springs retaining the cables to the rear axle.

Refer to **Section 8:3** and disconnect the rear end of the propeller shaft from the differential flange. Refer to **FIG 8:1**. Disconnect the Panhard rod from the bracket at the underbody, then disconnect the springs from the trailing arms. Lower the rear axle until the springs can be removed. Remove the screws retaining the rear axle to the trailing arms and reaction rods, then lower the axle fully and remove from beneath the car.

Removal of the drive shafts requires a slide hammer attached to the shaft flange and a special puller for renewal of the bearings and seals, this is a job for the service station and can also be carried out without removal of the rear axle assembly.

Refitting:

This is a reversal of the removal procedure, referring to **Chapter 11** for detailed instructions concerning braking system components and the final bleeding of the system which must be carried out on completion.

8:5 Rear suspension

The layout of rear suspension components is shown in **FIG 8:1**.

Damper removal:

Slacken the rear wheel nuts, then raise and safely support the rear of the car on floor stands located as

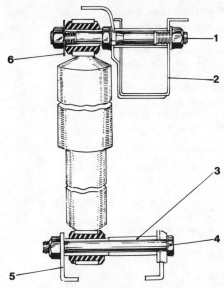

FIG 8:7 Damper installation

Key to Fig 8:7   1 Upper retaining bolt   2 Sidemember
3 Spacer sleeve   4 Lower retaining bolt   5 Trailing arm
6 Washer

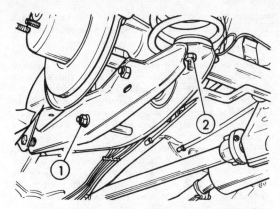

FIG 8:8 Damper and coil spring lower mountings

shown in **FIG 8:6**. Remove the road wheels. Raise a jack beneath the centre of the axle to slightly compress the coil springs and relieve the load from the dampers. Remove the upper and lower retaining nuts, then detach the damper from its mountings.

Refitting is a reversal of the removal procedure, noting the correct locations of damper components as shown in **FIG 8:7**.

Trailing arm and coil spring removal:

Slacken the rear wheel nuts, then raise the rear of the car and support safely on stands located as shown in **FIG 8:6**. Remove the wheels. Raise a jack beneath the centre of the axle to remove the load from the damper, the refer to **FIG 8:8** and remove the damper lower mounting bolt 1. Remove the coil spring lower retaining nut 2, then lower the jack until the coil spring can be removed. Remove the front and rear retaining bolts arrowed in **FIG 8:9**, then remove the trailing arm.

Examine the trailing arm for damage or distortion and renew if necessary. Check the front and rear bushes for damage or deterioration. If faults are found, new bushes should be fitted by a service station as special tools and press equipment are required.

Refitting is a reversal of the removal procedure, making sure that the spacer sleeve 3 (see **FIG 8:7**) is properly located when attaching the lower end of the damper. Check that the rubber upper spring seat is in good condition, renewing it if worn or damaged.

Reaction rod and Panhard rod:

The removal and refitting of reaction rods or the Panhard rod are straightforward operations. The car should be raised and safely supported on stands located as shown in **FIG 8:6**. If new bushes are required at any

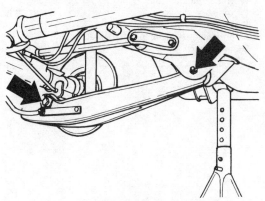

FIG 8:9 Trailing arm retaining bolts

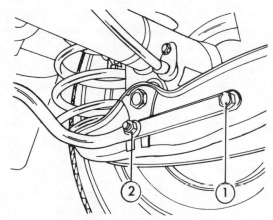

FIG 8:10 Anti-roll bar removal

location, the work should be carried out by a service station, as special tools and press equipment are needed.

Anti-roll bar removal:

Raise the rear of the car and support safely on floor stands located as shown in **FIG 8:6**. Raise a jack beneath the centre of the axle to slightly compress the coil springs and relieve the load on the dampers. Refer to **FIG 8:10** and remove the damper lower attachments 1 on each side. Remove nuts 2 on each side then detach the anti-roll bar.

When refitting, position the anti-roll bar in the brackets and install nuts 2 finger tight. Install the lower damper attachments, locating the spacer sleeve correctly as shown in **FIG 8:7**. Adjust the anti-roll bar correctly to the brackets and tighten the nuts and damper attachments fully.

8:6 Fault diagnosis

(a) Noisy axle

1 Incorrect or insufficient lubricant
2 Worn bearings
3 Worn gears
4 Damaged or broken gear teeth
5 Incorrect adjustments in differential
6 General wear

(b) Excessive backlash

1 Worn gears or bearings
2 Worn drive shaft splines
3 Worn universal joints
4 Loose wheel attachments

(c) Oil leaks

1 Defective oil seals
2 Defective gasket or distorted casing
3 Overfilled rear axle

(d) Vibration

1 Propeller shaft out of balance
2 Defective centre bearing
3 Worn universal joints

(e) Rattles

1 Worn universal joints
2 Worn suspension rubber bushings
3 Loose or worn damper mountings

(f) Knock

1 Check (a)
2 Badly worn splines on propeller or drive shaft
3 Worn universal joints

CHAPTER 9

FRONT SUSPENSION AND HUBS

9:1 Description

Independent front suspension is provided by means of MacPherson struts, controlled by lower control arms and an anti-roll bar. The layout of front suspension components is shown in **FIG 9:1**.

The suspension struts incorporate double-acting dampers and seats for the coil springs, and are integral with the steering knuckles. They are attached to the underside of the wheel arches and controlled at the lower ends by the control arms. The control arm inner mounting points are fitted with rubber bushes, the outer ends being fitted with ball joints to accommodate suspension movement. The anti-roll bar is connected to the outer ends of the control arms by means of short links and attached to the underbody with rubber bushed brackets.

The wheel hubs rotate on taper roller bearings which are adjustable to compensate for normal wear. The brake disc is bolted to the hub.

9:2 Front hubs

Checking bearing end play:

Slacken the wheel nuts, raise the front of the car and support safely on floor stands located as shown in **FIG 9:2**. Remove the road wheels. Grip the brake disc and hub by hand and press it in and out to check for axial play at the bearings. Rotate the hub and check that it spins freely without bearing noise, taking care not to confuse noise from the brake with that from a defective bearing. If end float is apparent or if roughness is noticed when the hub is turned, the bearings should be adjusted first and, if roughness is still apparent, the bearings should be dismantled for inspection.

Adjustment:

Carefully lever the grease cap from the centre of the wheel hub, then remove and discard the split pin which locks the slotted nut. Tighten the nut to a torque of 70Nm (50lb ft) while turning the disc and hub, to settle the bearings. Now slacken the nut by one-third of a turn, plus a fraction more if necessary to align the split pin hole with the slots in the nut. Without moving the nut, check that the hub rotates freely without noise or roughness, then fit and lock a new split pin. Half fill the grease cap with fresh grease, then carefully tap into place.

Removal:

Slacken the front wheel nuts, then raise the front of the car and safely support on floor stands placed beneath the

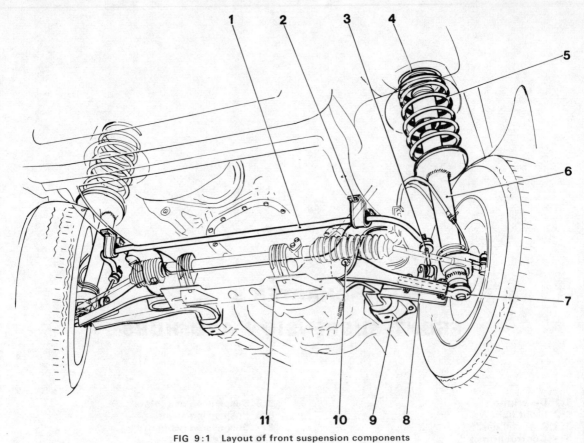

FIG 9:1 Layout of front suspension components

Key to Fig 9:1   1 Anti-roll bar   2 Bracket   3 Link   4 Strut upper mounting   5 Coil spring   6 Suspension strut assembly   7 Ball joint   8 Control arm   9 Rear bracket   10 Front bracket   11 Front axle crossmember

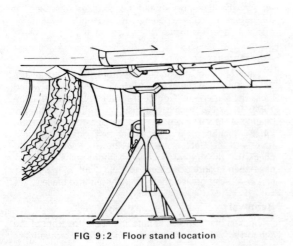

FIG 9:2 Floor stand location

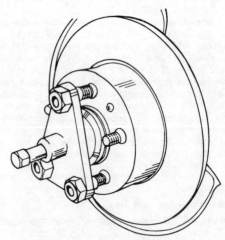

FIG 9:3 Front hub removal

lower control arms. Remove the road wheel. Refer to **Chapter 11** and remove the front brake caliper.

Carefully lever the grease cap from the centre of the wheel hub, then remove and discard the split pin and remove the slotted nut and the washer. Pull off the hub assembly, using a puller tool such as 2726 as shown in **FIG 9:3**. If the inner bearing remains in place on the stub axle when the hub is removed, carefully remove it from the axle, using a suitable puller if necessary. Discard the inner bearing grease seal. Remove the taper roller bearings from the hub.

Servicing:

Wipe the old grease from the hub and bearings, then thoroughly degrease the parts in petrol, paraffin or a similar solvent. Wash the bearing races separately by rotating them in a bowl of clean solvent. The brake disc must be thoroughly washed with solvent to remove all traces of grease or dirt.

Examine the surfaces of the stub axle on which the grease seal operates for scoring or nicks. Light damage can be smoothed over with fine grade emerycloth. Check the stub axle for hairline cracks or other damage.

Check the bearing outer races for fretting, scoring or wear. If damage is found, both bearing assemblies should be renewed complete. To remove the outer races from the hub, use special tools 2724 and 2725 in conjunction with driver 1801, if available. Alternatively, drive the races from the hub using a suitable drift, working evenly round the races to prevent jamming.

If inner and outer races appear in good condition, lubricate the taper roller bearings with light oil and press each firmly back into its outer race. Rotate the bearing to check for any roughness in operation. Dirt can be a cause of roughness, so wash the bearings again thoroughly before repeating the test. If a bearing is defective, both bearings must be completely renewed, including the outer races in the hub.

Reassembly:

If the outer races have been removed, installation should be carried out using tools 2724 and 5005 in conjunction with driver 1801, if available. Alternatively, drive the races fully and squarely into position using a suitable drift.

The wheel bearings must be lubricated with approved grease (see **FIG 9:4**). Pack the inside of the hub evenly to a depth equal to the inside diameters of the outer races. Pack the inner bearing with grease, working it well into the rollers. Install the inner bearing then press a new grease seal into the hub to retain the bearing in position, using tool 5005 in conjunction with driver 1801 as shown in **FIG 9:5**, if available. Alternatively, use a suitable tube or drift to install the seal, making sure that it seats fully and squarely.

Slide the hub assembly back onto the stub axle, taking care not to damage the seal. Pack the outer bearing fully with grease and fit into place, then fit the washer and slotted nut. Adjust the bearings as described previously.

On completion, make sure that the brake disc is completely free from grease and dirt, then refit the brake caliper as described in **Chapter 11**.

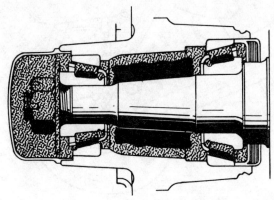

FIG 9:4   Front hub lubrication

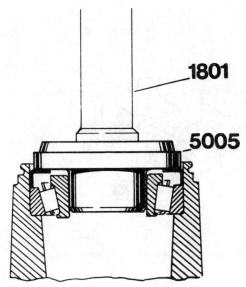

FIG 9:5   Grease seal installation

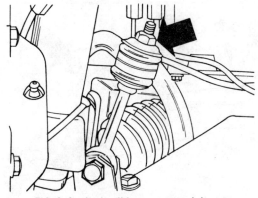

FIG 9:6   Anti-roll bar outer retaining nut

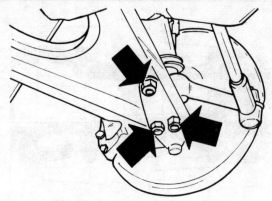

FIG 9:7 Ball joint to control arm attachments

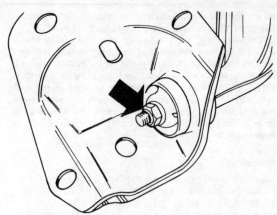

FIG 9:10 Control arm to bracket attachment

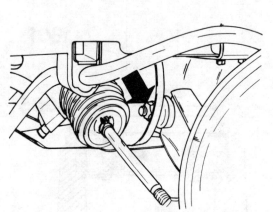

FIG 9:8 Control arm front retaining bolt

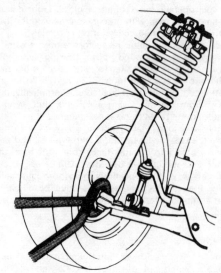

FIG 9:11 Checking suspension ball joint axial play

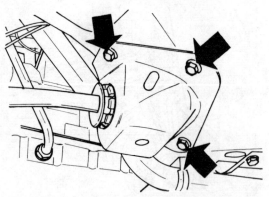

FIG 9:9 Control arm rear attachments

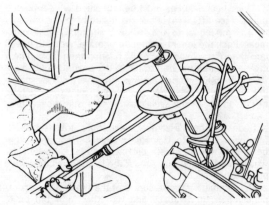

FIG 9:12 Slackening ball joint nut

9:3 Anti-roll bar

Removal:

Raise the front of the car and support safely on floor stands located as shown in **FIG 9:2**. Remove the nut arrowed in **FIG 9:6** on both sides to release the ends of the anti-roll bar from the links. Collect the rubber washers. Remove the brackets shown at 2 in **FIG 9:1** to detach the anti-roll bar from the underbody.

Refitting is the reversal of the removal procedure, after inspecting the rubber bushes and washers and renewing any found damage or deteriorated.

9:4 Control arms

Removal:

Slacken the front wheel nuts, then raise the front of the car and support safely on floor stands located as shown in **FIG 9:2**. Remove the road wheel. Disconnect the anti-roll bar from the link as shown in **FIG 9:6**.

Refer to **FIG 9:7** and disconnect the ball joint from the control arm. Remove the control arm front retaining bolt as shown in **FIG 9:8**, then remove the control arm rear attachments as shown in **FIG 9:9**. Separate the bracket from the body member and lower the control arm. Separate the bracket and the link for the anti-roll bar from the control arm.

Examine the control arm for damage or distortion and renew if any faults are found. Check the bushes in the arm and bracket for damage or deterioration. If faults are found, new brushes should be fitted by a service station, as special tools and press equipment are required.

Refitting:

This is a reversal of the removal procedure, noting the following points:

Connect the anti-roll bar link to the control arm, then fit the bracket to the control arm with the nut arrowed in **FIG 9:10** finger tight only. Install the control arm and loosely fit the bolts arrowed in **FIGS 9:8** and **9:9**. Attach the ball joint to the control arm as shown in **FIG 9:7**, then tighten the fixings to 95 to 130Nm (70 to 90lb ft). The road wheel must now be fitted and the car lowered to the ground, so that the weight rests on the wheels before finally tightening control arm fixings. Alternatively, raise the jack beneath the outer end of the control arm to compress the coil spring, but leave the floor stand in position as a safety precaution. With the suspension correctly compressed, connect the anti-roll bar to the link and tighten the mounting nut, then tighten the front retaining bolt arrowed in **FIG 9:8** to 55 to 95Nm (40 to 70lb ft), the rear bushing nut shown in **FIG 9:10** to 50 to 60Nm (36 to 43lb ft). Finally, tighten the bolts shown in **FIG 9:9** to 30 to 50Nm (22 to 36 lb ft.).

9:5 Suspension ball joints

Checking ball joint play:

To check suspension ball joint axial play, the car weight must be resting on the road wheels. Use a large adjustable wrench to grip the ball joint lower surface and upper mounting as shown in **FIG 9:11**, then compress and release the tool alternately to check free play. Maximum allowable play is 3mm (0.12in). If free play is excessive, or if the dust seal for the balljoint is damaged, the ball

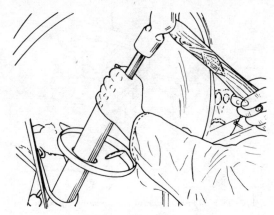

FIG 9:13   Releasing ball joint taper

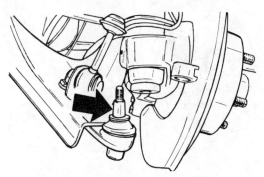

FIG 9:14   Early type ball joint installation

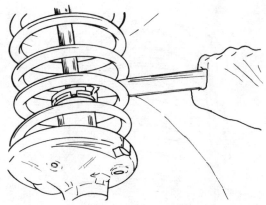

FIG 9:15   Slackening cap nut

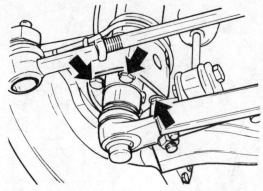

FIG 9:16 Later type ball joint mounting bolts

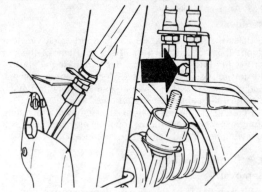

FIG 9:19 Brake line bracket bolt

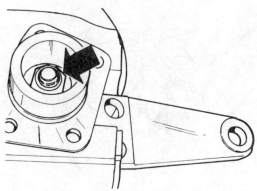

FIG 9:17 Ball joint retaining nut

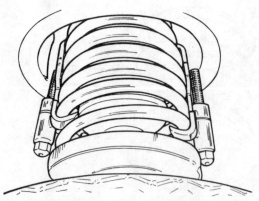

FIG 9:18 Compressor tool installation

joint must be renewed. Always renew the balljoint if the seal is damaged, as the entry of road dirt and grit causes rapid wear.

Ball joint renewal:

Early models:

Early models do not have a separate mounting for the ball joint attached to the lower end of the suspension strut, so the strut must be dismantled for access to the ball joint retaining nut.

Refer to **Section 9:6** and remove the damper unit from the suspension strut. Use a 19mm socket spanner with a long extension to turn the ball joint retaining nut as shown in **FIG 9:12**, counterholding the suspension strut with a large adjustable wrench gripping the strut at the weld. Loosen the nut by a few turns only, then solidly support the lower control arm and use a suitable drift and hammer to loosen the ball joint taper as shown in **FIG 9:13**. Now coat the inside of the socket with grease or vaseline and remove the nut completely to separate the ball joint from the strut. The coating will retain the nut in the socket so that it can be withdrawn.

Wire the suspension strut assembly to the upper mounting to prevent damage, then disconnect the ball joint from the lower control arm as shown in **FIG 9:7**.

Attach the new ball joint to the control arm, making sure that the taper arrowed in **FIG 9:14** is completely free of grease, otherwise the ball joint can be tightened too far into the mounting, causing the rubber seal to stick to the strut. Fit the ball joint into the strut, then stick the nut into the socket with grease and thread into place. Tighten to 95 to 130Nm (70 to 95lb ft). Refit the remaining components in the reverse order of removal, as described in **Section 9:6**.

Later type:

Slacken the front wheel nuts, then raise the front of the car and support safely on floor stands located as shown in **FIG 9:2**. Using tool 5039 or similar as shown in **FIG 9:15**, slacken the cap nut by a few turns. Refer to **FIG 9:16** and remove the four bolts retaining the ball joint attachment. Remove the ball joint from the control arm as shown in **FIG 9:7**.

Remove the ball joint retaining nut arrowed in **FIG 9:17**, then mount the attachment on suitable press plates

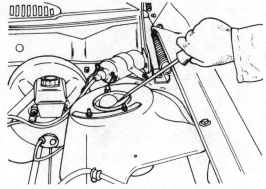

FIG 9:20 Removing upper cover

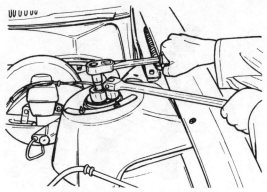

FIG 9:21 Removing central nut

and press out the ball joint. Alternatively, support the attachment securely and drive out the ball joint using a suitable drift. Take care to avoid damage to the ball joint attachment.

Fit the new ball joint to the attachment, making sure that the taper surface is completely free from grease. If not, the ball joint may seat too deeply and cause the rubber seal to stick to the suspension strut. Fit the nut and tighten to 50 to 70Nm (35 to 50lb ft). Refit the ball joint attachment to the suspension strut, tightening the fixings to 15 to 25Nm (11 to 18lb ft). Attach the ball joint assembly to the control arm, tightening to 95 to 130Nm (70 to 95lb ft). Tighten the cap nut as shown in **FIG 9:15**, then refit the road wheel and lower the car.

9:6 Suspension struts

The suspension struts can be dismantled for renewal of components without the need to disconnect the strut from the lower control arm, the method being as described in this section. However, if the suspension strut must be removed entirely, the brake caliper must be detached as described in **Chapter 11** and the suspension ball joint disconnected as described previously.

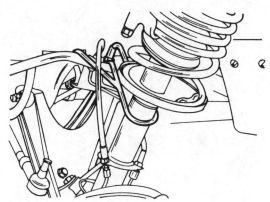

FIG 9:22 Supporting strut assembly

Dismantling:

With the weight of the car resting on the road wheels, use suitable spring compressor tools, such as 5040, to compress the spring as shown in **FIG 9:18**. The tools must be fitted to span five spring coils. This done, slacken the front wheel nuts then raise and safely support the car on floor stands located as shown in **FIG 9:2**. Place a stand, jack or other suitable support beneath the outer end of the control arm, to just support the weight of the assembly. Remove the road wheel.

Refer to **Chapter 10** and disconnect the tie rod from the steering arm. Disconnect the anti-roll bar from the link as shown in **FIG 9:6**. Remove the bolt for the brake line bracket, which is arrowed in **FIG 9:19**. Lever off the upper strut cover, using a screwdriver as shown in **FIG 9:20**. Use tools 5037 and 5036, or other suitable tools, to counterhold the suspension strut and remove the upper nut as shown in **FIG 9:21**. Hold the suspension strut while removing the support beneath the control arm, then carefully lower the strut out of the wheel arch and support

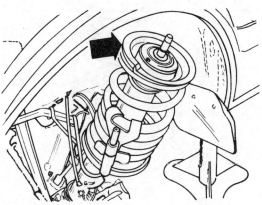

FIG 9:23 Spring seat removal

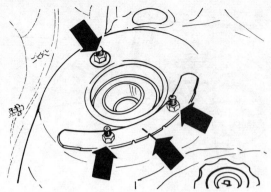

FIG 9:24 Upper spring mounting removal

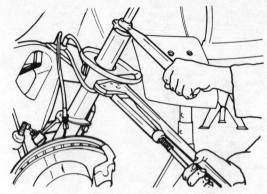

FIG 9:27 Removing damper retaining nut

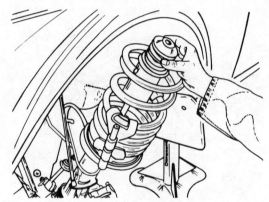

FIG 9:25 Damper protector removal

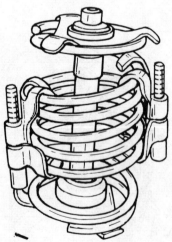

FIG 9:26 Releasing spring pressure

by wiring to the anti-roll bar or by using tool 5045 (see **FIG 9:22**). This operation must be carefully carried out to avoid damage or strain on the brake pipes and hoses. Remove the spring seat arrowed in **FIG 9:23**.

If the upper spring mounting is to be removed, carefully mark the position of the curved plate on the upper wheel arch as shown by the line arrowed in **FIG 9:24**. It is most important that the original position of the plate be retained, as this controls front wheel camber angle. Remove the three nuts shown by the remaining arrows to detach the upper mounting.

Remove the rubber bumper and damper protector as shown in **FIG 9:25**, then lift the compressed coil spring from the lower spring seat.

If the coil spring is to be renewed, the spring compressor must be released. If the type of compressor used has sufficient range of movement to allow spring pressure to be completely released before travel of the tool is complete, the tool can merely be slackened until the spring can be removed. However, if short compressor tools are used as shown in **FIG 9:18**, a second compressor tool such as 5041 must be fitted as shown in **FIG 9:26**. Tighten the second tool until the first tools can be removed, then slacken the second tool to release spring pressure completely. The new spring must be suitably compressed before installation. If the spring is not to be renewed, leave it compressed ready for installation.

To remove the damper, use tool 5039 or similar to slacken the upper damper nut as shown in **FIG 9:27**,

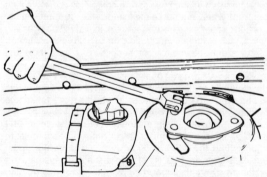

FIG 9:28 Front wheel camber adjustment

counterholding the strut assembly with a suitable large wrench, gripping the welded part of the unit, pull the damper vertically from the strut assembly.

Reassembly:

This is the reversal of the removal procedure, noting the following points:

Make sure that the compressed coil spring is fitted correctly into the lower spring seat and that the upper spring seat is correctly fitted to the top spring coil. If the upper spring mounting was removed, make sure that the curved plate is located accordingly to the marks made during removal, so that the original camber angle will be unchanged. Tighten the upper spring mounting nuts to 15 to 25Nm (11 to 18lb ft). On completion, it is recommended that the camber angle be checked.

9:7 Suspension geometry

Due to the need for special optical measuring equipment for accurate results, the checking of front wheel geometry should be carried out by a fully equipped service station.

The caster and camber angles are correctly set during production, it not being possible to adjust the caster angle. If caster is incorrect, it will be caused by damage or misalignment of front suspension components, so all parts should be checked and any found damaged or distorted renewed.

Camber angle is adjusted by rotating the strut upper mounting, after slackening the three nuts shown in **FIG 9:24**. The unit is turned with tool 5038 or similar, fitted to the threads above the nuts as shown in **FIG 9:28**. The camber angle was + 1° to + 1.5° but is changed on 1979 models to 0° to + 1°. When the camber is correct, the retaining nuts must be retightened to 15 to 25Nm (11 to 18lb ft).

9:8 Fault diagnosis

(a) Wheel wobble

1 Worn or loose hub bearings
2 Weak front springs
3 Uneven tyre wear
4 Worn suspension bushes
5 Loose wheel fixings

(b) Car pulls to one side

1 Unequal tyre pressures
2 Incorrect suspension geometry
3 Defective suspension bushes or damaged parts
4 Weak spring on one side
5 Fault in steering system

(c) Bottoming of suspension

1 Bump rubbers damaged or missing
2 Broken or weak front coil spring
3 Defective damper

(d) Excessive body roll

1 Check 2 and 3 in (c)
2 Anti-roll bar loose or defective

(e) Rattles

1 Broken front spring
2 Bump rubbers damaged or missing
3 Defective damper
4 Defective control arm or anti-roll bar bush

(f) Suspension hard

1 Tyre pressures too high
2 Suspension ball joints stiff
3 Dampers faulty

NOTES

CHAPTER 10

THE STEERING GEAR

10:1 Description

Rack and pinion steering gear is employed. The pinion shaft is turned by the lower end of the steering column shaft, through a universal joint assembly, and moves the rack to the left or right, transmitting the steering motion to the front wheels by means of the tie rods and the arms on the steering knuckles. The rack and pinion are held in mesh by a spring and piston, the spring pressure being adjustable to compensate for wear. The steering gear housing is held to the front suspension crossmember by means of U-bolts and nuts. The tie rod ends are connected to the steering arms by means of ball joint assemblies, threaded to allow for front wheel toe-in adjustment. Some models may be fitted with power assisted steering gear, in which a pump driven by a belt from the crankshaft pulley pressurises the hydraulic fluid in the system. Fluid pressure is transmitted to the rack and pinion assembly to assist the turning effort applied at the steering wheel. The power steering system is covered in **Section 10:7**.

Apart from regular checks on the general condition of the steering gear components and a check on the hydraulic fluid level for power steering gear, no routine maintenance is necessary as all components are factory lubricated. Additional lubrication will only be necessary after the steering gear has been overhauled, or if lubricant has been lost due to a damaged rubber bellows. The bellows on the steering gear and the rubber seals on the ball joints should be examined for splits, holes or other damage and parts renewed if any fault is found. At the same time, check the ball joints for excessive play. If evidence of looseness is found, or if a ball joint rubber seal is damaged, the ball joint in question must be renewed. A damaged seal will allow the entry of dirt and grit which will cause rapid wear. If excessive free play in the steering gear is evident, the assembly should be removed and adjusted as described at the end of **Section 10:5** or **10:6**, or overhauled completely if internal components are worn or damaged.

The manual steering gear may be either of cam gear or ZF manufacture, these being illustrated at A and B respectively in **FIG 10:1**.

10:2 Ball joints and tie rods

Ball joint renewal:

Raise the front of the car and support safely on floor stands located as shown in **Chapter 9, FIG 9:2**. Remove the nuts securing the outer ball joint to the steering arm,

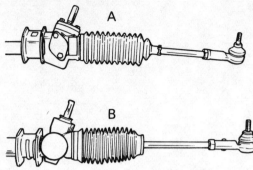

FIG 10:1 Cam gear steering assembly A and ZF assembly B

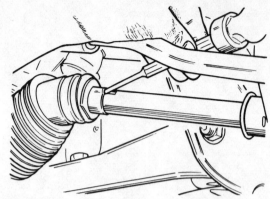

FIG 10:4 Releasing flange from locking groove, cam gear steering

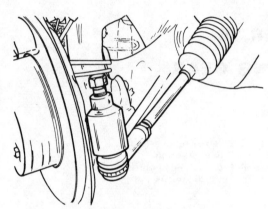

FIG 10:2 Ball joint removal

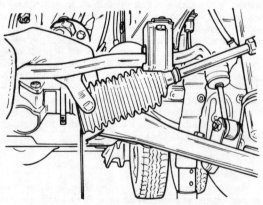

FIG 10:3 Draining cam gear steering oil

then use tool 5043 or other suitable remover tool to separate the ball joint from the arm (see **FIG 10:2**). Hold the tie rod against rotation with an 11mm spanner on the flats provided, then slacken the locknut securing the ball joint to the rod. Unscrew the ball joint from the end of the tie rod, carefully counting the number of turns taken to do so. When the new joint is fitted to the tie rod, screw it on by the same number of turns as previously counted. Tighten the locknut gently to temporarily secure the ball joint in this position, until the front wheel alignment is corrected later. Make sure that the tapered surfaces of ball joint and steering arm are clean and free from grease, then fit the ball joint and tighten the retaining nut securely. Check front wheel alignment as described in **Section 10:8**.

Tie rod and bellows removal:

Raise the front of the car and support safely on floor stands located as shown in **Chapter 9, FIG 9:2**. Disconnect the outer ball joint from the steering arm as described previously. Remove the fixing screws and detach the protective cover from beneath the engine. On cam gear steering, slacken the inner clamps for both rubber bellows and drain the steering gear oil as shown in **FIG 10:3**. This procedure is not necessary for ZF steering gear, as the unit is lubricated with grease.

On cam gear steering, use a suitable lever to prise the outer sleeve from the locking groove in the rod as shown in **FIG 10:4**. On ZF steering, use a suitable punch to bend back the lockwasher as shown in **FIG 10:5**. In all cases, use a 32mm spanner to remove the tie rod from the steering rack as shown in **FIG 10:6**.

Carefully clamp the outer ball joint in a vice, then slacken the locknut and unscrew the tie rod, carefully counting the number of turns taken to do so to allow for correct refitting. Remove the securing clamps and detach the rubber bellows from the tie rod. Renew the bellows if not in perfect condition.

Refitting:

This is a reversal of the removal procedure, carrying out the appropriate lubrication procedures as described next.

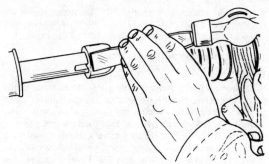

FIG 10:5 Releasing lockwasher, ZF steering

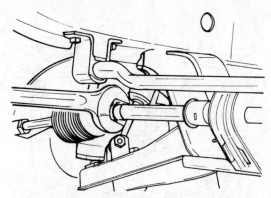

FIG 10:6 Disconnecting tie rod from steering rack

On ZF steering, before connecting the tie rod to the rack, turn the steering fully to the left for lefthand drive models, or to the right for righthand drive models, until the rack projects as far as possible from the housing. Wipe the old grease from the rack using a non-fluffy cloth, then lubricate with an approved grade of grease as described in the reassembly instructions given in **Section 10:6**. Fit a new lockwasher to the rack, making sure that the tongue engages in the rack groove, then refit and tighten the tie rod connection and lock by tapping the edge of the lockwasher over the flat provided. Before tightening the clamps to secure the rubber bellows to tie rod and housing, make sure that the ball joint is pointing upwards at the correct angle for installation to the steering arm.

On cam gear steering, attach the tie rod to the rack and tighten the connector securely, then lock by using a suitable punch to drive the flange into the groove provided. Before connecting the rubber bellows to the housing and tie rod, make sure that the ball joint is pointing upwards at the correct angle for installation to the steering arm. Fill a suitable syringe with 0.2 litre ($\frac{1}{3}$pt) (7fl oz) of SAE 20W-50 engine oil and inject this into the bellows as shown in **FIG 10:7**. Install and tighten the inner clamp. Reconnect the ball joint to the steering arm as described previously. Before lowering the car, turn the steering gently from lock to lock several times to ensure even distribution of lubricant through the steering gear assembly.

In all cases, on completion of the work, front wheel alignment must be checked and adjusted if necessary as described in **Section 10:8**.

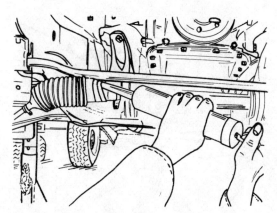

FIG 10:7 Lubricating cam gear steering

10:3 Steering column

Steering wheel removal:

Compress the steering wheel pad then unfold the upper edge to remove, as shown in **FIG 10:8**. Make sure that the steering is in the straightahead position, then remove the central retaining nut. Use tool 2263 or other suitable puller to remove the steering wheel from the column shaft (see **FIG 10:9**) Do not strike the steering wheel in an attempt to remove it, as this may damage the collapsible column assembly.

Refitting:

This is a reversal of the removal procedure. Make sure that the steering wheel spokes are horizontal and that the

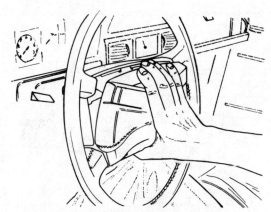

FIG 10:8 Removing steering wheel pad

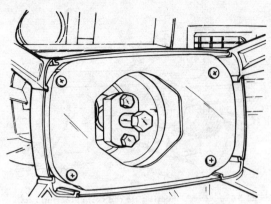

FIG 10:9 Steering wheel removal

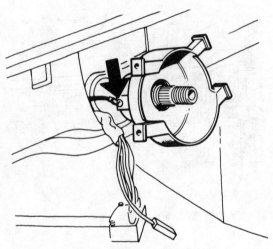

FIG 10:10 Column switch housing

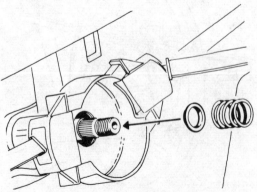

FIG 10:11 Spring and bearing race

turn signal activator is to the left. Tighten the central retaining nut to 30 to 40Nm (23 to 29lb ft). After pressing the pad into place, check the operation of the horn.

Upper steering shaft and column:

Removal:

Disconnect the battery earth cable, then remove the clamping screw for the upper steering shaft joint which is accessible from inside the engine compartment. Remove the steering wheel as described previously.

Remove the upper column covers, then remove the turn signal switch and wiper switch and disconnect the associated wiring. Refer to **FIG 10:10** and remove the switch housing, noting the earth wire connection arrowed. Remove the spring and upper bearing from the steering shaft as shown in **FIG 10:11**.

FIG 10:12 shows the location of the steering lock shearhead bolts. These bolts must be centre punched, then drilled to a suitable depth and diameter and removed with a screw extractor tool. Remove the rubber grommet for the steering column in the engine compartment rear bulkhead, then remove the steering column lower attachment. Push the steering shaft in through the bulkhead until it clears the lower part of the instrument panel, then pull the shaft back into the passenger compartment to remove. If necessary, disconnect the steering lock assembly from the column.

Refitting:

Install the steering lock assembly, if removed. Position the rubber grommet on the lower end of the column, then push the column in through the bulkhead. Position the unit beneath the dashboard, with the steering lock protruding through the hole in the panel. Attach the upper steering shaft joint and firmly tighten the bolt and nut. Install new shearhead bolts, but do not tighten as later adjustments may be required.

Install the rubber bush and clamp for the lower attachment, but do not tighten the screw fully. Install the rubber grommet in the bulkhead. Fit the switch bracket, making sure that the earth wire is correctly connected (see **FIG 10:10**).

Install the turn signal switch, wiper switch and ignition switch, then connect the horn wire. Install the race and spring for the upper bearing and refit the column covers. Check that the front wheels are in the straightahead. position and refit the steering wheel as described previously.

Turn the steering wheel in both directions and check that it rotates freely. Adjust the position of components if necessary, then tighten the lower attachment bolts fully. Check again that the steering wheel turns freely, then tighten the shearhead bolts until the heads break off. Reconnect the battery, then check the operation of horn, turn signals and wiper.

10:4 Steering gear removal and refitting

Removal:

From inside the engine compartment, remove the clamp bolt and nut arrowed in **FIG 10:13**. Use a suitable screwdriver to lever open the clamp slightly, so that the shaft will slide from the clamp easily. Raise the front of the car and support safely on floor stands located as shown in **Chapter 9, FIG 9:2**. Disconnect the outer tie rod ball joints from the steering arms as described in **Section 10:2**.

Remove the fixing screws and detach the protection cover from beneath the engine, then remove the nuts arrowed in **FIG 10:14** to disconnect the steering gear from the front axle crossmember. Carefully pull the steering gear downwards to disconnect from the universal joint assembly, then remove the gear from the car. Remove the rubber spacers and plates for the steering gear attachment points. Renew the rubber parts if worn or damaged.

Refitting:

This is a reversal of the removal procedure. On completion, front wheel alignment should be checked and if necessary adjusted as described in **Section 10:8**.

10:5 Cam gear steering overhaul

Dismantling:

Remove the steering gear as described in **Section 10:4**. Slacken the clamps and detach the inner ends of the bellows on each side and drain the oil into a suitable container. Remove the tie rods and, if necessary, the outer ball joints and rubber bellows, as described in **Section 10:2**.

Refer to **FIG 10:15**. Remove screws 17 and detach cover 18 and gasket 19. Remove spring 20, 'O' ring 21 and piston 22.

Remove screws 6 and detach cover 8 with seal 7 and gasket 9, complete with shim(s), if fitted. Lift out pinion 13 complete with spacer 10, shim(s) 11 and bearing 12. Carefull pull out rack 24 to the pinion side of the housing.

Remove the rack bush using tool 4078 or other suitable puller and slide hammer assembly (see **FIG 10:16**). Remove the lower pinion bearing, using tool 5047 or other suitable puller and slide hammer assembly.

Clean all metal parts in a suitable solvent and dry them, then inspect for wear or damage. Renew any faulty parts. Always renew the rack bush and all seals and gaskets.

Reassembly:

This is a reversal of the dismantling procedure, noting the following points:

Install the new rack bush as shown in **FIG 10:17**, using tool 2993 or similar. The bush lock must align with the slot in the housing as shown by the arrows. Lubricate all internal parts with SAE 20W-50 engine oil during the remaining assembly procedures. Install the lower bearing, using tool 5048 or other suitable driver, and make sure that the bearing seats fully. Install the pinion complete with upper bearing into the housing, but do not fit the shims at this stage. Fit the spacer sleeve into the housing, then install the pinion cover complete with gasket but without the seal.

Install a suitable dial gauge assembly so that the button rests against the end of the pinion shaft as shown in **FIG 10:18**. Move the pinion shaft up and down to check free play. A shim or shims having a total thickness equal to the measured free play must now be selected, using a suitable micrometer. This done, an additional shim must be added to increase the measured thickness by 0.1 to 0.25mm (0.004 to 0.010in) to correctly preload the pinion.

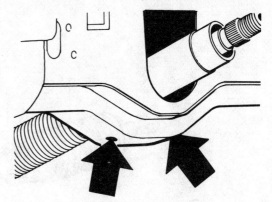

FIG 10:12   Locations of shearhead bolts

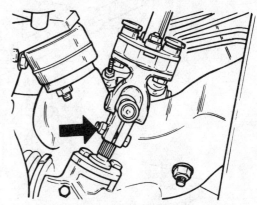

FIG 10:13   Clamp bolt location

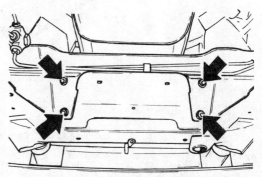

FIG 10:14   Steering gear clamp nuts

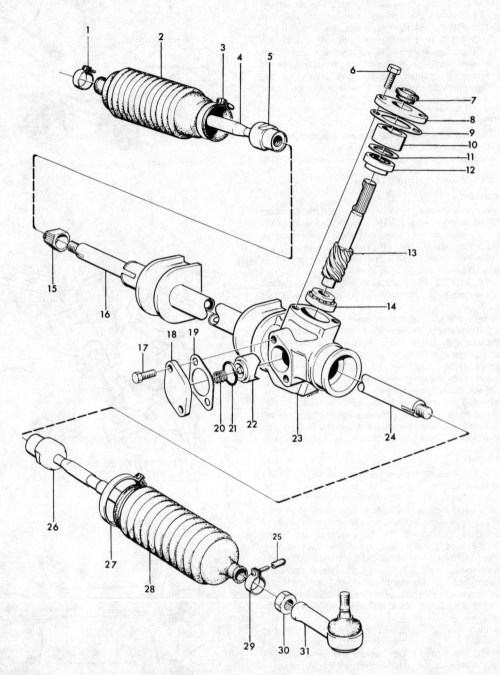

FIG 10:15   Cam gear steering components

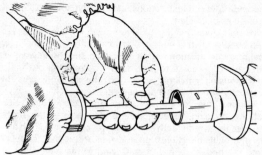

FIG 10:16 Rack bush removal

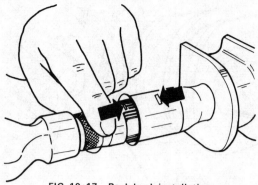

FIG 10:17 Rack bush installation

Remove the pinion cover, gasket and spacer again, then install the new seal to the pinion cover. The seal should be smeared with a non-setting gasket compound and installed with driver 2734 or other suitable tool, tapping with a soft-faced hammer until the seal is fully installed (see **FIG 10:19**).

Remove the pinion again, then install the rack from the pinion side so that the teeth do not damage the bush. Refit the pinion, together with the shims previously selected and the spacer sleeve. Install the pinion cover and gasket and tighten the fixing screws.

Install the piston in the housing without the 'O' ring and spring, then use a metal straightedge and feeler gauges to check the play between piston and housing as shown in **FIG 10:20**. Now measure the pinion cover gasket, together with any matching shims removed, using a suitable micrometer. A suitable shim or shims must be selected so that their thickness together with the gasket, equals the previously measured piston end play. A further shim 0.02 to 0.15mm (0.0008 to 0.006in) thick should be added, to provide the necessary piston preload.

Fit the spring and 'O' ring to the piston, then install the shims previously selected and the gasket and refit the cover and tighten the fixing screws. This procedure should set the steering gear preloads correctly, but checks should be made using a torque meter such as tool 5053 as shown in **FIG 10:21**. Use the tool to turn the rack from one end position to the other and check the torque required to do so, which should be 0.6 to 1.7Nm (5 to 15lb in). If outside limits, the pinion and piston setting procedures should be repeated to check that they are correct. Then, if turning torque is still incorrect, shims must be removed or added as necessary to bring the figure to within limits.

On completion, the steering gear should be lubricated as described in **Section 10:2**, noting that this can be carried out before the gear is installed, if preferred. Refit the steering gear as described in **Section 10:4** then check and if necessary adjust front wheel alignment as described in **Section 10:8**.

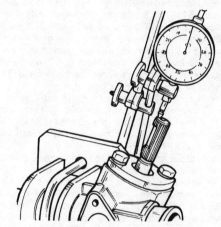

FIG 10:18 Checking pinion end play

10:6 ZF steering overhaul

Dismantling:

Remove the steering gear as described in **Section 10:4**. Remove the tie rods and, if necessary, the outer ball joints and rubber bellows, as described in **Section 10:2**.

Refer to **FIG 10:22**. Use a small screwdriver to carefully lever off dust seal 17. Straighten the legs of

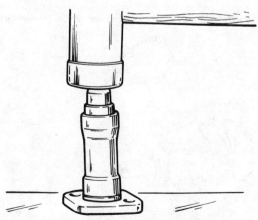

FIG 10:19 Pinion cover seal installation

FIG 10:20 Checking piston free play

splitpin 18 and remove towards the centre of the housing. Discard the splitpin and obtain a new one for use when reassembling. Remove cover 19 and spring 20, using tool 5119 or similar as shown in **FIG 10:23**. Remove the piston 22 complete with seal 21 (see **FIG 10:22**), knocking the rack with the palm of the hand to help release the components. Remove pinion dust seal 6, then carefully lever out pinion nut lock ring 7 using a small screwdriver. Remove the pinion nut 8, using 5119 or other suitable tool, remove 'O' ring 9.

Remove pinion 13 complete with thrust washer 10, circlip 11 and bearing 12. To do this, carefully clamp the end of the pinion shaft in the padded jaws of a vice and tap downwards on the housing with a soft-faced hammer (see **FIG 10:24**). Remove the rack from the pinion side of the housing. If the bearing is to be renewed, remove the thrust washer and circlip, then carefully press or drive the bearing from the pinion shaft. If necessary, remove the bearing shown at 14 in **FIG 10:22**, using a suitable puller and slide hammer assembly. Remove the rack bush from the housing by pressing in the locking tabs and levering the bush outwards.

Clean all metal parts in a suitable solvent and dry them, then inspect for wear or damage. Renew any faulty parts. Always renew all gaskets and rubber seals.

Reassembly:

This is a reversal of the dismantling procedure, noting the following points. Lubrication should be carried out

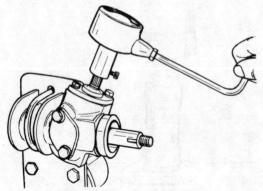

FIG 10:21 Checking pinion turning torque

according to the instructions, using Calypsol D 4024-OK grease or equivalent.

Install lower bearing 14, if removed. If the bearing was removed from the pinion shaft, carefully press the new bearing into position and fit the circlip and thrust washer. Fit new 'O' rings 16 to rack bush 15. Press the bush into the housing, making sure that the locking tabs fit correctly into the housing recesses.

Grease the rack and insert from the pinion side of the housing, taking care not to damage the bush. Grease the pinion teeth and the lower end of the shaft and fill the ballbearing with grease, then insert the assembly into the housing. Fit a new 'O' ring to the pinion nut as shown in **FIG 10:25**. Install and tighten the pinion nut, then fit lock ring 7 (see **FIG 10:22**), pressing it firmly down against the nut. Fill the cavity above the bearing with grease, then install dust cover 6.

Fit a new 'O' ring 21 to piston 22, then grease the piston and install together with spring 20. Install cover 19, but do not tighten completely. Use a suitable torque meter to check pinion turning torque, in the manner shown in **FIG 10:21** for cam gear steering. Turn the pinion shaft with the tool so that the rack traverses from one end of its travel to the other and check the reading. This should be 0.6 to 1.7Nm (5 to 15lb in). Adjust to the correct figure by turning the cover inwards to increase or outwards to decrease. When correct, lock the cover in position with a new splitpin. Install the dust cover.

The rack should be finally lubricated with Calypsol D 4024-OK grease or equivalent, after turning the pinion shaft until the rack is extended from the pinion side of the housing as far as possible (see **FIG 10:26**). If the steering gear is installed on the car, this can be done by turning the steering wheel until the rack is in the correct position for lubrication. Apply sufficient grease to fill the spaces between the teeth as shown, then turn the pinion shaft to wind the rack fully to the opposite end of its travel. Now wind the rack out again and repeat the grease application procedure. The total amount of grease required for this operation will be approximately 25g (1oz).

Refit the tie rods as described in **Section 10:2**. Install the steering gear as described in **Section 10:4**, then check and if necessary adjust front wheel alignment as described in **Section 10:8**.

10:7 Power steering

The main assemblies of the power steering gear are similar in design and operation to the cam gear unit covered previously, but an integral power unit is incorporated. The power unit is supplied with hydraulic fluid from a pressure pump mounted on the engine and belt driven from the crankshaft pulley. Those items of maintenance and overhaul which can be carried out by a reasonably competent owner/mechanic are given in this section, but it is not recommended that any further work be attempted. When the steering gear is refitted, checks on the operation of the hydraulic circuits must be carried out using special test equipment and gauges, and special tools and equipment are needed for all internal servicing operations. For these reasons, all such operations should be carried out only by a fully equipped Volvo service station.

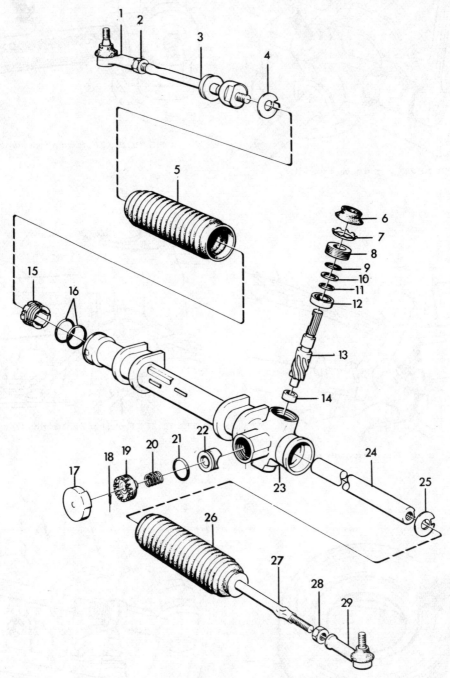

FIG 10:22   ZF steering components

Key to Fig 10:22   1 Outer ball joint   2 Locknut   3 Tie rod   4 Lockwasher   5 Bellows   6 Dust cover   7 Lock ring
8 Pinion nut   9 Seal   10 Thrust washer   11 Circlip   12 Bearing   13 Pinion   14 Bearing   15 Bush   16 'O' rings
17 Dust cover   18 Splitpin   19 Cover   20 Spring   21 Seal   22 Piston   23 Housing   24 Rack   25 Lockwasher
26 Bellows   27 Tie rod   28 Locknut   29 Outer ball joint

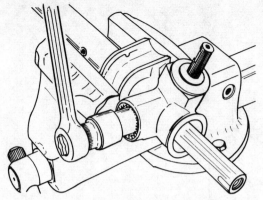

FIG 10:23 Piston cover removal

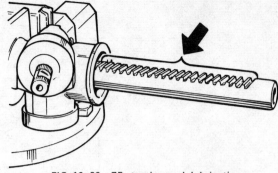

FIG 10:26 ZF steering rack lubrication

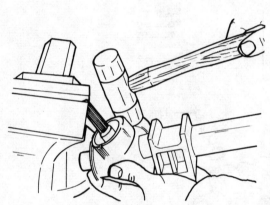

FIG 10:24 Pinion assembly removal

FIG 10:27 Typical power steering fluid reservoir

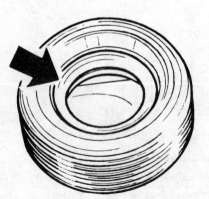

FIG 10:25 Pinion nut 'O' ring

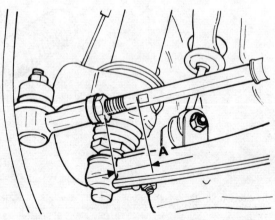

FIG 10:28 Toe-in adjustment

Ball joints and tie rods:

Servicing of the power steering gear tie rods, outer ball joints and rubber bellows, and the final lubrication of the steering gear with 20W-50 oil, should be carried out in the manner described for cam gear steering units in **Section 10:2**.

Checking system fluid level:

Refer to **FIG 10:27**. Wipe away any dirt which could fall inside, then remove the cap from the fluid reservoir. Start the engine and allow it to idle. Under these conditions, the level should be stabilised at the mark in the reservoir. If not, top up using Automatic Transmission Fluid type A, or Dexron. **Never use anything but the recommended fluid in the hydraulic system.**

If the fluid level has been allowed to drop too low and air has entered the system, it will be necessary to bleed out the air. To do this, raise the front of the car and support safely on floor stands placed beneath the lower suspension control arms. Start the engine and allow it to idle, then turn the steering wheel slowly from lock to lock several times. Continue doing this until the fluid in the reservoir is almost free from air bubbles. topping up the level in the reservoir as necessary. When the level stabilises at the mark in the reservoir, switch off the engine, refit the cap and lower the car.

Pump drive belt tensioning:

The power steering pump drive belt tension is correct when the belt can be deflected 5 to 10mm ($\frac{3}{16}$ to $\frac{3}{8}$in) with firm hand pressure at the centre of the longest run. If incorrect, slightly slacken the bolts securing the pump to the mounting bracket, swing the pump away from the engine until tension is correct, then firmly retighten the bolts. If the belt is worn or damaged, it must be renewed. To do this, slacken the pump mounting bolts as just described, swing the unit towards the engine as far as possible, then remove the belt from the pulleys. Note that it may be necessary to remove the drive belts for other units before the steering pump drive belt can be removed, as described in the appropriate instructions elsewhere in this manual. Fit the new belt, then set to the correct tension as described previously. Tension should be reset after a short period of driving, to take up the initial stretch of the new belt.

10:8 Front wheel alignment

When correctly adjusted, the front wheels will converge slightly at the front when viewed vertically from above. The amount of convergence, known as toe-in, should be 4.5 ± 1.5mm (0.177 ± 0.06in) for manual steering, or 3.0 ± 1.5mm (0.120 ± 0.06in) for power steering. Measurement is carried out as follows:

The car must be at kerb weight and the tyres inflated to the recommended pressures. Set the steering to the straightahead position and check wheel alignment with an approved track setting gauge. Push the car forward until the wheels have turned through 180° and recheck. If adjustment is required, refer to **FIG 10:28**. Slacken the locknut securing the outer ball joint to the tie rod at each side, then slacken the outer clamps for the rubber bellows at each tie rod to prevent the bellows from being twisted as the rods are turned. Rotate the tie rods equally on each side, using an 11mm spanner on the flats provided, until front wheel alignment is correct, then tighten outer ball joint locknuts and recheck. Note that the length of the tie rods must not differ by more than 2mm (0.08in), as measured between the tightened locknut and outer edge of the flat on the rod (see A in **FIG 10:28**). If necessary, readjust to bring tie rods lengths to within specifications. On completion, retighten the bellows clamps.

If the correct measuring equipment is not available, it is recommended that the work be carried out by a fully equipped service station, as incorrect settings can result in steering faults and rapid tyre wear.

10:9 Fault diagnosis

(a) Wheel wobble

1 Unbalanced wheels and tyres
2 Slack steering connections
3 Incorrect steering geometry
4 Excessive play in steering gear
5 Faulty suspension
6 Worn or loose hub bearings

(b) Wander

1 Check 2, 3 and 4 in (a)
2 Uneven tyre pressures
3 Ineffective dampers
4 Uneven tyre wear

(c) Heavy steering

1 Check 3 in (a)
2 Very low tyre pressures
3 Lack of lubrication
4 Wheels out of track
5 Steering gear adjustment incorrect
6 Inner steering shaft bent
7 Steering column bearings tight
8 Power steering fault (where fitted)

(d) Lost motion

1 Loose steering wheel connection
2 Worn rack and pinion teeth
3 Worn steering ball joints
4 Worn suspension ball joints
5 Slack pinion bearings
6 Steering gear out of adjustment

NOTES

CHAPTER 11

THE BRAKING SYSTEM

11 : 1 Description

Hydraulically operated disc brakes are fitted at all four wheels. The independent handbrake mechanism consists of brake shoe assemblies operating in drums which are integral with the rear brake discs, actuated by cable from the lever in the car.

The footbrake system has two separate circuits, the pressure generated in the master cylinder by pedal action being transmitted simultaneously but independently to each circuit. The primary circuit operates both front brakes and the righthand rear brake, the secondary circuit both front brakes and the lefthand rear brake. Thus, if the system is damaged and a brake fluid leak results, breaking power will be lost only in one rear wheel. Should this occur, very little braking power will be lost, but longer pedal travel will be noticed and, due to the operation of the pressure warning valve, a warning light on the dashboard will operate. Should failure of one of the braking circuits become apparent in this manner, the fault should be traced and rectified as soon as possible.

A vacuum servo unit to assist the pressure applied at the brake pedal is a standard fitment. Brake pressure regulating valves fitted in the hydraulic circuits reduce pressure supplied to the rear brakes according to the load on the pedal, to minimise the possibility of the rear wheels locking under heavy braking.

The master cylinder which draws fluid from the reservoir is operated from the brake pedal via the servo unit by a short pushrod and coupling. Fluid pressure from the master cylinder is conveyed to the brake units by means of brake pipes and hoses.

11 : 2 Routine maintenance

Regularly check the level of fluid in the master cylinder reservoir and replenish if necessary. Wipe dirt from around the cap before removing it and check that the vent hole in the cap is unobstructed. The fluid level should be maintained at the mark provided on the side of the reservoir. If frequent topping up is required, the system should be checked for leaks, but it should be noted that with disc brake systems the fluid level will drop gradually over a period of time due to the movement of caliper pistons compensating for friction pad wear. The recommended brake fluid is one conforming to specification SAE J.1703 or DOT 3 or 4. **Never use anything but the recommended fluid.**

At the intervals recommended in the manufacturer's service schedule, the brake fluid in the system should be

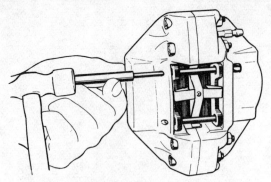

FIG 11:1 Brake pad removal, ATE caliper

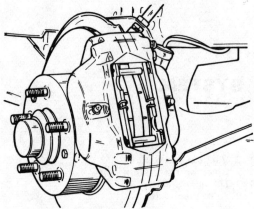

FIG 11:2 Brake pad removal, Girling caliper

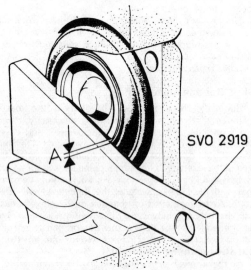

FIG 11:3 Checking piston installation, ATE caliper

completely changed. This can be carried out by opening all the bleed screws and pumping out the old fluid by operating the brake pedal. The system should then be filled with fresh brake fluid of the correct type and the brakes bled as described in **Section 11:7**. Alternatively, the work can be carried out very quickly by pressure bleeding at a service station.

Checking brake pads and linings:

Regularly check the thickness of friction lining material on front and rear brake pads. To check brake pad thickness, raise the front of the car as appropriate and remove the road wheels. Look into the caliper recess and examine the friction pads. It may be necessary to remove the pad retaining spring on some Girling caliper units to obtain a clear view of the friction linings, as described in **Section 11:3**.

If any lining is worn to a thickness of 3mm ($\frac{1}{8}$in) or if any lining is cracked or oily, all four friction pads at the front or rear brakes, whichever is the case, must be renewed. **Do not renew pads singly or on one side of the car only, as uneven braking will result.**

Under normal conditions the handbrake will only be used to lock the wheels against rotation when the car is stationary, so the linings will be subject to little or no frictional wear. For this reason, the need for handbrake lining renewal will be rare, unless the linings have become contaminated or unless incorrect adjustment has caused lining wear through brake binding. Handbrake servicing is described in **Section 11:8**.

Brake adjustment:

No adjustments are required for the service brake. The disc brakes are self-adjusting, due to the action of the operating pistons in the calipers. These pistons are returned to the rest position after each brake application by the piston seals, the seals being slightly stretched during brake application. As the friction pads wear, the piston stroke is increased and the piston will travel further than before and move through the stretched seal a little, the seal returning the piston to a new position nearer to the pad when the brakes are released. In this manner, the piston stroke remains constant regardless of the thickness of friction pads.

If handbrake lever travel is excessive, or if the handbrake will not hold the car propperly on a gradient, adjustment should be carried out as described in **Section 11:8**. If handbrake operational faults persist after adjustment, the brake units should be dismantled for examination of the shoe linings as described in the same section.

Additional maintenance:

The pedal pivots for both brake and clutch should occasionally be lubricated with grease. Wipe off excess lubricant to prevent contamination of the carpets.

Additional long-term maintenance items include renewal of the vacuum servo air filter as described in **Section 11:6**, and the complete overhaul of the brake hydraulic system. All components in the system should be dismantled, checked for wear or damage, then reassembled using new seals throughout. Both items should be carried out at the intervals recommended in the manufacturer's service schedule.

11:3 Disc brakes

Brake pad removal and installation:

Raise and safely support the front or rear of the car as appropriate. Apply the handbrake firmly when working on front brakes, or chock the front wheels against rotation when working on the rear brakes. Remove the road wheels for access to the calipers. Syphon sufficient brake fluid from the reservoir to bring the level down to the halfway mark. If this is not done, fluid may overflow when the new pads are fitted and the pistons pressed back into position. Note that brake fluid is poisonous and that it can damage paintwork. If brake pads are being removed as part of caliper servicing and are to be refitted, mark them for installation in their original positions.

For ATE calipers, use a 3mm (0.12in) diameter drift to drive out the retaining pins as shown in **FIG 11:1**. Remove the retaining spring, then pull the pads from the caliper, collecting any shims which may be fitted between the pads and the caliper pistons.

On Girling calipers, remove the spring clips then drive out the retaining pins, remove the retaining springs and pull out the pads (see **FIG 11:2**). Collect any shims or round damper washers which may be fitted between the pads and the caliper pistons.

In all cases, check that the new pads are of the correct type and that they are free from grease, oil and dirt. Clean dirt and rust from the caliper recesses before fitting the pads. To enable the new pads to be fitted, use a suitable flat wooden lever to push the four caliper pistons for front brakes, or the two caliper pistons for rear brakes, down into their bores to allow for the extra thickness of the new pads. Note that this operation will cause the level of fluid in the master cylinder reservoir to rise, this being the reason for syphoning off some of the fluid.

On ATE calipers having pistons provided with cutouts, check that the pistons are correctly located in the caliper as shown in **FIG 11:3**. The shoulders of the piston recess should incline 20° in relation to the lower face of the caliper. Check with tool 2919 or other suitable gauge. When one piston shoulder touches the angled part of the gauge, the opposite shoulder must not be less than 1mm (0.04in) away from the gauge as shown at A. If necessary, use 2918 or other suitable tool to carefully rotate the piston to the correct position.

Fit the new pads, together with any shims or damper washers removed, ensuring that the components are correctly fitted. Note that, on Girling calipers, shims must not be fitted if damper washers are used. Damper washer installation is shown in **FIG 11:4**.

On ATE calipers, fit the retaining pins and new retaining spring, driving the pins fully home. If any retaining pin is a loose fit or damaged in any way, it must be renewed. On Girling calipers, install the new retaining springs then fit the retaining pins and lock in place with new spring clips.

On completion, operate the brake pedal several times to bring the pads close to the disc. If this is not done, the brakes may not function the first time that they are used. Check that the pads are free to move slightly, this indicating that the pads are not binding against the retaining pins or caliper surfaces. Refit the road wheels and lower the car, then check and if necessary top up fluid in the reservoir as described in **Section 11:2**. Road test to check the brakes.

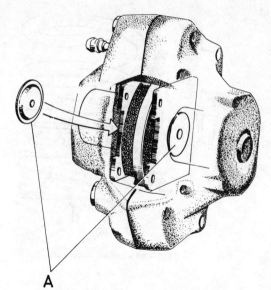

FIG 11:4   Girling damper washer installation

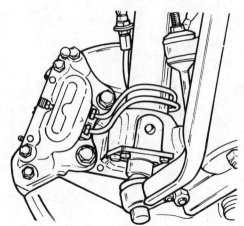

FIG 11:5   Front brake caliper installation

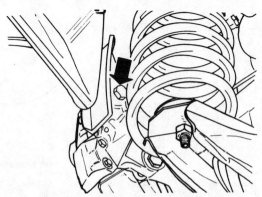

FIG 11:6   Guard plate mounting bolt

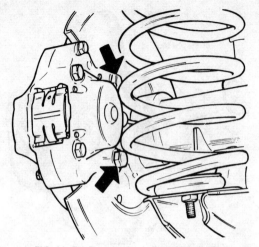

FIG 11:7   Rear brake caliper installation

Removing and refitting a caliper:

Front brake caliper:

Raise the front of the car and support safely on floor stands located as shown in **Chapter 9, FIG 9:2**. This allows the front suspension to hang free so that the brake hoses can be refitted correctly without strain. Remove the brake pads from the caliper as described previously. Refer to **FIG 11:5**. Disconnect the brake pipes from the caliper and plug the ends of the pipes to prevent fluid loss. If the caliper is being removed for attention to the brake disc or wheel bearings, the hydraulic pipes need not be disconnected. The caliper can be detached from the strut and very carefully moved aside without excessive bending of the pipes. Keep the pipes close to the strut assembly. Remove the two mounting bolts and lift off the caliper. Note that, if a brake pipe should stick in the union, it should be renewed.

Refit the caliper in the reverse order of removal, making sure that the mating surfaces of the caliper and mounting are clean. Before installing the pads, check the location of the caliper in relation to the brake disc. To do this, use feeler gauges to check the distance between the disc and the caliper support nib on each side. The difference between the measurements must not exceed 0.25mm (0.01in). Repeat the check at the opposite end of the caliper to check that it is mounted parallel to the disc. If the caliper is not correctly aligned with the disc, adjust the position using suitable shims, which are available in thicknesses of 0.2 and 0.4mm (0.008 and 0.016in). It is recommended that the brake caliper securing bolts be locked in place by the application of Loctite AV to the threads, and that new bolts are used each time the caliper is refitted.

Reconnect the brake lines then refit the brake pads as described previously. On completion, bleed the brakes as described in **Section 11:7**.

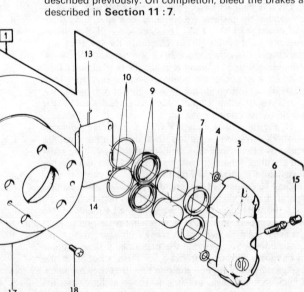

FIG 11:8   Front brake caliper components, Girling shown

Key to Fig 11:8   1 Caliper components   2 Inner caliper half   3 Outer caliper half   4 Seals   5 Bolt securing caliper halves   6 Bleed screw   7 Seals   8 Pistons   9 Dust seals   10 Retaining rings   11 Retaining pin   12 Spring clip   13 Retaining spring   14 Brake pad   15 Dust cap   16 Caliper retaining bolt   17 Brake disc   18 Screw

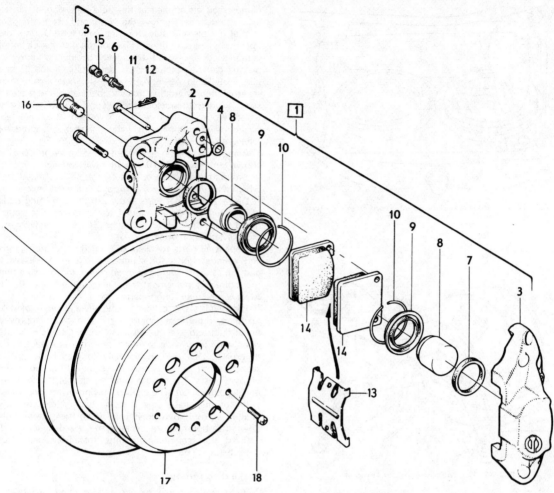

FIG 11 :9 Rear brake caliper components, Girling shown

Key to Fig 11 :9 1 Caliper components 2 Inner caliper half 3 Outer caliper half 4 Seal 5 Caliper half securing bolt
6 Bleed screw 7 Seal 8 Piston 9 Dust seal 10 Retaining ring 11 Retaining pin 12 Spring clip 13 Retaining
spring 14 Brake pad 15 Dust cap 16 Caliper retaining bolt 17 Brake disc and drum assembly 18 Screw

Rear brake caliper:

Chock the front wheels against rotation, then raise the rear of the car and support safely on floor stands placed beneath the rear axle on each side. Remove the brake pads as described previously. Release the handbrake fully.

If a guard plate is fitted as shown in **FIG 11 :6**, detach the plate after removing the bolt arrowed. Disconnect the brake pipe from the attachment at the rear axle, then remove the caliper retaining bolts arrowed in **FIG 11 :7**. Carefully remove the caliper from the mounting, then disconnect the brake pipe and plug to prevent loss of fluid. Note that, if the brake pipe should stick in the union, it should be renewed.

Refitting is a reversal of the removal procedure, making sure that the mating surfaces of caliper and mounting are clean. Check caliper alignment and lock the mounting bolts as described in the previous instructions for front

brake units. On completion, bleed the brakes as described in **Section 11 :7**.

Caliper overhaul:

Remove the caliper as described previously. Wipe grease and dirt from the outside of the caliper to avoid contamination of the internal components. Typical brake caliper components are shown in **FIG 11 :8** for front units, **FIG 11 :9** for rear units. The caliper halves are shown separated in the illustrations for clarity, but calipers must never be separated in this manner during overhaul. If any part of the caliper body is damaged, or if there is leakage from the internal seals between caliper halves, the caliper assembly should be renewed complete.

Remove retaining ring 10, if fitted, then remove dust seals 9 from the pistons. Place a suitable thin block of wood into the caliper between the pistons, then use

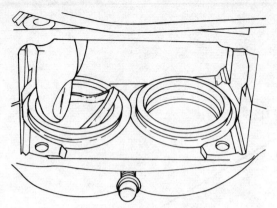

FIG 11:10   Piston seal removal, front brake shown

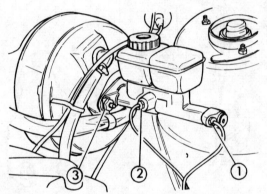

FIG 11:11   Master cylinder removal

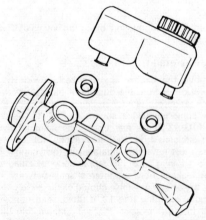

FIG 11:12   Removing reservoir and seals

compressed air applied at the fluid pipe connection to eject the pistons. Remove the wood and use the fingers to pull the pistons fully from the cylinders. During this operation, keep the fingers clear of the pistons while the compressed air is used, to prevent accidental injury, as pistons can be ejected with considerable force. If one piston sticks in position, remove the first piston then seal the open cylinder with a suitable clamp and piece of sheet rubber, then eject the second piston against a wood block as before. If any piston is completely seized in its cylinder, the caliper assembly should be renewed complete.

Remove the piston seals from the cylinder grooves, as shown in **FIG 11:10**. If removal proves difficult, use a pointed wooden or plastic tool, never a metal tool which may damage the seal groove in the cylinder.

Discard all rubber parts and wash the remaining parts in commercial alcohol, methylated spirits or clean approved brake fluid. Use no other cleaner or solvent on brake system components.

Inspect all parts for wear or damage and the pistons and cylinder bores for scoring or pitting. Renew any part found worn, damaged or corroded, making sure that the correct replacement part is obtained and fitted. Always renew all rubber parts.

Reassemble the caliper in the reverse order of dismantling, dipping all internal parts in clean approved brake fluid and assembling them wet. Observe absolute cleanliness to prevent the entry of dirt or any trace of oil or grease. Use the fingers only to install the piston seals, making sure that they are squarely located in the grooves. Install the pistons carefully so that the seals are not dislodged. On ATE calipers having pistons provided with cutouts, make sure that the pistons are correctly aligned as described previously. Push the pistons fully down their bores before installing the new dust seals and, if fitted, the seal retaining rings. Install the caliper as described previously.

Brake disc removal:

Remove the brake caliper as described previously, then remove the two attachment screws and detach the brake disc from the wheel hub assembly. If the disc sticks in position, tap it free with light blows of a soft-faced hammer. On the rear brake units, the disc is in unit with the handbrake drum, so the handbrake must be fully released to prevent the shoes from binding against the drum and preventing removal. Refit in the reverse order of removal, making sure that the mating surfaces of wheel hub and brake disc are clean and dry.

Inspect the surfaces of the brake disc where the pads make contact, checking for damage or distortion. Slight scoring of the surface is unimportant, but deep scores can reduce the braking effect and increase pad wear. Brake disc thickness should not vary by more than 0.03mm (0.0012in) between any two points. Measure at several points around the disc. Disc distortion must not exceed 0.1mm (0.004in) for front brakes, or 0.15mm (0.006in) for rear brakes. Measurements should be taken with the disc installed on the hub and rotated through a full turn, using a suitable dial guage mounted on the brake caliper with the gauge button resting against the outer circumference of the disc. Minor surface damage or distortion can be cured by resurfacing at a service station, but note

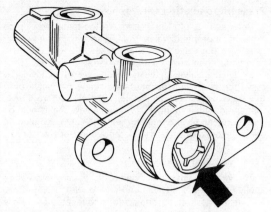

FIG 11:13 Location of retaining circlip

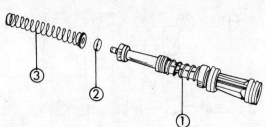

FIG 11:14 Piston assembly 1, spring seat 2 and return spring 3

that disc thickness must not be reduced by more than 1.2mm (0.05in) during this operation. If damage or distortion is too serious for this remedial treatement to be effective, or if the disc is cracked, a new brake disc should be installed.

11:4 The master cylinder

Removal:

Refer to **FIG 11:11**. Place suitable rags beneath the master cylinder to catch any fluid spillage. Note that brake fluid is poisonous and that it can damage paintwork. Disconnect brake pipes at unions 1 and 2, then remove mounting nuts 3 and detach the master cylinder assembly from the vacuum servo unit. Empty the contents of the fluid reservoir into a waste container. Do not touch the brake pedal while the master cylinder is removed, otherwise vacuum servo components may be damaged.

Refitting is a reversal of the removal procedure. On completion, refill the reservoir with new approved brake fluid and bleed the system as described in **Section 11:7**.

Overhaul:

Wipe dirt and grease from the outside of the unit to prevent contamination of internal components. Carefully pull the reservoir from the cylinder and collect the sealing rings (see **FIG 11:12**). Remove the circlip arrowed in **FIG 11:13**, then remove the piston assembly 1 (see **FIG 11:14**), spring seat 2 and return spring 3.

Discard piston 1 complete with seals, as these components must be renewed as an assembly. Wash the remaining parts thoroughly in commercial alcohol, methylated spirits or clean approved brake fluid. Use no other cleaner or solvent on brake system components. Check the return spring and spring seat and renew if damaged or distorted. If the cylinder bore shows any trace of scoring or corrosion, the master cylinder assembly should be renewed complete. Ensure that the feed and compensating ports in the cylinder body are clear by blowing through with compressed air.

Observe absolute cleanliness when reassembling to prevent the entry of dirt or any trace of oil or grease. Dip the internal components in new approved brake fluid and assemble them wet. Fit the spring seat and return spring

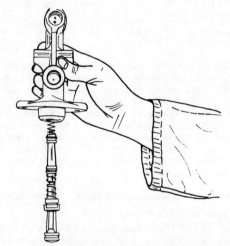

FIG 11:15 Installing master cylinder internal components

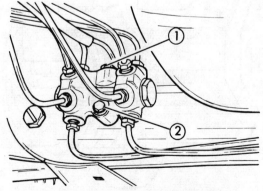

FIG 11:16 Pressure warning valve installation

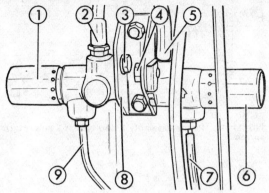

FIG 11:17 Regulating valve installation

Key to Fig 11:17   1 Lefthand circuit valve   2 Hose to lefthand rear brake   3, 4 Attachment screws   5 Hose to righthand rear brake   6 Righthand circuit valve   7 Pipe from master cylinder   8 Mounting bracket   9 Pipe from master cylinder secondary circuit

to the new piston and stand the assembly on a flat surface. Lower the master cylinder over the components, as shown in **FIG 11:15**, so that they are not displaced during the operation. Make sure that the piston seals enter the bore correctly so that they are not damaged or turned back. Press the piston into the bore slightly against spring pressure with a screwdriver, then fit the retaining circlip and release the piston. Smear the reservoir seals with clean brake fluid and fit to the master cylinder, then push the reservoir into place.

11:5 Pressure warning and regulating valves

Pressure warning valve renewal:

Refer to **FIG 11:16**. Remove screw 2 and electric wire 1. Place a suitable container beneath the valve to catch spillage of fluid, then disconnect the brake pipes from the valve.

Install the valve in the reverse order of removal. On completion, bleed the braking system as described in **Section 11:7**, then check for fluid leakage at the pipe connections to the valve while an assistant holds heavy pressure on the brake pedal.

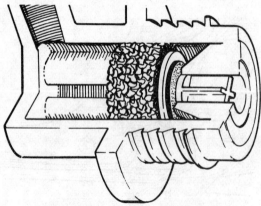

FIG 11:18 Brake servo non-return valve

Pressure regulating valve renewal:

Refer to **FIG 11:17**. Disconnect the metal brake pipe from the appropriate valve, then remove the fixing screw to release the valve from the bracket. Slacken the hose connector, then unscrew the valve from the hose.

Install the valve in the reverse order of removal. To avoid strain on the flexible hose, screw the valve onto the hose connector as far as possible before finally tightening with a spanner. Note that a new seal should be used between hose connector and valve. On completion, bleed the braking system as described in **Section 11:7**.

11:6 Vacuum servo unit

The vacuum servo unit operates to assist the pressure applied at the brake pedal and so reduce braking effort. The vacuum cylinder in the servo is connected by a hose to the vacuum pump, which operates to maintain a partial vacuum in the system. A vacuum reservoir and connection to the inlet manifold are also incorporated in the system. It is possible to overhaul the pump assembly as described later, but the servo unit itself is a sealed assembly and, if it is faulty or inoperative, must be renewed complete.

Testing:

To test the servo unit, switch off the engine and pump the brake pedal several times to clear all vacuum from the unit. Hold a steady light pressure on the brake pedal and start the engine. If the pump and servo are working properly, the brake pedal will move further down without further foot pressure, due to increasing vacuum in the system.

With the brakes off, run the engine to medium speed and turn off the ignition, immediately closing the throttle. This helps to build up a vacuum in the system. Wait one to two minutes, then try the brake action with the engine still switched off. If not vacuum assisted for two or three operations, a servo non-return valve is faulty. Three non-return valves are fitted, at the hose connections to the servo unit, inlet manifold and vacuum reservoir. Note that poor overall performance of the vacuum servo unit can be caused by a clogged air filter.

Non-return valve renewal:

With the engine switched off, depress the brake pedal several times to clear all vacuum from the servo. Refer to **FIG 11:18**. Pull the vacuum hose from the valve, then prise out the valve using two screwdrivers. Remove and discard the seal.

Fit the new seal, making sure that the flange is properly positioned in the cylinder. Coat the seal internally with the special grease supplied in the repair kit, then carefully press the new valve into place. Make sure that seal remains correctly fitted during this operation. Reconnect the vacuum hose so that its highest point is at the attachment to the valve.

Air filter renewal:

Remove the panel from beneath the dashboard for access to the rear of the servo unit. Refer to **FIG 11:19**. Pull back the rubber gaiter and remove the end cap, then pull out filter elements 11 and 12. Carefully cut the new

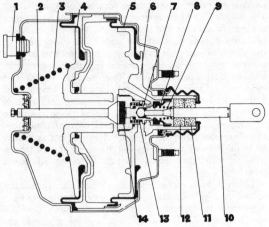

FIG 11:19 Section through vacuum servo assembly

Key to Fig 11:19   1 Non-return valve   2 Front pushrod
3 Return spring   4 Front diaphragm   5 Rear diaphragm
6 Guide housing   7 Valve piston seat   8 Seal assembly
9 Spring   10 Pedal pushrod   11, 12 Filter elements
13 Spring   14 Reaction disc

filter elements from centre to outer edge to allow for
installation over the pushrod, if not supplied in this condition. Install the elements with the cuts on opposite
sides, then install the end cap and relocate the rubber
gaiter.

Vacuum servo removal:

Remove the master cylinder as described in **Section
11:4**, then pull the vacuum hose from the servo. Refer
to **FIG 11:20**. Remove the panel from beneath the dashboard, then disconnect the pushrod from the brake
pedal. Remove the fixing nuts, then detach the servo
from the engine compartment bulkhead.

Refitting is a reversal of the removal procedure, but
note that two beads of a suitable sealing compound
should be applied to the contact surface of the servo
unit as shown by the arrow in **FIG 11:21**.

Vacuum pump overhaul:

Disconnect the hoses from the pump unit, then remove
the pump from the engine. Refer to **FIG 11:22** and

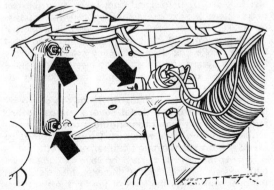

FIG 11:20 Vacuum servo removal

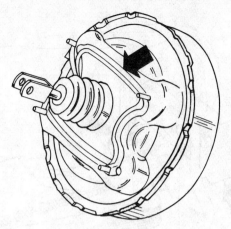

FIG 11:21 Sealant application on servo unit

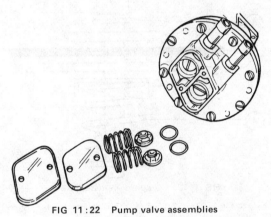

FIG 11:22 Pump valve assemblies

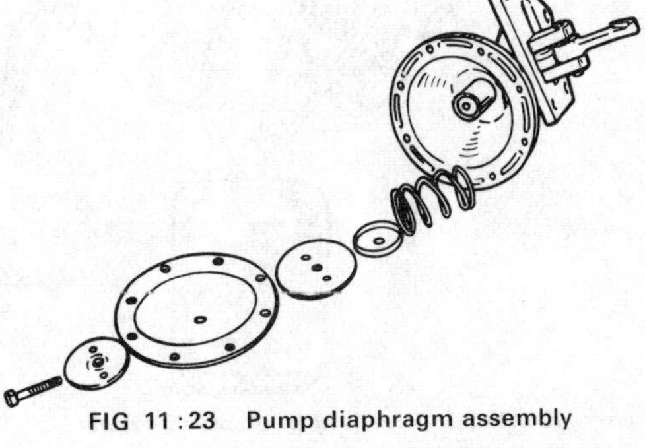

FIG 11:23 Pump diaphragm assembly

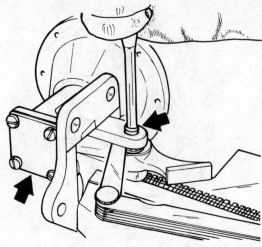

FIG 11:24   Pivot pin removal

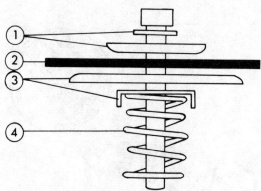

FIG 11:25   Diaphragm installation

Key to Fig 11:25   1 Washers   2 Diaphragm   3 Washers
4 Spring

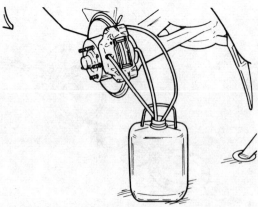

FIG 11:26   Bleeding front brake caliper

remove the cover, gasket, valve springs, valves and seals. The valves should be marked for correct refitting if they are not to be renewed, as they are installed facing in opposite directions. Mark the upper and lower parts of the pump housing so that they can be refitted in their original relative positions, then remove the fixing screws and separate the two parts. Refer to **FIG 11:23** and remove the screw, washer, diaphragm, lower washer and spring. Mount the lower part of the pump in a vice as shown in **FIG 11:24**, then insert a feeler gauge as shown to support the bearing bracket and prevent distortion. Use a suitable punch to drive out the pivot pin as shown by the righthand arrow. Renove the cover shown by the lefthand arrow, then remove the internal rod and the pump lever.

Clean all parts and examine them carefully. Inspect the valves, springs and seals for damage or distortion and the diaphragm for damage or deformation. Check that the needle bearing in the pump lever is in good condition. Renew any faulty components.

Reassemble the pump in the reverse order of dismantling, using a drop of suitable locking fluid to retain the lever pivot pin in the bearing bracket. Install the diaphragm assembly, noting the correct positions of the washers as shown in **FIG 11:25**. Fit all components to the screw, then hold the pump unit inverted while installing and tightening the screw. Fit together the pump upper and lower parts, indexing the alignment marks made previously, then fit the screws and tighten alternately and evenly. Install the valve assemblies, making sure that each is fitted the correct way up. With the hose connections facing the operator, the lefthand valve should be fitted cone side down, the righthand valve cone side up. Use a new gasket when installing the cover.

Refit the pump, making sure that the pad at the end of the lever rides on the cam in the engine. Reconnect the hoses to the pump.

11:7 Bleeding the system

This is not routine maintenance and is only necessary if air has entered the hydraulic system due to parts being dismantled, or because the level in the master cylinder supply reservoir has been allowed to drop too low. The need for bleeding is indicated by a spongy feeling at the brake pedal accompanied by poor breaking performance. The front brake nearest the master cylinder must be bled first followed by the second front brake, then the rear brake nearest the master cylinder and lastly the opposite rear brake. If a rear caliper only has been disconnected with little loss of fluid, it will usually be sufficient to bleed that rear brake unit only, but if any other part of the hydraulic system has been disconnected the entire system must be bled according to the following instructions.

Vacuum must be exhausted from the servo by depressing the brake pedal several times before starting the work and the engine must not be run whilst bleeding is carried out. Do not attempt to bleed the brakes with any caliper removed.

Remove the reservoir cap and top up to the correct level with approved brake fluid. At frequent intervals during the operation, check the level of the fluid in the reservoir and top up as needed. If the level drops too low air will enter the system and the operation will have to be restarted.

Remove the dust caps from the three bleed screws on the first front brake caliper, then fit lengths of rubber or plastic tube to the bleed screws and lead the free ends of the tubes into a clean container as shown in **FIG 11 :26**. Pour sufficient brake fluid into the container to cover the ends of the tubes.

Unscrew each bleed screw on the front caliper by approximately half a turn, pump the brake pedal steadily through five complete strokes, then tighten the bleed screws. Repeat this operation on the second front caliper. This done, connect a hose in a similar manner to the single bleed screw at the first rear brake unit. Open the bleed screw and leave open until no air bubbles can be seen in the fluid flowing into the container, then tighten the bleed screw. Repeat this operation at the second rear brake unit.

Now repeat the operation at the front brake units, this time pumping the pedal through three full strokes only. Repeat the procedure at the rear brakes, then refit the dust caps to all bleed screws. Check that all air has been bled from the system by pressing the brake pedal down with a force of about 20kg (44lb). Under this load, pedal travel must not exceed 60mm (2.36in), and the warning lamp on the dashboard must not light. If necessary, repeat the procedures described to bleed the remaining air from the system.

On completion, top up the fluid to the correct level. Discard all used fluid. Always store brake fluid in clean sealed containers to avoid air or moisture contamination.

Adjusting brake pedal position:

Brake pedal position can only be checked when all brake bleed screws in the system are opened, so the work is best carried out when changing the brake fluid as described in **Section 11 :2**. With all bleed screws open, refer to **FIG 11 :27** and check that distance A between the pedal at full stroke and the floor mat is a minimum of 5mm (0.20in), or a minimum of 15mm (0.59in) from the bulkhead plate B. From this initial position, pedal travel C should be 155 ± 10mm (6.1 ± 0.4in) for lefthand drive cars, or 160± 10mm (6.3 ± 0.4in) for righthand drive. When the pedal is released, it should be at the same height as the clutch pedal. If adjustments are necessary, slacken the pushrod locknut, disconnect the clevis at the brake pedal, then turn the clevis fork as necessary. On completion, reconnect the clevis and tighten the locknut.

Adjusting brake warning light switch:

Refer to **FIG 11 :28**. With the brake pedal fully released, distance A should be approximately 4mm (0.16in). To adjust, release the retaining screws and move the warning switch bracket as necessary. Tighten the retaining screws on completion.

11 :8 The handbrake

Adjustment:

The handbrake should hold the car firmly against movement when the lever in the car is applied by three or four notches. Always check the adjustment at ratchet first, as described later. To adjust cable remove the rear

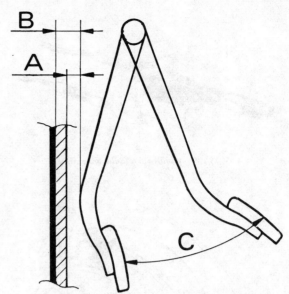
FIG 11 :27   Checking brake pedal position

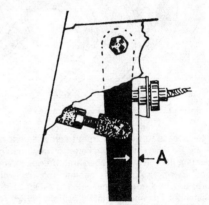
FIG 11 :28   Brake warning light switch adjustment

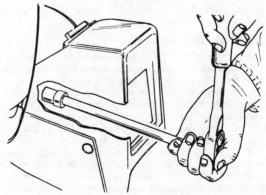
FIG 11 :29   Handbrake cable adjustment

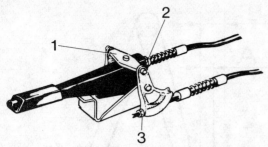

FIG 11:30   Handbrake lever assembly

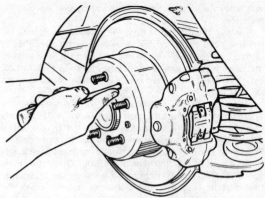

FIG 11:32   Handbrake shoe adjustment

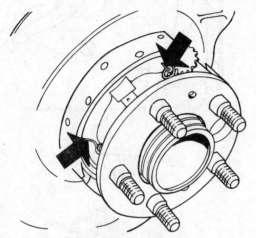

FIG 11:31   Handbrake shoe removal

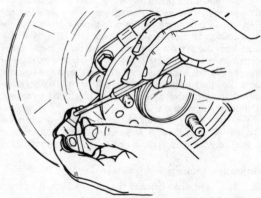

FIG 11:33   Lockpin removal

ashtray for access to the adjustment screw as shown in **FIG 11:29**. Release the handbrake lever fully, then make adjustments a little at a time, checking after each adjustment until correct. A 17mm socket spanner will be required to turn the screw. Now refer to **FIG 11:30** and check that yoke 1 is approximately at right angles to the lever. If necessary, adjust nuts 3 at each of the cables until correct, then recheck the original adjustment. If the adjustment nuts 2 or 3 are near the end of their travel, it indicates that the handbrake shoe linings are worn, so checks should be carried out after removing the drum as described next.

Handbrake shoe removal:

Remove the rear brake caliper and brake disc as described previously, but do not disconnect the brake pipe from the caliper. Instead, support the caliper by wiring to the rear suspension springs so that the brake pipe is not strained. As the pipe remains connected, it will not be necessary to bleed the systems when the caliper is refitted.

Unhook the return springs arrowed in **FIG 11:31** and remove the brake shoes and adjuster.

If the shoe linings are worn, damaged or contaminated with grease or oil, all four handbrake shoes should be renewed. If oil contamination is evident, checks should be made for oil leaks from the rear axle and any necessary repairs carried out before new shoes are installed. The

brake disc and drum assembly should be renewed if the part of the drum on which the shoes operate is badly scored, or if it is out of round by more than 0.2mm (0.008in).

Refitting:

Clean the sliding surfaces for the brake shoes on the backplate and apply a thin smear of heat resistant graphite grease to these points. Apply a small amount of similar grease to the levers and adjusters. Take care to ensure that no grease can contact the brake shoe linings or the inside of the drum. Install the brake shoes with lower return spring, then install the upper return spring and adjuster. Turn the adjuster so that the shoes are fully contacted. Install the disc and drum assembly as described previously, then turn the drum so that the hole provided is aligned with the adjuster in the brake unit.

Release the handbrake fully. Insert a screwdriver through the hole and into the adjuster teeth as shown in **FIG 11:32**. Turn the adjuster until resistance to turning can be felt, then check that the brake drum can be turned without binding. If the shoes are contacting the drum, slacken the adjuster a little at a time until the drum is just free to turn. Repeat the adjustment operation on the opposite brake unit. This done, adjust the handbrake cables as described previously. Refit the remaining components in the reverse order of removal.

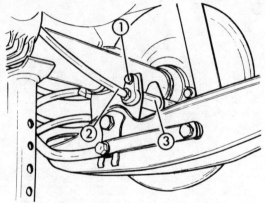

FIG 11:34   Handbrake cable removal

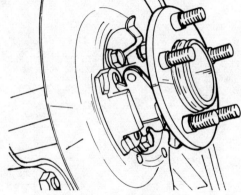

FIG 11:35   Cable lever location

Handbrake cable renewal:

Note that the cables cross over beneath the car, so that the cable connected to the righthand side of the lever operates the lefthand brake unit, and vice versa. Remove the handbrake lever cover and disconnect the wire for the ashtray light. Slacken the screw shown at 2 in **FIG 11:30** to release the cable tension. Slacken the nut 3 on the cable to be renewed, holding the end of the cable against rotation with a small screwdriver. Disconnect the cable from the lever.

Raise the front end of the rear seat cushion, then move the floor mat to the side and loosen the clamp securing the cable to the floor panel. Disconnect the sleeve and rubber grommet from the rear seat support. Remove the hand-brake shoes as described previously.

Refer to **FIG 11:33** and press out the lock pin which retains the cable in the operating lever. Refer to **FIG 11:34** and remove screw 1. Pull out cable 2 and plastic tube 3 with rubber seal. Pull the cable assembly from the centre support and floor passage. Realign the plastic tube to the bracket and install the rubber seal.

Route the new cable through the centre support and the hole in the floor, noting that the lefthand cable should be routed through the hole to the right of the propeller shaft, and vice versa. Note that, where the cables cross, the righthand wheel cable must be on top. Route the cable through the plastic tube and connect it to the bracket. Lubricate the lever pivot and the sliding surfaces for the brake shoes with a thin layer of heat resistant graphite grease. Attach the lever to the cable then push in the cable and locate the lever behind the rear axle flange (see **FIG 11:35**).

Refit the remaining components in the reverse order of removal. Connect the new cable at the handbrake lever so that the yoke shown at 1 in **FIG 11:30** is at right angles to the lever when it is applied. Release the lever fully then adjust the handbrake shoes as described previously, noting that adjustments must be carried out at both rear brakes even if only one cable has been renewed. Adjust the cables by turning the screw shown at 2 in **FIG 11:30**, as described previously.

11:9   Fault diagnosis

(a)   Spongy pedal

1 Leak in the system
2 Worn master cylinder
3 Leaking caliper cylinder
4 Air in the fluid system
5 New pads not bedded-in

(b)   Excessive pedal movement

1 Check 1 and 4 in (a)
2 Very low fluid level in reservoir
3 Brake pedal position incorrect

(c)   Brakes grab or pull to one side

1 Distorted discs
2 Wet or oily friction pads
3 Loose caliper
4 Disc or hub loose
5 Worn suspension or steering connection
6 Mixed friction pads of different grades
7 Uneven tyre pressures
8 Broken handbrake shoe return spring
9 Seized handbrake cable
10 Seized caliper piston

(d)   Brake failure

1 Empty fluid reservoir
2 Broken hydraulic pipeline
3 Ruptured master cylinder seal
4 Ruptured caliper seal

(e)   Pedal yields under continuous pressure

1 Faulty master cylinder seals
2 Faulty caliper seals
3 Leak in brake pipe or hose

NOTES

CHAPTER 12

THE ELECTRICAL SYSTEM

12:1 Description

All models covered by this manual have 12-volt electrical systems in which the negative terminal of the battery is earthed to the car bodywork.

There is a wiring diagram in **Technical Data** at the end of this manual which will enable those with electrical experience to trace and correct faults.

Instructions for servicing the items of electrical equipment are given in this chapter, but it must be pointed out that it is not sensible to try to repair units which are seriously defective, electrically or mechanically. Such faulty equipment should be replaced by new or reconditioned units.

12:2 The battery

To maintain the performance of the battery, it is essential to carry out the following operations, particularly in winter when heavy current demands must be met.

Keep the top and surrounding parts of the battery dry and clean, as dampness can cause current leakage. Clean off corrosion from the metal part of the battery mounting with diluted ammonia and coat them with anti-sulphuric paint. Clean the terminal posts and smear them with petroleum jelly, tightening the terminal clamps securely. High electrical resistance due to corrosion at the battery terminals can be responsible for a lack of sufficient current to operate the starter motor.

Regularly remove the screw caps or the cover from the battery and check the electrolyte level in each cell, topping up with distilled water if necessary to the level of the marker provided in each cell.

If a battery fault is suspected, test the condition of the cells with a hydrometer. Never add neat acid to the battery. If it is necessary to prepare new electrolyte due to loss or spillage, add sulphuric acid to distilled water. It is highly dangerous to add water to acid. It is safest to have the battery refilled with electrolyte, if it is necessary, by a service station.

The indications from the hydrometer readings of the specific gravity are as follows:

	Specific gravity
For climates below 27°C or 80°F:	
Cell fully charged	1.270 to 1.290
Cell half discharged	1.190 to 1.210
Cell discharged ..	1.110 to 1.130
For climates above 27°C or 80°F:	
Cell fully charged	1.210 to 1.230
Cell half discharged	1.130 to 1.150
Cell discharged	1.050 to 1.070

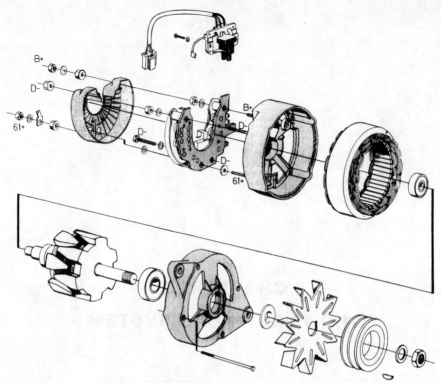

FIG 12 : 1   Components of the SEV Marchal alternator D14/70A

These figures assume electrolyte temperature of 60°F or 16°C. If the temperature of the electrolyte exceeds this, add 0.002 to the readings for each 5°F or 3°C rise. Subtract 0.002 for any corresponding drop below 60°F or 16°C.

If the battery is in a low state of charge, take the car for a long daylight run or put the battery on a charger at 5amp, with the vents in place, until it gases freely. Do not use a naked light near the battery as the gas is inflammable. If the battery is to stand unused for long periods,

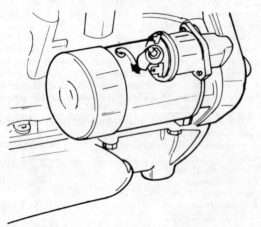

FIG 12 : 2   Starter motor installation

give a refreshing charge every month. It will be ruined if it is left uncharged.

12 : 3 The alternator

The alternator provides current for the various items of electrical equipment and to charge the battery, the unit operating at all engine speeds. The current produced is alternate, this being rectified to direct current supply by diodes mounted in the alternator casing. Alternator drive is by belt from the crankshaft pulley. Very little maintenance is needed, apart from the occasional check on belt tension as described in **Chapter 4**, **Section 4 : 3**, and on the condition and tightness of the wiring connections.

The alternator must never be run with the battery disconnected, nor must the battery cables be reversed at any time. Test connections must be carefully made, and the battery and alternator must be completely disconnected before any electric welding is carried out on any part of the car. The engine must never be started with a battery charger still connected to the battery. These warnings must be observed, otherwise extensive damage to the alternator components, particularly the diodes, will result.

The alternator is designed and constructed to give many years a trouble-free service. If a fault should develop in the unit, it should be checked and serviced by a fully equipped service station or a reconditioned unit obtained and fitted. **FIG 12 : 1** shows alternator components.

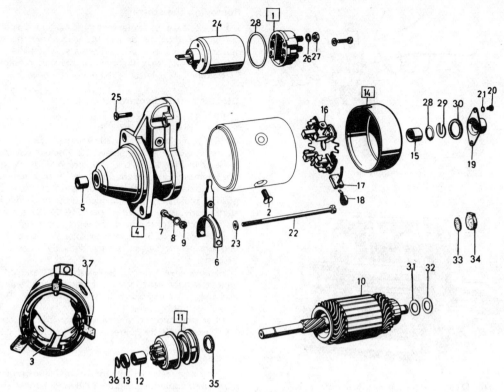

FIG 12:3   Starter motor components

Key to Fig 12:3   1 Solenoid end housing   2 Screw   3 Field coils   4 End bracket   5 Bush   6 Engagement lever
7 Bolt   8 Washer   9 Nut   10 Armature   11 Drive pinion   12 Spacer bush   13 Stop ring   14 Brush cover   15 Bush
16 Brush holder   17 Brush   18 Spring   19 End cover   20 Screw   21 Washer   22 Through bolt   23 Washer
24 Solenoid   25 Screw   26 Washer   27 Nut   28 Spacer ring   29 Lock ring   30 Seal   31, 32 Washers   33 Metal
washer   34 Rubber washer   35 Seal   36 Circlip   37 Starter body

Alternator testing:

A simple check on alternator charging can be carried out after dark by switching on the headlamps and starting the engine. If the alternator is charging, the headlamps will brighten considerably as the system voltage rises from the nominal battery voltage to the higher figure produced by the alternator.

If the alternator is not charging, check the wiring and connections in the charging circuit. If these are in order, the alternator unit is at fault and must be checked and repaired by a service station.

12:4 The starter

The starter is a brush type series wound motor with an overrunning clutch and operated by a solenoid. The armature shaft is supported in metal bushes which require no routine servicing.

When the starter is operated from the switch, the engagement lever moves the pinion into mesh with the engine ring gear. When the pinion meshes with the gear teeth, the solenoid contact closes the circuit and the starter motor operates to turn the engine. When the engine starts, the speed of the rotating ring gear causes the pinion to overrun the clutch and armature. The

pinion continues in engagement until the switch is released, when the engagement lever returns it to the rest position under spring pressure.

Tests for a starter which does not operate:

Check that the battery is in good condition and fully charged and that its connections are clean and tight. Switch on the headlamps and operate the starter switch. Current is reaching the starter if the lights dim when the starter is operated, in which case it will be necessary to remove the starter for servicing. If the lights do not dim significantly, switch them off and operate the starter switch while listening for a clicking sound at the starter motor, which will indicate that the starter solenoid is operating.

If no sound can be heard at the starter when the switch is operated, check the wiring and connections between the battery and the starter switch and between the switch and the solenoid. If the solenoid can be heard operating, check the wiring and connections between the battery and the main starter motor terminal, taking care not to accidentally earth the main battery to starter motor lead which is live at all times. If the wiring is not cause of the trouble, the fault is internal and the starter motor must be removed and serviced.

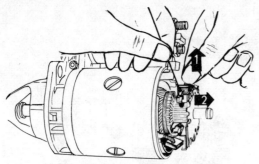

FIG 12:4   Brush holder removal

FIG 12:5   Starter motor lubrication

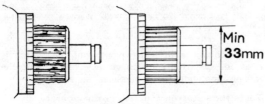

FIG 12:6   Commutator resurfacing

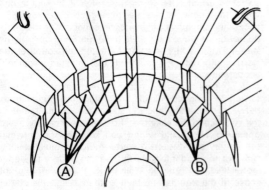

FIG 12:7   Undercutting mica insulation

Removing the starter:

FIG 12:2 shows starter motor installation. Disconnect the battery, then disconnect the leads from the starter motor terminals. Remove the bolts securing the starter motor to the housing, then remove the starter motor.

Refitting is a reversal of the removal procedure.

Starter motor dismantling:

FIG 12:3 shows the starter motor components. Remove the two screws 20 with washers 21 and detach cover 19 with seal 30. Remove lock ring 29 and spacer ring 28. Remove screws 22. Remove cover 14.

Refer to FIG 12:4. Use a suitable wire hook to raise the brushes in the direction of arrow 1, then remove the brush holder assembly in the direction of arrow 2. The positive brushes remain attached to the field coils in the starter body. Remove nut 27 (see FIG 12:3) and washer 26 to disconnect the field coil wiring from the solenoid Remove screws 25 and detach solenoid assembly from end bracket 4. Detach starter body 37 from the end bracket.

Remove steel and rubber washers 33 and 34, then remove engagement lever pivot bolt 7. Remove armature assembly 10 and lever 6 from end bracket 4. Remove pinion assembly as described later.

After servicing the internal components as described later, reassemble the starter in the following manner.

Reassembly:

This is a reversal of the dismantling procedure, lubricating components in the following manner:

Refer to FIG 12:5. Apply a thin layer of grease to the insulation washers, shaft bearing surfaces, spacer washers and lock ring shown at 1. New bushes 2 and 5 should be immersed in oil for half an hour before installation, as described later. If the original bushes are retained, they should be lubricated sparingly with oil. A generous application of grease should be applied to the armature guides and the engagement lever groove as shown at 3. Apply a thin layer of grease to the shaft bearing surfaces shown at 4. Lubricate the engagement lever pivot and the iron core of the solenoid with a thin layer of grease as shown at 6.

Care should be taken to avoid lubricant contamination of parts other than those shown in the illustration, otherwise electrical faults may develop. Take particular care to keep lubricant away from the commutator and brush gear.

Starter motor servicing:

Cleaning:

Blow away all loose dust and dirt with an airline. Use a small brush to clean out crevices. Petrol or methylated spirits may be used to help clean the metal parts, but the field coils, armature and drive pinion assembly must under no circumstances be soaked with solvent.

Brush gear:

Check the brushes for wear or contamination. Clean the brushes and holder assembly with a petrol moistened cloth and check that the brushes move freely in the holder. Brushes must be renewed if they have worn to a length of 13mm (0.52in) or less. To check brush spring pressure, fit a brush in place with the top flush with the holder. Hook a suitable spring balance to the end of the brush spring while it is bearing against the brush, then check the pressure needed to lift the spring. This should be 14 to 16N (3.1 to 3.5lb). Any spring which is weakened or distorted should be renewed.

If a brush sticks in its holder, remove it and ease the sides against a smooth file. When soldering new brushes into position, hold the connecting wire with a pair of flat-nosed pliers to prevent solder from flowing down the wire, which would render the brush unserviceable.

The commutator:

The commutator on which the carbon brushes operate should have a smooth polished surface which is dark in appearance. Wiping over with a piece of cloth moistened with methylated spirits or petrol is usually sufficient to clean the surface. Light burn marks or scores can be polished off with fine grade glasspaper (do not use emerycloth as this leaves particles embedded in the copper). Deeper damage may be skimmed off in a lathe, at high speed and using a very sharp tool. A diamond tipped tool should be used for a light final cut. Note that the commutator must not be reduced below the minimum diameter of 33mm (1.3in) as shown in **FIG 12:6**, and that maximum permitted out of round is 0.08mm (0.0032in).

The mica between commutator segments should be undercut to a depth of 0.4mm (0.016in), using a hacksaw blade ground to the thickness of the insulation. Mica must be undercut to its full width and to a constant depth, incorrect examples being shown at **A** and correct examples at **B** in **FIG 12:7**. On completion, clean away all dust from the commutator.

The armature:

Check the armature for charred insulation, loose segments or laminations and for scored laminations. Shortcircuited windings may be suspected if individual commutator segments are badly burned. If the armature is damaged in any way it should be renewed. If an electrical fault in the armature is suspected, have it tested on special equipment at a service station.

Field coils:

Test the continuity with a 12-volt supply and test lamp between the terminal post and each field brush in turn. Test for insulation breakdown by connecting a test lamp between the connector which attaches to the solenoid terminal and the outer body of the starter. This test is best made with a 40-volt AC supply. If the lamp lights, defective insulation is indicated. As special equipment is needed to press out and to accurately install field coils, the work should be carried out by a service station.

Drive pinion assembly:

The starter drive pinion and clutch assembly must not be washed in solvents, as this would wash away the internal lubricant. Cleaning should be confined to wiping away dirt with a cloth. Light damage to the pinion teeth can be cleaned off with a fine file or oilstone, but deeper damage necessitates renewal of the complete drive

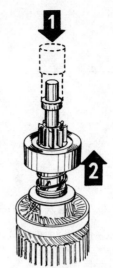

FIG 12:8   Drive pinion removal

assembly. Check that the clutch takes up the drive instantaneously but slips freely in the opposite direction. The complete assembly must be renewed if the clutch is defective.

To remove the drive pinion assembly, obtain a suitable length of metal tube which will bear on the outer circumference of the stop ring 13 (see **FIG 12:3**) without fouling circlip 36. Place the tube against the stop ring as shown in **FIG 12:8** and tap downwards in the direction of arrow 1. The circlip will then be exposed and can be removed from the groove. Remove circlip, stop ring, spacer and pinion assembly from the armature shaft. When refitting, fit the stop ring with open side towards shaft end, pushing it past the shaft groove, then prise a new circlip into the groove. Always use a new circlip as the original will have been weakened by removal. Force the stop ring over the circlip to secure, using a suitable puller if necessary.

Bearings:

The bearing bushes shown at 5 and 15 in **FIG 12:3** should be renewed if worn or damaged. Clearance A between shaft and bush should not exceed 0.12mm

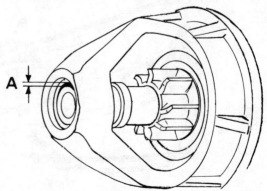

FIG 12:9   Checking bearing clearance

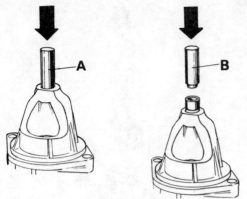

FIG 12:10 Bush removal A and installation B

(0.005in), as shown in **FIG 12:9**. If suitable mandrels are not available, have the work carried out at a service station.

Refer to **FIG 12:10**. Use Bosch special tool EF.2649, or other suitable mandrel having a polished pilot the same diameter as the bush internal bore, to remove and install bushes. New bushes must be soaked in thin engine oil for at least half an hour before fitting. Make sure that the bore for the bush is clean and free from burrs before fitting the new bush.

Solenoid:

No attempt should be made to service a faulty solenoid unit. Any mechanical or electrical faults will dictate renewal of the assembly.

12:5 Fuses

The fuses which protect the main electrical circuits are mounted in a fuse box located beneath the dashboard on the lefthand side.

If a fuse blows, briefly check the circuit that it protects and install a new fuse. Check each circuit in turn and if

the new fuse does not blow, it is likely that the old one had weakened with age. If the new fuse blows, carefully check the circuit that was live at the time and do not fit another fuse until the fault has been found and rectified. A fuse that blows intermittently will make it more difficult to correct the fault, but try shaking the wiring loom, as the fault is likely to be caused by chafed insulation making intermittent contact.

Never fit a fuse of higher rating than that specified, and never use anything as a substitute for a fuse of the correct type. The fuse is designed to be the weak link in the circuit and if a higher rated fuse or an incorrect substitute is installed, the wiring may fail instead, possibly causing a fire.

12:6 Windscreen wipers and washers

Wipers:

The windscreen wipers are operated by a two-speed electric motor incorporating a self-parking switch. 245 models are additionally equipped with a wiper for the tailgate window, this being a single-speed unit. If a wiper motor does not operate, check the fuse and wiring first. It is recommended that a wiper motor having internal mechanical or electrical faults be replaced by a new or exchange unit.

Windscreen wiper mechanism removal:

Refer to **FIG 12:11**. Disconnect the battery earth cable. Remove the side panel and the panel beneath the dashboard. Remove the defroster hoses and the glove box.

Remove the wiper arms from the spindles and disconnect the linkage from the motor crank. Remove the bolts securing the wiper linkage pivots, then lift out the assembly through the glove box opening. Disconnect the wiring from the wiper motor then detach the motor from the mountings.

Refitting is a reversal of the removal procedure, making sure that the linkage and motor are in the parked positions before installing the wiper arms. Wet the screen and

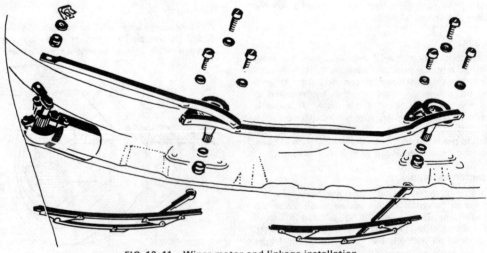

FIG 12:11 Wiper motor and linkage installation

check the operation of the wipers, repositioning the arms on the spindles if the blades contact the windscreen surround.

Tailgate wiper motor removal:

Refer to **FIG 12:12**. Disconnect the battery earth cable then remove the panel from the inside of the tailgate. Remove the retaining screws securing the wiper motor protection plate. Disconnect the link arm at the wiper motor 1, then fold the protection plate aside and lift out the wiper motor. Mark the wires so that they can be refitted to the correct terminals, then disconnect them from the motor.

Refitting is a reversal of the removal procedure.

Windscreen washers:

The washer unit is located in the lefthand front corner of the engine compartment and is controlled by the wiper switch. The unit comprises an electrically driven pump, the fluid container and hoses and jets. If any part of the motor and pump assembly is faulty or damaged, the unit should be renewed complete.

12:7 Instrument panel

The instrument panel is an independent unit containing the instruments and warning lights and is enclosed in a plastic housing. Electrical connections from the car wiring harness to the printed circuit at the back of the panel is by means of a multi-connector plug. Note that, on some later models, the speedometer is sealed at the factory by a plastic cover over the speedometer cable connection. This seal must be broken in order to remove the cable or speedometer. The purpose of the seal is to prevent unauthorised tampering with the instrument readings by giving visual indication that the cable has been disconnected. A new seal is not needed when the cable is reconnected, but if work is carried out by an authorised service station the connection should be resealed with a suitable device, these being supplied by the factory for servicing purposes.

Instrument panel removal:

Remove the covers from the steering column then remove the bracket retaining screws. Allow the bracket to slide down the steering column. Remove the instrument panel retaining screws, then reach behind the panel and disconnect the speedometer cable.

Grip the reverse side of the speedometer and press the unit upwards and outwards until the snap lock at the instrument panel upper edge is released. Lift out the instrument panel and disconnect the terminal plug from the reverse side. The individual warning lights and instrument assemblies can then be removed from the reverse side of the panel.

Refitting is a reversal of the removal procedure.

12:8 Headlamps

The headlamps may be of either the sealed beam or separate bulb type, according to year of vehicle manufacture and specification. Sealed beam units must be renewed complete if either main or dipped beam filament should fail.

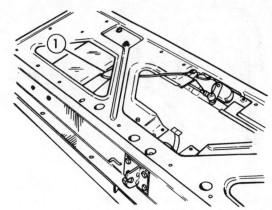

FIG 12:12   Tailgate wiper motor

FIG 12:13   Headlamp wiper and lock pins

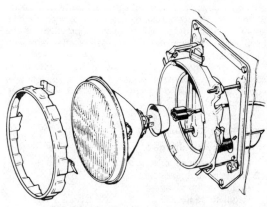

FIG 12:14   Headlamp components

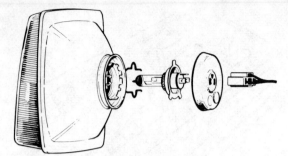

FIG 12:15   Replacing a headlamp bulb

Headlamp removal and refitting:

If a headlamp wiper system is fitted, move the wiper arm outwards until it locks in position as shown in **FIG 12:13**. Rotate the lock pins half a turn in the direction of the arrows, then lift them out. Remove the headlamp rim.

Turn the outer chromed ring slightly anticlockwise, then remove the ring and carefully lift out the headlamp unit (see **FIG 12:14**). Disconnect the plug from the rear of the unit. Remove the dust cover and either change the bulb or the complete lamp unit, according to type, if a filament is defective. Refit the dust cover and install the headlamp assembly in the reverse order of removal.

Headlamp removal and refitting (1979 models):

These models may be fitted with either square or rectangular headlamps.

Remove the contact and hinge out the wiper arm. Remove the radiator grille and the headlamp rim. Slacken the nut securing the wiper motor to the headlamp bracket and remove the motor. Unscrew the four screws and withdraw the bracket and headlamp. The bulb is retained by a spring clip as shown in **FIG 12:15**.

After reassembly check the beam alignment.

Headlamp beam setting:

Headlamp main beams should be set so that, when the car is normally loaded, the main beams are parallel to each other and to the road. The dipped beams should provide a good spread of light to the front and nearside of the car without dazzling oncoming drivers. Vertical and horizontal adjustment screws are provided at the headlamp mounting and are accessible after removing the headlamp rim.

It is recommended that headlamp beam setting be carried out at a service station having special optical equipment, this method giving the most accurate results.

12:9 Fault diagnosis

(a) Battery discharged

1 Terminal connections loose or dirty
2 Shorts in lighting circuits
3 Alternator not charging
4 Regulator faulty
5 Battery internally defective

(b) Insufficient charge rate

1 Check 1 and 4 in (a)
2 Drive belt slipping
3 Alternator defective

(c) Battery will not hold charge

1 Low electrolyte level
2 Battery plates sulphated
3 Electrolyte leakage from cracked case
4 Battery internally defective

(d) Battery overcharged

1 Regulator faulty

(e) Alternator output low or nil

1 Drive belt broken or slipping
2 Regulator faulty
3 Brushes sticking, springs weak or broken
4 Faulty internal windings
5 Defective diode(s)

(f) Starter motor lacks power or will not turn

1 Battery discharged, loose cable connections
2 Starter switch or solenoid faulty
3 Brushes worn or sticking, leads detached or shorting
4 Commutator dirty or worn
5 Starter shaft bent
6 Engine abnormally stiff to turn

(g) Starter runs but does not turn engine

1 Pinion engagement mechanism faulty
2 Broken teeth on pinion or engine ring gear

(h) Starter motor rough or noisy

1 Mounting bolts loose
2 Pinion engagement mechanism faulty
3 Damaged pinion or engine ring gear teeth

(j) Noisy starter when engine is running

1 Pinion return mechanism faulty
2 Mounting bolts loose

(k) Starter motor inoperative

1 Check 1 and 3 in (f)
2 Armature or field coils faulty

(l) Lamps inoperative or erratic

1 Battery low, bulbs burned out
2 Faulty earthing of lamps or battery
3 Lighting switch faulty, loose or broken connection

(m) Wiper motor sluggish, taking high current

1 Wiper motor internally defective
2 Linkage worn or binding

CHAPTER 13

THE BODYWORK

13:1 Bodywork finish

Large scale repairs to body panels are best left to expert panel beaters. Even small dents can be tricky, as too much hammering will stretch the metal and make things worse instead of better. If panel beating is to be attempted, use a dolly on the opposite side of the panel. The head of a large hammer will suffice for small dents, but for large dents a heavy block of metal will be necessary. Use light hammer blows to reshape the panel, pressing the dolly against the opposite side of the panel to absorb the blows. If this method is used to reduce the depth of dents, final smoothing with a suitable filler will be easier, although it may be better to avoid hammering minor dents and just use the filler alone.

Clean the area to be filled, making sure it is free from paint, rust and grease, then roughen the area with emerycloth or a file to ensure a good bond. Use a proprietary filler paste mixed according to the instructions and press it into the dent with a putty knife or similar. Allow the filler to stand slightly proud of the surrounding area to allow for rubbing down after hardening. Use a file and emerycloth or a disc sander to blend the repaired area to the surrounding bodywork, using finer grade abrasives as the work nears completion. Apply a coat of primer surfacer and, when it is dry, rub down with 'Wet-or-Dry'

paper lubricated with soapy water, finishing with 400 grade. Apply more primer and repeat the operation until the surface is perfectly smooth. Take time on achieving the best finish possible at this stage as it will control the final effect.

The touching up of paintwork can be carried out with self-spraying cans of paint, these being available in a wide range of colours. Use a piece of newspaper or board as a test panel to practice on first, so that the action of the spray will be familiar when it is used on the panel. Before spraying the panel, remove all traces of wax polish. Mask off large areas such as windows with newspaper and masking tape. Small areas such as trim strips or door handles can be wrapped with masking tape or carefully coated with grease or petroleum jelly. Apply the touching-up paint, spraying with short bursts and keeping the spray moving. Do not attempt to cover the area in one coat, applying several successive coats with a few minutes drying time between each. If too much paint is applied at one time, runs will develop. If so, do not try to remove the run by wiping but wait until it is dry and rub down as before.

After the final coat has been applied, allow a few hours of drying time before blending the new finish to the old with fine cutting compound and a cloth, buffing with a

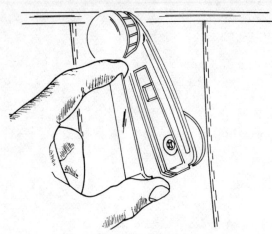

FIG 13:1   Regulator handle removal

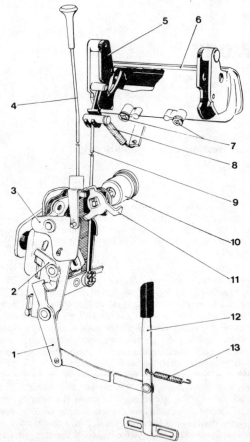

FIG 13:2   Front door lock components, early models

Key to Fig 13:2   1, 2, 3 Levers   4 Pull rod   5 Outer handle   6 Cover   7 Fixing screws   8 Return spring   9 Pull rod   10 Lock cylinder   11 Lock mechanism   12 Inner lock release lever   13 Return spring

light circular motion. Leave the paint to harden for a period of weeks rather than days before applying wax polish.

13:2 Door components

Complete door removal:

Remove the bolts securing the door check strap to the door pillar. Support the weight of the door, then remove the bolts attaching the hinges to the door panel and lift the door assembly away.

If it is necessary to remove the hinges, the panel in front of the door must be removed first for access to the hinge attachment bolts.

Install the door in the reverse order of removal, adjusting its position as necessary for correct fit in the aperture. The holes in the hinges and attachment between door and hinges are oval to allow for lateral adjustment. To allow adjustment up and down or fore and aft, the holes in the door post are larger than the diameter of the attachment bolts. Slacken the appropriate bolts, move the door to the required position, then firmly retighten the bolts. If it is necessary to adjust the distance between the lower door hinge and the door to ensure squareness, this should be carried out using shims which are available as spare parts.

Door trim removal:

To remove an armrest from a front door, remove the two plastic plugs using a narrow screwdriver, then remove the attaching screws which are covered by the plugs. Turn the plastic ring at the front edge of the armrest several turns to the left, then push the armrest forward and disengage the hook at the front edge.

To remove the armrest from a rear door, remove the two fixing screws.

Insert a finger behind the window regulator handle and push against the catches which secure the front cover, then lever off the cover using a suitable screwdriver (see **FIG 13:1**). Remove the single fixing screw and detach the regulator handle, noting its position for correct refitting.

Remove the lock button and the screws securing the top edge of the trim panel to the door. Insert a screwdriver or other flat-bladed tool between the trim panel and the door and lever out the retaining clips.

Refitting is the reversal of the removal procedure.

Door lock removal:

Later models are fitted with modified door lock assemblies. If a lock on an earlier model is to be renewed and the original type is unavailable, the door panel must be modified as described later to allow the later type of lock assembly to be fitted.

Front door, early models:

Remove the door trim panel as described previously, then refer to **FIG 13:2**. Remove the attachment screws located at the rear edge of the door and remove lock cylinder 10. Remove pull rod 4 after disconnecting from the lock mechanism. Disconnect pull rod 9 and pushrod for lever 12. Take out the three retaining screws located at the rear end of the door then detach the lock from the door panel.

Refitting is a reversal of the removal procedure.

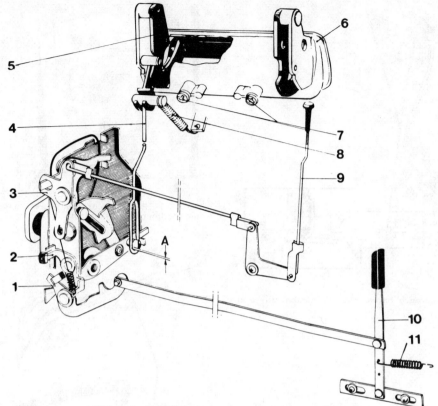

FIG 13:3 Rear door lock components, early models

Key to Fig 13:3   1 Remote control lever   2 Lever for childproof lock   3 Lever plate   4 Pull rod   5 Outer handle
6 Cover   7 Fixing screws   8 Return spring   9 Pull rod   10 Inner release lever   11 Return spring

Rear door, early models:

Remove the trim panel as described previously, then refer to **FIG 13:3**. Disconnect pull rod 9 from lever assembly 3, then disconnect pull rod 4. Disconnect lever 10 pushrod from lock. Remove the lock retaining screws which are located at the rear edge of the door, then remove the lock assembly from the door panel.

Refit in the reverse order of removal, checking that there is a clearance at **A** of $1 \pm 1mm$ ($\frac{1}{32} \pm \frac{1}{32}$in) between lower eye of pull rod 4 and the pin on the lock lever. If not, adjust to within limits by screwing the pull rod in or out as necessary.

All doors, later models:

FIG 13:4 shows the later type of door lock assembly. If only the outer part of the lock, which engages the striker plate, is to be renewed, use a suitable Allen key to remove the two fixing screws and detach the outer part of the lock from the door panel. Refit in the reverse order of removal and tighten the fixing screws alternately and evenly. If the complete lock assembly is to be removed, first remove the three screws and detach the stowage compartment from the lower part of the door, then remove the trim panel as described previously. Peel the plastic

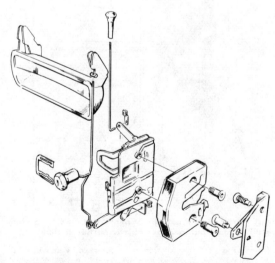

FIG 13:4 Later type of door lock assembly

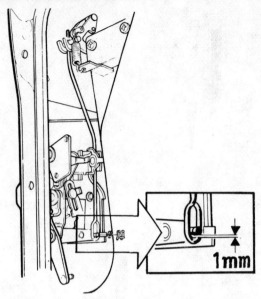

FIG 13:5 Clearance between outer handle stay and the pin

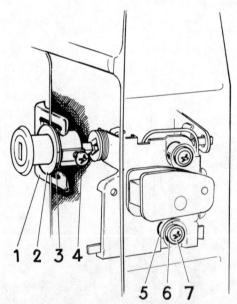

FIG 13:6 Additional components required when installing modified lock assembly to earlier models

Key to Fig 13:6   1 Clip   2 Sleeve for lock cylinder
3 Washer   4 Screw for lock cylinder   5 Spacer washer
6 Countersunk washer   7 Screw for lock

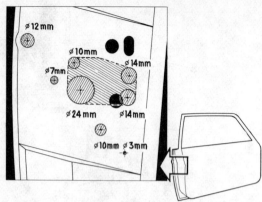

FIG 13:7 Positions of new holes to be drilled for installation of modified lock

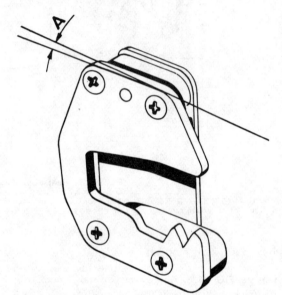

FIG 13:8 Door lock striker plate

FIG 13:9 Door glass removal

sheet away from the inner door panel as necessary. Remove the lock stays for outer and inner controls and for the lock button. Remove the outer part of the lock as described previously then remove the inner part of the lock assembly from the door panel.

Refit in the reverse order of removal. After securing all lock stays, check to make sure that there is a gap of 1mm (0.04in) between the pin and the outer handle lock stay, as shown in **FIG 13:5**. If necessary, adjust until the clearance is as specified. Refit the remaining components and check the operation of the door lock.

To renew a lock cylinder, remove the stowage compartment and trim panel as described previously, peel back the waterproofing sheet as necessary, then use a screwdriver to remove the spring clip and detach lock cylinder from door panel. Refit in the reverse order of removal, using a new seal for the lock cylinder. Refit the remaining components in the reverse order of removal.

Installing modified door lock:

If the later type of door lock is to be fitted to earlier models, the additional components shown in **FIG 13:6** will be required for front door, or items 5, 6 and 7 for rear door. The door panel must also be modified by drilling holes to the correct diameters as shown in **FIG 13:7**. Punchmarks, at the correct locations for these holes, will be found in the door panel. The hole required should be cut as indicated by the broken line and the edges should be adjusted by filing to provide the correct fit.

When the door panel has been prepared, refer to **FIG 13:6** and place spacer washers 5 for the upper and lower screws between the lock and door. Fit countersunk washers 6 on upper and lower screws 7 then tighten the lock into position. Use one of the original screws to fit in the third screw hole. Fit a washer 3 onto sleeve 2 for lock cylinder on front doors. Insert the sleeve in the door and secure with clip 1. Insert the lock cylinder in the sleeve and at the same time guide the square pin into the hole. Secure the lock cylinder with screw 4. On completion, check the operation of the lock assembly.

Door lock striker plates:

FIG 13:8 shows a typical door lock striker plate. The position of the plate is adjustable, as the holes in the plate are larger than the mounting screws. The plate should have an inward inclination 1.5° for front doors and 2.5° for rear doors, as shown at **A** in the illustration. To check striker plate position, open the door and hold the outside door handle in the open position while closing the door. The latch should slide smoothly into the striker plate. If adjustment is necessary, first scribe round the striker plate so that it can be moved back to the original position if necessary. Slacken the fixing screws, move the plate as necessary, then firmly retighten the screws.

If sufficient movement cannot be obtained for correct adjustment, check that the door is properly located in the aperture and adjust if necessary as described previously.

Door glass and regulator mechanism:

Removal:

Instructions given in this section apply to both front and rear doors.

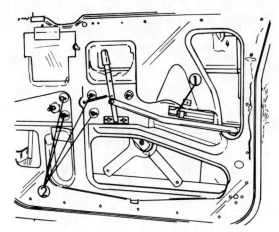

FIG 13:10   Removing regulator mechanism

Wind door glass down fully, then remove the door trim panel as described previously. Carefully peel the waterproof sheet from the door panel.

Remove the lock springs and washers on the inside of the regulator arms, then bend the arms outward and remove them from the door glass channel, the glass can now be removed by lifting and tilting forwards as shown in **FIG 13:9**.

To remove the regulator mechanism, refer to **FIG 13:10** and remove clip 1 at the regulator arm retaining point. Remove retaining screws 2, then withdraw the mechanism through the large aperture at the bottom of the door panel.

Refitting:

This is a reversal of the removal procedure, noting the following points:

Check that the door glass is correctly installed in the channel, as shown in **FIG 13:11** and **13:12**. For either door on two-door models, and front doors on four-door models, dimension **A** should be 263 ± 2mm (10.275 to 10.443in) and angle **B** should be 89° ± 1°. For rear doors on four-door models, dimension **A** should be 169 ± 2mm (6.575 to 6.732in) and angle **B** should be 90° ± 1°.

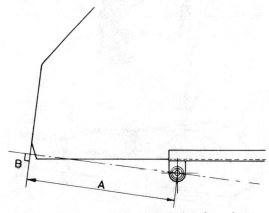

FIG 13:11   Glass channel installation, front doors

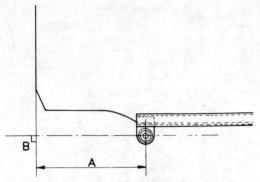

FIG 13:12 Glass channel installation, rear doors

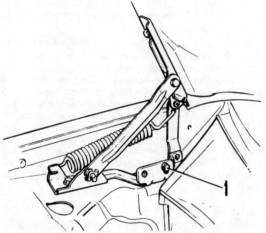

FIG 13:13 Bonnet hinge mounting bolts

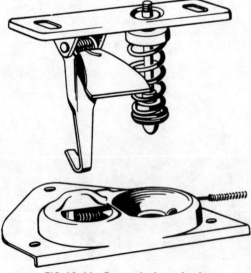

FIG 13:14 Bonnet lock mechanism

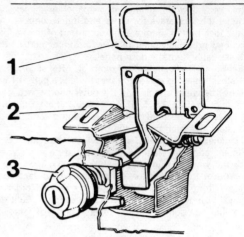

FIG 13:15 Boot lock mechanism

Key to Fig 13:15   1 Striker plate   2 Lock mechanism
3 Lock knob

When refitting the waterproof sheet, make sure that it is properly smoothed into place and that it is sealing effectively against the door panel.

13:3 The bonnet

Adjustment:

Fore and aft adjustment is carried out by slackening the bolts securing the bonnet panel to the hinges, moving the panel as necessary, then retightening the bolts firmly. Up and down adjustment at the rear is carried out by slackening the hinge mounting bolts shown at 1 in **FIG 13:13**, moving the assembly up or down, then firmly retightening the bolts. If necessary, the position of the bonnet at the front corners can be adjusted by screwing the rubber stops in or out.

If the bonnet rattles when closed, or if it closes too tightly, adjustment can be carried out at the dovetail bolt shown in **FIG 13:14**. Slacken the locknut securing the bolt to the upper plate, rotate the bolt in or out as necessary, then firmly retighten the locknut.

Bonnet removal:

Open the bonnet fully, then scribe round the bonnet hinges so that it can be refitted in its original position. Disconnect windscreen washer hoses from connection beneath the bonnet. Slacken the bolts securing the bonnet panel to the hinge plates. Have an assistant steady the bonnet panel while the bolts are completely removed, then carefully lift off the bonnet taking care not to damage the surrounding bodywork.

Refitting is a reversal of the removal procedure, adjusting bonnet procedure as described previously.

13:4 Boot lid or tailgate

Boot lid, Saloon models:

Adjustment:

Fore and aft adjustment of the boot lid is carried out by slackening the bolts securing the panel to the hinge plates and moving the panel within the limits allowed by the oval mounting holes. On completion, firmly retighten the bolts. To adjust the lid position vertically, slacken the bolts securing the hinges to the bodywork and adjust within the limits allowed by the oval mounting holes. On completion, firmly retighten the bolts.

If the boot lid closes too tightly or too loosely, the position of the striker plate 1 shown in **FIG 13:15** can be adjusted up or down as necessary.

Boot lock removal:

Refer to **FIG 13:15**. Remove the curved securing plate and pull off the lock knob 3. Remove the two bolts located beneath the upper edge of the boot lid and detach lock assembly 2. Refit in the reverse order of removal, adjusting the position of the lock within the limits allowed by the slotted mounting holes until the lock striker enters the lock correctly. When correct, firmly retighten the bolts.

A new type of boot lock was introduced on 1979 models. This does not have an opening knob and is operated by key only. Renewal requires tool No 999 5174-1, with magnetic head, to be inserted through the adjacent aperture to remove the lock retaining clip.

Boot lid removal:

Open the boot lid fully and scribe round the hinge plates to ensure refitting in the original position. Have an assistant steady the panel, then remove the bolts securing the hinge plates to the panel and lift off the lid, taking care not to damage the surrounding bodywork. Refit in the reverse order of removal, adjusting the position of the lid, if necessary, as described previously.

If the boot spring stay is to be removed, the use of a suitable clamp such as tool 2739 will be necessary

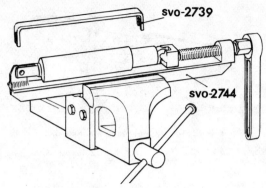

FIG 13:16   Spring stay compressor tools

(see **FIG 13:16**). A compressor tool such as 2744 will be necessary to compress the spring stay for installation.

To remove, open the boot fully, then close it slightly until the clamping tool can be fitted over the stay and remove the fixing bolts to detach the stay, leaving the clamp installed if the stay is to be refitted. If a new stay is to be installed, use a suitable compressor to compress the stay until the clamp can be removed, then compress the new stay in a similar manner to install the clamp. Refit the stay in the reverse order of removal.

If the boot hinges are to be removed, remove first the stay, then the boot lid, as described previously. Scribe round the hinge plates for correct refitting, then unscrew the fixing bolts and remove the hinges. Refit in the reverse order of removal, adjusting the hinge positions on the bodywork if necessary before retightening the mounting bolts.

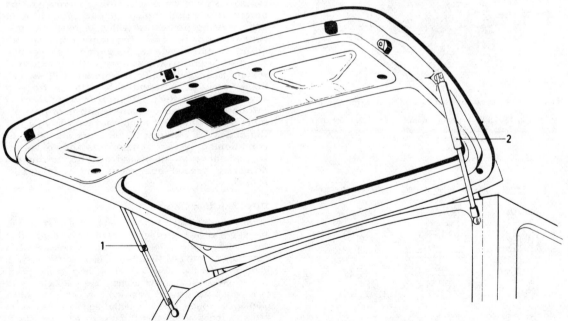

FIG 13:17   Tailgate support strut 1 and gas strut 2

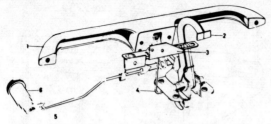

FIG 13:18   Tailgate lock mechanism

Key to Fig 13:18   1 Outer handle   2 Inside release lever
3 Latch   4 Latch control   5 Lever   6 Lock cylinder

Tailgate, Estate models:
Removal:

Remove the trim panel from the inside of the tailgate,
then remove the lefthand licence plate light and disconnect the wire. Disconnect the remaining wires from
the connections inside the tailgate. Refer to **FIG 13:17**
and disconnect stay 1 and gas strut 2 from the tailgate.
Have an assistant support the tailgate, then remove the
screws securing the hinge plate to the panel and lift off
the tailgate. Refit in the reverse order of removal.

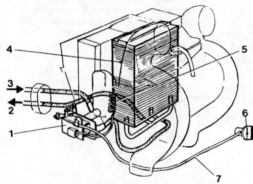

FIG 13:19   Layout of heating and ventilation system

Key to Fig 13:19   1 Heater control valve   2 Water hose,
output   3 Water hose, input   4 Heater radiator   5 Capilliary
tube   6 Temperature control   7 Control cable

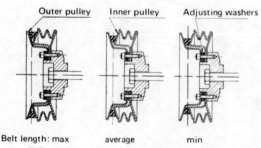

Belt length: max   average   min
     FIG 13:20   AC compressor belt tensioning

Tailgate lock removal:

Remove the trim panel from the inside of the tailgate.
Refer to **FIG 13:18**. Disconnect the link rod from lever 5
and remove the screws securing the lock assembly to the
panel. Move the lock to the left then remove through the
opening in the panel. Refit in reverse order of the removal procedure.

13:5 Heating and air conditioning
Heating system:

The heating and ventilation unit is situated behind the
dashboard and consists of a heat exchanger connected
to the engine cooling system, an electrically operated
double rotor cooling fan, a temperature control valve and
vacuum operated shutters which control the flow of
fresh or recirculated air to the system. Ducts from the
unit pass into adjustable vents in the dashboard, and to
floor level outlets for the front and rear seats. The changing
of air in the car interior is assisted by air extractor vents
fitted at the lower edge of the rear window.

Temperature control is by means of a control valve 1
(see **FIG 13:19**) in the coolant inlet line which reacts to
temperatures above the present requirements to reduce
the coolant flow or, conversely, to increase the flow if
the temperature falls.

Air flow into the heater will be induced to a limited
extent by the forward motion of the car, but operation of
the electric fan will ensure adequate air supply for all
conditions and vehicle speeds.

Air conditioning system:

An air conditioning (refrigeration) system is available
as an optional extra on some models.

**Owners of vehicles fitted with air conditioning
systems should consult a Volvo service station
before attempting engine removal procedure, or
any servicing procedure which involves the dis-
connection or removal of system components or
hoses, so that advice can be obtained concerning
the discharging of the system. If the pressurised
system is opened, liquid refrigerent will escape,
immediately evaporating and instantly freezing
anything in contact. Uncontrolled release of
refrigerent will cause severe frostbite or possibly
more serious injury if in contact with any part of
the body. For this reason, all work involving air
conditioning system components should be entrusted only to a Volvo service station having the
necessary special equipment and trained personnel.**

Drive belt tensioning:

Tension is correct if the belt can be deflected by 5 to
10mm ($\frac{3}{16}$ to $\frac{3}{8}$in) when firm hand pressure is applied at
the centre of the longest belt run. If adjustment is
necessary, refer to **FIG 13:20** and add or remove washers
from between the outer and inner drive pulleys. One
washer gives approximately 5mm ($\frac{3}{16}$in) adjustment to
belt length. To prevent clamping the belt tight when
refitting the outer pulley turn the engine occasionally
while the bolts are tightened progressively. Use five or
six washers between the pulleys when fitting a new belt.

APPENDIX

TECHNICAL DATA

HINTS ON MAINTENANCE AND OVERHAUL

GLOSSARY OF TERMS

INDEX

Inches	Decimals	Milli-metres	Inches to Millimetres — Inches	Inches to Millimetres — mm	Millimetres to Inches — mm	Millimetres to Inches — Inches
1/64	.015625	.3969	.001	.0254	.01	.00039
1/32	.03125	.7937	.002	.0508	.02	.00079
3/64	.046875	1.1906	.003	.0762	.03	.00118
1/16	.0625	1.5875	.004	.1016	.04	.00157
5/64	.078125	1.9844	.005	.1270	.05	.00197
3/32	.09375	2.3812	.006	.1524	.06	.00236
7/64	.109375	2.7781	.007	.1778	.07	.00276
1/8	.125	3.1750	.008	.2032	.08	.00315
9/64	.140625	3.5719	.009	.2286	.09	.00354
5/32	.15625	3.9687	.01	.254	.1	.00394
11/64	.171875	4.3656	.02	.508	.2	.00787
3/16	.1875	4.7625	.03	.762	.3	.01181
13/64	.203125	5.1594	.04	1.016	.4	.01575
7/32	.21875	5.5562	.05	1.270	.5	.01969
15/64	.234375	5.9531	.06	1.524	.6	.02362
1/4	.25	6.3500	.07	1.778	.7	.02756
17/64	.265625	6.7469	.08	2.032	.8	.03150
9/32	.28125	7.1437	.09	2.286	.9	.03543
19/64	.296875	7.5406	.1	2.54	1	.03937
5/16	.3125	7.9375	.2	5.08	2	.07874
21/64	.328125	8.3344	.3	7.62	3	.11811
11/32	.34375	8.7312	.4	10.16	4	.15748
23/64	.359375	9.1281	.5	12.70	5	.19685
3/8	.375	9.5250	.6	15.24	6	.23622
25/64	.390625	9.9219	.7	17.78	7	.27559
13/32	.40625	10.3187	.8	20.32	8	.31496
27/64	.421875	10.7156	.9	22.86	9	.35433
7/16	.4375	11.1125	1	25.4	10	.39370
29/64	.453125	11.5094	2	50.8	11	.43307
15/32	.46875	11.9062	3	76.2	12	.47244
31/64	.484375	12.3031	4	101.6	13	.51181
1/2	.5	12.7000	5	127.0	14	.55118
33/64	.515625	13.0969	6	152.4	15	.59055
17/32	.53125	13.4937	7	177.8	16	.62992
35/64	.546875	13.8906	8	203.2	17	.66929
9/16	.5625	14.2875	9	228.6	18	.70866
37/64	.578125	14.6844	10	254.0	19	.74803
19/32	.59375	15.0812	11	279.4	20	.78740
39/64	.609375	15.4781	12	304.8	21	.82677
5/8	.625	15.8750	13	330.2	22	.86614
41/64	.640625	16.2719	14	355.6	23	.90551
21/32	.65625	16.6687	15	381.0	24	.94488
43/64	.671875	17.0656	16	406.4	25	.98425
11/16	.6875	17.4625	17	431.8	26	1.02362
45/64	.703125	17.8594	18	457.2	27	1.06299
23/32	.71875	18.2562	19	482.6	28	1.10236
47/64	.734375	18.6531	20	508.0	29	1.14173
3/4	.75	19.0500	21	533.4	30	1.18110
49/64	.765625	19.4469	22	558.8	31	1.22047
25/32	.78125	19.8437	23	584.2	32	1.25984
51/64	.796875	20.2406	24	609.6	33	1.29921
13/16	.8125	20.6375	25	635.0	34	1.33858
53/64	.828125	21.0344	26	660.4	35	1.37795
27/32	.84375	21.4312	27	685.8	36	1.41732
55/64	.859375	21.8281	28	711.2	37	1.4567
7/8	.875	22.2250	29	736.6	38	1.4961
57/64	.890625	22.6219	30	762.0	39	1.5354
29/32	.90625	23.0187	31	787.4	40	1.5748
59/64	.921875	23.4156	32	812.8	41	1.6142
15/16	.9375	23.8125	33	838.2	42	1.6535
61/64	.953125	24.2094	34	863.6	43	1.6929
31/32	.96875	24.6062	35	889.0	44	1.7323
63/64	.984375	25.0031	36	914.4	45	1.7717

UNITS	Pints to Litres	Gallons to Litres	Litres to Pints	Litres to Gallons	Miles to Kilometres	Kilometres to Miles	Lbs. per sq. In. to Kg. per sq. Cm.	Kg. per sq. Cm. to Lbs. per sq. In.
1	.57	4.55	1.76	.22	1.61	.62	.07	14.22
2	1.14	9.09	3.52	.44	3.22	1.24	.14	28.50
3	1.70	13.64	5.28	.66	4.83	1.86	.21	42.67
4	2.27	18.18	7.04	.88	6.44	2.49	.28	56.89
5	2.84	22.73	8.80	1.10	8.05	3.11	.35	71.12
6	3.41	27.28	10.56	1.32	9.66	3.73	.42	85.34
7	3.98	31.82	12.32	1.54	11.27	4.35	.49	99.56
8	4.55	36.37	14.08	1.76	12.88	4.97	.56	113.79
9		40.91	15.84	1.98	14.48	5.59	.63	128.00
10		45.46	17.60	2.20	16.09	6.21	.70	142.23
20				4.40	32.19	12.43	1.41	284.47
30				6.60	48.28	18.64	2.11	426.70
40				8.80	64.37	24.85		
50					80.47	31.07		
60					96.56	37.28		
70					112.65	43.50		
80					128.75	49.71		
90					144.84	55.92		
100					160.93	62.14		

UNITS	Lb ft to kgm	Kgm to lb ft	UNITS	Lb ft to kgm	Kgm to lb ft
1	.138	7.233	7	.967	50.631
2	.276	14.466	8	1.106	57.864
3	.414	21.699	9	1.244	65.097
4	.553	28.932	10	1.382	72.330
5	.691	36.165	20	2.765	144.660
6	.829	43.398	30	4.147	216.990

TECHNICAL DATA

Dimensions are in millimetres with inch equivalents in brackets unless otherwise stated

ENGINE

Type	In-line, inclined at 20°
Number of cylinders	4

Designation:

B20E	Pushrod with fuel injection
B21A	OHC with carburetter
B21E	OHC with fuel injection

Bore and stroke:

Pushrod	88.9 × 80.0 (3.500 × 3.150)
OHC	92 × 80 (3.622 × 3.150)

Capacity:

Pushrod	1986cc (121cu in)
OHC	2127cc (130cu in)

Compression ratio:

B20E	8.7:1
B21A, 1975	9.5:1
B21A, 1976 on	8.5:1
B21E	9.3:1
Firing order	1–3–4–2
No 1 cylinder	Front

Specifications, pushrod engine:

Pistons:

Material	Light alloy
Weight, standard	507 ± 5gr (17.90 ± 0.18oz)
Permitted piston weight differential	10gr (0.35oz)
Piston clearance in bore	0.01 to 0.03 (0.0004 to 0.0012)

Piston rings:

Fitted gap, upper ring	0.40 to 0.55 (0.016 to 0.022)
lower ring	0.30 to 0.45 (0.012 to 0.018)
scraper ring	0.25 to 0.45 (0.010 to 0.018)

Compression rings (two on each piston):

Height	1.98 (0.078)
Clearance in groove	0.040 to 0.072 (0.0016 to 0.0028)

Oil scraper rings (one on each piston):

Height	4.74 (0.186)
Clearance in groove	0.040 to 0.072 (0.0016 to 0.0028)

Gudgeon pins:

Diameter:

Standard	24.00 (0.945)
Oversize	24.05 (0.947)

Crankshaft:

End float	0.047 to 0.137 (0.0018 to 0.0054)

Main journal diameter:

Standard	63.451 to 63.464 (2.4981 to 2.4986)
0.010 in undersize	63.197 to 63.210 (2.4881 to 2.4886)
0.020 in undersize	62.943 to 62.956 (2.4781 to 2.4786)
Main bearings, radial clearance	0.028 to 0.083 (0.0011 to 0.0033)

Crankpin diameter:

Standard	53.987 to 54.000 (2.1255 to 2.1260)
0.010 undersize	53.733 to 53.746 (2.1155 to 2.1160)
0.020 undersize	53.479 to 53.492 (2.1055 to 2.1060)
Big-end bearings, radial clearance	0.029 to 0.071 (0.0012 to 0.0028)

Camshaft:
Number of bearings	..	..	..	3
Radial clearance ..	..	..	..	0.020 to 0.075 (0.0008 to 0.0030)
End float ..	..	..	..	0.020 to 0.060 (0.0008 to 0.0024)

Valves:
Inlet:
Disc diameter ..			..	44 (1.732)
Stem diameter ..	..	..	..	7.955 to 7.970 (0.3132 to 0.3138)
Valve seat angle	..	..	..	44.5°
Seat angle in head	..	..		45°
Seat width in head	..	..	..	2 (0.08)
Clearance, hot or cold ..		..		0.40 to 0.45 (0.016 to 0.018)

Exhaust:
Disc diameter ..		..	..	35 (1.378)
Stem diameter ..	..	..	..	7.925 to 7.940 (0.3120 to 0.3126)
Valve seat angle	..	..	..	44.5°
Seat angle in head	..	..	..	45°
Seat width in head	..	..	..	2 (0.08)
Clearance, hot or cold ..		..	..	0.40 to 0.45 (0.016 to 0.018)

Valve guides:
Length, inlet ..	..	..	..	52 (2.047)
Length, exhaust	..	..	..	59 (2.323)
Inner diameter ..	..	..	..	8.000 to 8.022 (0.315 to 0.316)
Height above head upper face..		..		17.9 (0.705)
Stem to guide clearance (inlet)		..	..	0.030 to 0.068 (0.0012 to 0.0026)
Stem to guide clearance (exhaust)		..		0.060 to 0.097 (0.0024 to 0.0038)

Valve springs:
Free length ..	..	..	..	46 (1.81)
With a loading of 295 ± 23N (66 ± 5lb)		..		40 (1.57)
With a loading of 825 ± 43N (185 ± 9.5lb)		..		30 (1.18)

Specifications OHC engine:
Pistons:
Material	..	..	..	Light alloy
Weight..	..	..	..	555 ± 5gr (19.5 ± 18oz)
Permitted piston weight differential		..		10gr (0.35oz)
Piston clearance in bore		..	..	0.01 to 0.03 (0.0004 to 0.0012)

Piston rings:
Compression rings (two on each piston):
Fitted gap ..	..	..	..	0.35 to 0.55 (0.0138 to 0.0217)
Height ..	..	..	..	1.978 to 1.990 (0.0779 to 0.0783)
Clearance in groove..		..	..	0.0400 to 0.072 (0.0016 to 0.0028)
Oversizes ..	..	..	..	0.5 and 1.0 (0.0197 and 0.0394)

Oil scraper rings (one on each piston):
Fitted gap ..	..	..	..	0.25 to 0.40 (0.010 to 0.016)
Height ..	..	..	..	3.978 to 3.990 (0.1566 to 0.1571)
Clearance in groove..		..	..	0.030 to 0.062 (0.0012 to 0.0024)
Oversizes ..	..	..	..	0.5 and 1.0 (0.0197 and 0.0394)

Gudgeon pins:
Diameter:
Standard	..	..	..	24.00 (0.945)
Oversize	..	..	..	24.05 (0.947)

Crankshaft:
End float ..	..	..	..	0.037 to 0.147 (0.0015 to 0.0058)
Big-end bearings, radial clearance		..		0.024 to 0.070 (0.0009 to 0.0028)
Main bearings, radial clearance ..		..		0.028 to 0.083 (0.0011 to 0.0033)

Main bearing journals:
Diameter:
Standard	63.451 to 63.464 (2.4981 to 2.4986)
First undersize	63.197 to 63.210 (2.4881 to 2.4886)
Second undersize	62.943 to 62.956 (2.4781 to 2.4786)

Width on crankshaft for flange bearing shell:
Standard	38.958 to 38.991 (1.5338 to 1.5351)
First Oversize	39.212 to 39.245 (1.5438 to 1.5451)
Second oversize	39.466 to 39.499 (1.5538 to 1.5551)

Big-end bearing journals:
Diameter:
Standard	53.987 to 54.000 (2.1255 to 2.1260)
First undersize	53.733 to 53.746 (2.1155 to 2.1160)
Second undersize	53.479 to 53.492 (2.1055 to 2.1060)
Seat width	29.95 to 30.05 (1.179 to 1.183)

Connecting rods:
End float on crankshaft	0.15 to 0.35 (0.006 to 0.014)
Length (centre to centre)	145 ± 0.1 (5.71 ± 0.0039)
Permitted weight differential	10gr (0.35oz)

Flywheel:
Maximum run-out	0.005 (0.0002) at 150 (5.9) diameter
Ring gear (bevel forwards)	142 teeth

Camshaft:
Marking/maximum lift height:
B21A, 1975	A/9.8 (A/0.39)
B21A, 1976	A/10.5 (A/0.41)
B21E	D/11.2 (D/0.44)
Bearings	5
Bearing journal diameter	29.050 to 29.070 (1.1437 to 1.1445)
Radial clearance	0.030 to 0.071 (0.0012 to 0.0028)
Axial clearance	0.1 to 0.4 (0.004 to 0.016)
Bearing diameter	30.000 to 30.021 (1.1811 to 1.1819)

Intermediate shaft:
Bearings	3

Bearing journal diameter:
Front	46.975 to 47.000 (1.8494 to 1.8504)
Intermediate	43.025 to 43.050 (1.6939 to 1.6949)
Rear	42.925 to 42.950 (1.6899 to 1.6909)
Radial clearance	0.020 to 0.076 (0.0008 to 0.0030)
Axial clearance	0.20 to 0.46 (0.008 to 0.018)

Valves:
Inlet:
Disc diameter	44 (1.732)
Stem diameter	7.955 to 7.970 (0.3132 to 0.3138)
Valve seat angle	45.5°
Seat angle in head	45°
Seat width in head	2 ± 0.3 (0.08 ± 0.012)

Inlet valve clearance:
Cold engine, when adjusting	0.35 to 0.40 (0.014 to 0.016)
when checking	0.30 to 0.45 (0.012 to 0.018)
Hot engine, when adjusting	0.40 to 0.45 (0.016 to 0.018)
when checking	0.35 to 0.50 (0.014 to 0.020)

Exhaust:

Disc diameter	35 (1.378)
Stem diameter	7.925 to 7.940 (0.3120 to 0.3126)
Valve seat angle	45.5°
Seat angle in head	45°
Seat width in head	2 ± 0.3 (0.08 ± 0.012)

Exhaust valve clearance:

Cold engine, when adjusting	0.35 to 0.40 (0.014 to 0.016)
when checking	0.30 to 0.45 (0.012 to 0.018)
Hot engine, when adjusting	0.40 to 0.45 (0.016 to 0.018)
when checking	0.35 to 0.50 (0.014 to 0.020)

Valve guides:

Length, inlet	52 (2.047)
Length, exhaust	52 (2.047)
Inner diameter	8.000 to 8.022 (0.3150 to 0.3158)
Height above head upper face (inlet) ..	15.4 to 15.6 (0.606 to 0.614)
Height above head upper face (exhaust) ..	17.9 to 18.1 (0.705 to 0.713)
Stem to guide clearance (inlet)	0.030 to 0.060 (0.0012 to 0.0024)
Stem to guide clearance (exhaust) ..	0.060 to 0.090 (0.0024 to 0.0035)

Valve springs:

Free length	45 (1.77)
With a loading of 300 ± 20N (66 ± 4.4lb) ..	38 (1.50)
With a loading of 750 ± 40N (165 ± 8.8lb) ..	27 (1.06)

Tappets:

Diameter	36.975 to 36.995 (1.4557 to 1.4565)
Adjuster to tappet clearance	0.009 to 0.064 (0.0004 to 0.0025)
Tappet to head clearance	0.030 to 0.075 (0.0012 to 0.0030)
Adjuster thickness	3.3 to 4.5 (0.13 to 0.18) in steps of 0.05 (0.002)
Adjuster diameter	32.980 to 33.000 (1.2984 to 1.2992)

Lubricating system:

Oil capacity:

Including filter	3.85 litres (6.8 pints)
Excluding filter	3.35 litres (5.9 pints)
Filter type	Full flow
Pump type	Gear
Relief valve spring length (unloaded)	39.2 (1.54)

FUEL SYSTEM

Injection:

Fuel filter:

Type	Paper
Change interval	80,000km (50,000 miles)

Fuel pump:

Type	Electric, roller type
Capacity	100 litres/hr (22 Imp gal/hr; 26.5 US gal/hr at 71lb/sq in
Current draw	Max 8.5 amps

Auxiliary air valve:

Completely open	At − 30°C (− 22°F)
Completely closed	At + 70°C (+ 158°F)
Line pressure	4.5 to 5.2kg/sq cm (64 to 74lb/sq in)
Rest pressure	1.7 to 2.4kg/sq cm (24 to 34lb/sq in)
Control pressure, hot engine	3.5 to 3.9kg/sq cm (50 to 55lb/sq in)

Air filter:
Type	Paper
Change interval	40,000km (25,000 miles)

CO value:
Warm engine and idle	0.5 to 3.5%
USA	1.5%

Carburetters:

SU-HIF 6:
Damper piston axial clearance	1.1 to 1.7 (0.043 to 0.067)
Damper fluid	ATF type F

Idle speed:
B20A	700rev/min
B21A	850rev/min

Fast-idle speed:
B20A	1100 to 1500rev/min
B21A	1200 to 1600rev/min

CO content:
B20A, 1975 and all B21A	2.5%
B20A, 1976–77	1.5%

175 CD-2SE, 1977 and earlier models:
Damper piston axial clearance	1.0 to 1.8 (0.04 to 0.07)
Damper fluid	ATF type F

Idle speed:
B20A	700rev/min
B21A	850rev/min

Fast-idle speed:
B20A	1100 to 1500rev/min
B21A	1200 to 1600rev/min

CO content:
B20A and all B21A	2.5%
B20A, 1976–77	1.5%

175 CD-2SE from 1978 on and all DVG 175 CDSU:
Damper piston axial clearance	0.5 to 1.5 (0.02 to 0.06)
Damper fluid	ATF type F
Idle speed	900rev/min
Fast-idle speed	1400 to 1600rev/min
CO content	1.5 to 3.0%

IGNITION SYSTEM

Conventional system (B20A, B21A):
Distributor	Bosch JFU4

Direction of rotation:
B20A	Anticlockwise
B21A	Clockwise

Contact points gap:
B20A	0.35 (0.014)
B21A	0.40 (0.016)
Dwell angle at 500rev/min	62 ± 3°

Ignition setting at 700 to 800rev/min with vacuum
unit disconnected:
B20A	10° BTDC
B21A, 1975	12° BTDC
B21A, 1976 on	15° BTDC *Correct for RUW48R*
B21A, 1979	12° BTDC

Sparking plugs:
B20A	Bosch W175T35 or equivalent
B21A	Bosch W175T30 or equivalent
Plug electrode gap	0.7 to 0.8 (0.028 to 0.031)

Electronic system (B21E):

Distributor:

B21E, 1975–76	Bosch JGFU4
B21E, 1977 on	Bosch JGFT4
Direction of rotation	Clockwise
Ignition setting at 700 to 800rev/min with vacuum unit disconnected	8° BTDC
Sparking plugs	Bosch W200T30 or equivalent
Plug electrode gap	0.7 to 0.8 (0.028 to 0.031)

COOLING SYSTEM

Type:

Capacity			9.5 litres (16.7 pints Imp, 20 US pints)	
Thermostat:	*B20, type 1*	*B20, type 2*	*B21A, B20, type 3*	*B21E*
Starts				
opening	75° to 78°C	81° to 83°C	91° to 93°C	81° to 83°C
Fully open	89°C	92°C	102°C	92°C

TRANSMISSION

Clutch:

Type	Single dry plate, diaphragm spring
Diameter	216 (8.5)
Total friction area	440sq cm (68.2sq in)

Manual gearbox:

Type	M40 or M45 (M41 or M46 with overdrive)

Ratios:

	M40/41	*M45/46*
First	3.41:1	3.71:1
Second	1.99:1	2.16:1
Third	1.36:1	1.37:1
Fourth	1.00:1	1.00:1
Overdrive..	0.797:1	0.797:1
Reverse	3.25:1	3.68:1

Automatic gearbox

Type	Borg Warner Type 35 or Type 55

Ratios:

	Type 35	*Type 55*
Torque converter	2:1 to 1:1	2:1 to 1:1
First	2.31:1	2.45:1
Second	1.45:1	1.45:1
Third	1.00:1	1.00:1
Reverse	2.09:1	2.21:1

Final drive ratio:

Depending on year and model	3.73:1, 3.91:1, 4.10:1, 4.30:1

SUSPENSION

Front	Coil springs and struts
Rear..	Coil springs, live axle

STEERING

Type	Cam gear or ZF rack and pinion
Camber	+ 1° to + 1.5° (0° to + 1°, 1979 on)
Caster	+ 2° to + 3°
Kingpin inclination at 0° camber	12°

Toe-in at middle of tread:
    Manual steering ..   ..   4.5 ± 1mm (0° 24′ ± 0° 8′ total)
    Power steering ..   ..   3.0 ± 1mm (0° 16′ ± 0° 8′ total)
All figures given for unladen vehicle

BRAKES

Front	Girling disc
Diameter	263 (10.35)
Thickness	14.3 (0.563), 13.14 (0.52) minimum
Rear..	Girling or ATE disc with integral drum for handbrake
Diameter	281 (11.06)
Thickness	9.6 (0.38), 8.4 (0.33) minimum
Drum diameter	160.45 (6.32)

ELECTRICAL EQUIPMENT

Alternator:

	Before 1979	From 1979
Type	Bosch K1, 14V 55A 20	SEV Marchal D14/70A
Output	770W	980W
Stator coil resistance	0.14 ohm + 10%	0.10 ohm
Rotor coil resistance	4 ohms + 10%	3.5/4.3 ohms
Output test (at 3000rev/min) ..	48A	64A

Starter motor:

Type	Bosch GF 12V 1.1PS
Output	810W (1.1hp)
Brushes	4
Armature end float	0.05 to 0.30 (0.002 to 0.012)
Brush spring tension	14 to 16N (3.1 to 3.6lb)
Minimum brush length	13 (0.52)
Battery	12V, 60 Ah negative earth

TORQUE WRENCH SETTINGS

	Nm	lb ft
Engine:		
Cylinder head (lubricated thread)	90	65
Main bearings	120 to 130	87 to 94
Big-end bearings..	70 to 78	51 to 57
Flywheel	65 to 70	47 to 51
Spark plugs	35 to 40	25 to 29
Camshaft nut	130 to 150	94 to 108
Oil pan bolts	8 to 11	6 to 8
Automatic transmission:		
Converter drive plate	35 to 41	25 to 30
Converter housing to transmission case ..	11 to 18	8 to 13
Extension housing to transmission case ..	41 to 76	30 to 55
Oil pan bolts	11 to 18	8 to 13
Manual transmission:		
Clutch housing to transmission case ..	35 to 50	25 to 36
Gearlever carrier bolts	20 to 25	14 to 18
Top cover	15 to 25	11 to 18
Rear axle:		
Flange	280 to 300	200 to 220
Caps	50 to 70	35 to 50
Crownwheel	65 to 90	45 to 65

Steering:

Nut for ball joint (in strut)	..	..	50 to 70	35 to 50
Ball joint retaining bolts (late type)	..	..	18 to 28	15 to 20
Steering wheel retaining nut	..	..	40 to 60	30 to 45

Brakes:

Front caliper retaining bolts	..	..	90 to 100	65 to 70
Rear caliper retaining bolts	..	..	60 to 70	45 to 50
Road wheel nuts ..	..	..	100 to 130	70 to 95
Master cylinder retaining bolts	..	..	30 to 50	20 to 35
Bleed nipples	..	..	3.5 to 5.5	2.5 to 4
Brake pipe connections ..	..	..	8 to 12	6 to 9
Hoses to reducer valve ..	..	..	12 to 16	9 to 12

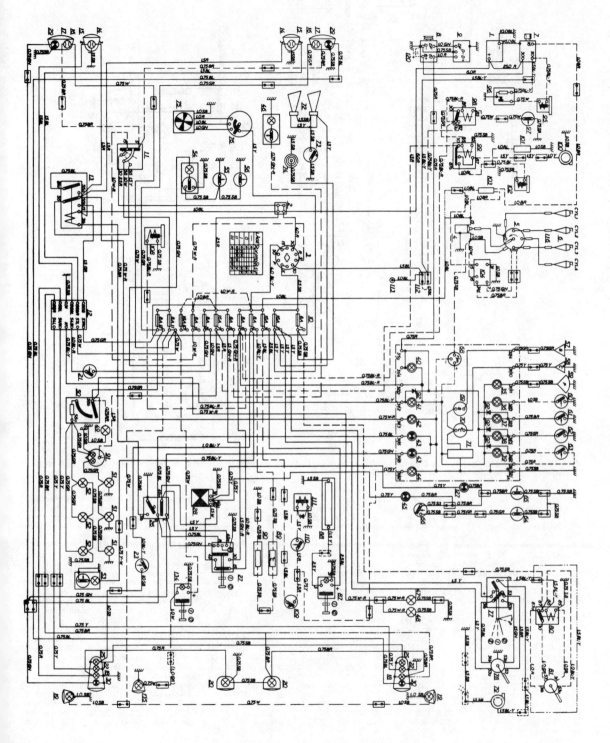

FIG 14:1   Typical basic wiring diagram

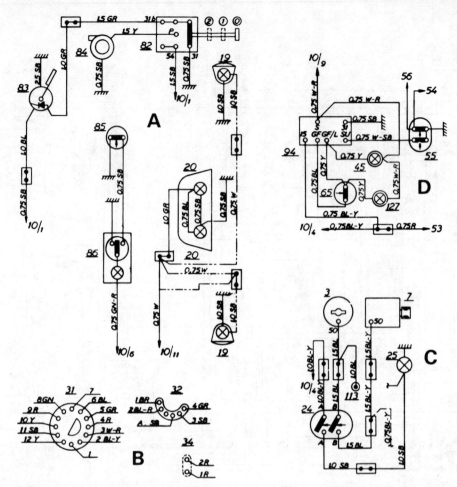

FIG 14:2 Wiring diagrams, additional and alternative details. A: Estate models. B: instrument panel connector. C: automatic transmission. D: seat belt reminder system

Key to Wiring diagrams: 1 Battery   2 Terminal box   3 Ignition switch   4 Ignition coil   5 Distributor   6 Spark plugs   7 Starter motor   8 Alternator   9 Charging regulator   10 Fuse box   11 Light switch   12 Bulb failure warning light   13 Headlamp relay   14 Headlamps   15 Dipped beams   16 Parking lamp   17 Day running lights   18 Rear lamp   19 Side marking lamp   20 Number plate lamp   21 Brake light contact   22 Brake lamp   23 Contact on manual transmission   24 Contact on automatic transmission   25 Reversing lights   26 Direction indicator lever   27 Hazard warning light switch   28 Flasher unit   29 Front direction indicators   30 Rear direction indicators   31, 32, 34 Instrument connector   35 Oil pressure warning light   36 Choke indicator light   37 Parking brake warning light   38 Brake warning light   39 EGR/EXH warning light   40 Battery charging warning light   41 Bulb failure warning light   42 Full beams indicator light   43 Direction indicator light   44 Overdrive indicator light   45 Fasten seat belt light, front   46 Engine compartment light   47 Seat belt lock light   48 Ashtray light   49 Gear position light   50 Instrument panel light dimmer   51 Instrument panel light   52 Control panel light   53 Glove locker light   54 Courtesy light   55 Door switch   56 Door switch   57 Fuel tank level sender   58 Temperature sender   59 Oil pressure sensor   60 Choke control contact   61 Parking brake contact   62 Brake warning light contact   63 EGR/EXH contact   64 Contact, seat belt, passenger seat   65 Contact, seat belt, driver's seat   66 Contact, passenger seat   67 Headlamps-on warning buzzer   68 Speedometer   69 Fuel gauge   70 Thermometer   71 Voltage stabiliser   72 Horn   73 Horn pad   74 Cigar lighter   75 Fan   76 Fan switch   77 Windscreen wiper/washer switch   78 Windscreen wipers   79 Windscreen washers   80 Headlamp wiper relay   81 Headlamp wipers   82 Switch for tailgate wiper/washer   83 Tailgate wiper   84 Tailgate washer   85 Rear door contact   86 Cargo space courtesy light   87 Switch for heated rear window   88 Heated rear window   89 Heater with thermostat, driver's seat cushion   90 Heater, driver's backrest   91 Clock   92 Diode   93 Connector   94 Fasten seat belt reminder   95 Start valve   96 Thermal timer contact   97 Air flow sensor   98 Main relay, fuel injection   99 Fuel pump relay   100 Fuel pump   101 Pressure regulating valve   102 Auxiliary air valve   103 Resistor   104 Control unit, ignition system   105 Solenoid on compressor   106 Solenoid valve   107 Switch for air conditioning   108 Solenoid valve, carburetter   109 Overdrive switch M46   110 Overdrive contact on gearbox M46   111 Overdrive solenoid on gearbox M46   112 Bridge connector   113 Under bonnet start terminal   116 Suppression resistor   117 Loudspeakers, front doors   118 Antenna, windscreen   119 Top dead centre sensor   120 Capacitor   126 Thermostat, air conditioning   127 Fasten seat belt light, rear   128 Relay for lambda probe   129 Frequency valve   130 Control unit, lambda system   131 Lambda probe   132 Test point, lambda probe   134 Switch for rear fog lamp   135 Rear fog lamp

Wiring colour code   SB Black   **W** White   **BR** Brown   **BL** Blue   **GR** Grey   **R** Red   **Y** Yellow   **GN** Green

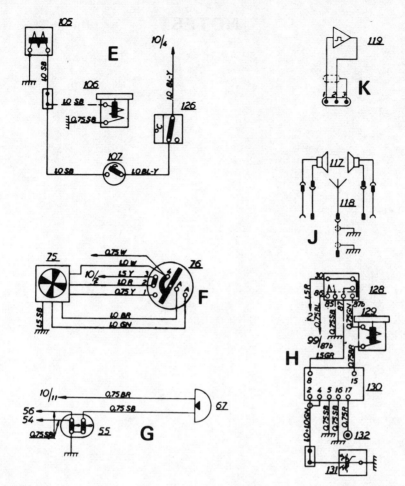

FIG 14:3 Wiring diagrams, additional and alternative details. E: air conditioning system. F: combined heater unit. G: headlamp warning buzzer. H: Lambda emission control system (California). J: radio (USA). K: top dead centre sensor

NOTES

HINTS ON MAINTENANCE AND OVERHAUL

There are few things more rewarding than the restoration of a vehicle's original peak of efficiency and smooth performance.

The following notes are intended to help the owner to reach that state of perfection. Providing that he possesses the basic manual skills he should have no difficulty in performing most of the operations detailed in this manual. It must be stressed, however, that where recommended in the manual, highly-skilled operations ought to be entrusted to experts, who have the necessary equipment, to carry out the work satisfactorily.

Quality of workmanship:

The hazardous driving conditions on the roads to-day demand that vehicles should be as nearly perfect, mechanically, as possible. It is therefore most important that amateur work be carried out with care, bearing in mind the often inadequate working conditions, and also the inferior tools which have to be used. It is easy to counsel perfection in all things, and we recognise that it may be setting an impossibly high standard. We do, however, suggest that every care should be taken to ensure that a vehicle is as safe to take on the road as it is humanly possible to make it.

Safe working conditions:

Even though a vehicle may be stationary, it is still potentially dangerous if certain sensible precautions are not taken when working on it while it is supported on jacks or blocks. It is indeed preferable not to use jacks alone, but to supplement them with carefully placed blocks, so that there will be plenty of support if the car rolls off the jacks during a strenuous manoeuvre. Axle stands are an excellent way of providing a rigid base which is not readily disturbed. Piles of bricks are a dangerous substitute. Be careful not to get under heavy loads on lifting tackle, the load could fall. It is preferable not to work alone when lifting an engine, or when working underneath a vehicle which is supported well off the ground. To be trapped, particularly under the vehicle, may have unpleasant results if help is not quickly forthcoming. Make some provision, however humble, to deal with fires. Always disconnect a battery if there is a likelihood of electrical shorts. These may start a fire if there is leaking fuel about. This applies particularly to leads which can carry a heavy current, like those in the starter circuit. While on the subject of electricity, we must also stress the danger of using equipment which is run off the mains and which has no earth or has faulty wiring or connections. So many workshops have damp floors, and electrical shocks are of such a nature that it is sometimes impossible to let go of a live lead or piece of equipment due to the muscular spasms which take place.

Work demanding special care:

This involves the servicing of braking, steering and suspension systems. On the road, failure of the braking system may be disastrous. Make quite sure that there can be no possibility of failure through the bursting of rusty brake pipes or rotten hoses, nor to a sudden loss of pressure due to defective seals or valves.

Problems:

The chief problems which may face an operator are:
1 External dirt.
2 Difficulty in undoing tight fixings.
3 Dismantling unfamiliar mechanisms.
4 Deciding in what respect parts are defective.
5 Confusion about the correct order for reassembly.
6 Adjusting running clearance.
7 Road testing.
8 Final tuning.

Practical suggestions to solve the problems:

1 Preliminary cleaning of large parts—engines, transmissions, steering, suspensions, etc,—should be carried out before removal from the car. Where road dirt and mud alone are present, wash clean with a high-pressure water jet, brushing to remove stubborn adhesions, and allow to drain and dry. Where oil or grease is also present, wash down with a proprietary compound (Gunk, Teepol etc,) applying with a stiff brush—an old paint brush is suitable—into all crevices. Cover the distributor and ignition coils with a polythene bag and then apply a strong water jet to clear the loosened deposits. Allow to drain and dry. The assemblies will then be sufficiently clean to remove and transfer to the bench for the next stage.

On the bench, further cleaning can be carried out, first wiping the parts as free as possible from grease with old newspaper. Avoid using rag or cotton waste which can leave clogging fibres behind. Any remaining grease can be removed with a brush dipped in paraffin. If necessary, traces of paraffin can be removed by carbon tetrachloride. Avoid using paraffin or petrol in large quantities for cleaning in enclosed areas, such as garages, on account of the high fire risk.

When all exteriors have been cleaned, and not before, dismantling can be commenced. This ensures that dirt will not enter into interiors and orifices revealed by dismantling. In the next phases, where components have to be cleaned, use carbon tetrachloride in preference to petrol and keep the containers covered except when in use. After the components have been cleaned, plug small holes with tapered hard wood plugs cut to size and blank off larger orifices with greaseproof paper and masking tape. Do not use soft wood plugs or matchsticks as they may break.

2 It is not advisable to hammer on the end of a screw thread, but if it must be done, first screw on a nut to protect the thread, and use a lead hammer. This applies particularly to the removal of tapered cotters. Nuts and bolts seem to 'grow' together, especially in exhaust systems. If penetrating oil does not work, try the judicious application of heat, but be careful of starting a fire. Asbestos sheet or cloth is useful to isolate heat.

Tight bushes or pieces of tail-pipe rusted into a silencer can be removed by splitting them with an open-ended hacksaw. Tight screws can sometimes be started by a tap from a hammer on the end of a suitable screwdriver. Many tight fittings will yield to the judicious use of a hammer, but it must be a soft-faced hammer if damage is to be avoided, use a heavy block on the opposite side to absorb shock. Any parts of the steering system which have been damaged should be renewed, as attempts to repair them may lead to cracking and subsequent failure, and steering ball joints should be disconnected using a recommended tool to prevent damage.

3 It often happens that an owner is baffled when trying to dismantle an unfamiliar piece of equipment. So many modern devices are pressed together or assembled by spinning-over flanges, that they must be sawn apart. The intention is that the whole assembly must be renewed. However, parts which appear to be in one piece to the naked eye, may reveal close-fitting joint lines when inspected with a magnifying glass, and, this may provide the necessary clue to dismantling. Lefthanded screw threads are used where rotational forces would tend to unscrew a righthanded screw thread.

Be very careful when dismantling mechanisms which may come apart suddenly. Work in an enclosed space where the parts will be contained, and drape a piece of cloth over the device if springs are likely to fly in all directions. Mark everything which might be reassembled in the wrong position, scratched symbols may be used on unstressed parts, or a sequence of tiny dots from a centre punch can be useful. Stressed parts should never be scratched or centre-popped as this may lead to cracking under working conditions. Store parts which look alike in the correct order for reassembly. Never rely upon memory to assist in the assembly of complicated mechanisms, especially when they will be dismantled for a long time, but make notes, and drawings to supplement the diagrams in the manual, and put labels on detached wires. Rust stains may indicate unlubricated wear. This can sometimes be seen round the outside edge of a bearing cup in a universal joint. Look for bright rubbing marks on parts which normally should not make heavy contact. These might prove that something is bent or running out of truth. For example, there might be bright marks on one side of a piston, at the top near the ring grooves, and others at the bottom of the skirt on the other side. This could well be the clue to a bent connecting rod. Suspected cracks can be proved by heating the component in a light oil to approximately 100°C, removing, drying off, and dusting with french chalk, if a crack is present the oil retained in the crack will stain the french chalk.

4 In determining wear, and the degree, against the permissible limits set in the manual, accurate measurement can only be achieved by the use of a micrometer. In many cases, the wear is given to the fourth place of decimals; that is in ten-thousandths of an inch. This can be read by the vernier scale on the barrel of a good micrometer. Bore diameters are more difficult to determine. If, however, the matching shaft is accurately measured, the degree of play in the bore can be felt as a guide to its suitability. In other cases, the shank of a twist drill of known diameter is a handy check.

Many methods have been devised for determining the clearance between bearing surfaces. To-day the best and simplest is by the use of Plastigage, obtainable from most garages. A thin plastic thread is laid between the two surfaces and the bearing is tightened, flattening the thread. On removal, the width of the thread is compared with a scale supplied with the thread and the clearance is read off directly. Sometimes joint faces leak persistently, even after gasket renewal. The fault will then be traceable to distortion, dirt or burrs. Studs which are screwed into soft metal frequently raise burrs at the point of entry. A quick cure for this is to chamfer the edge of the hole in the part which fits over the stud.

5 **Always check a replacement part with the original one before it is fitted.**

If parts are not marked, and the order for reassembly is not known, a little detective work will help. Look for marks which are due to wear to see if they can be mated. Joint faces may not be identical due to manufacturing errors, and parts which overlap may be stained, giving a clue to the correct position. Most fixings leave identifying marks especially if they were painted over on assembly. It is then easier to decide whether a nut, for instance, has a plain, a spring, or a shakeproof washer under it. All running surfaces become 'bedded' together after long spells of work and tiny imperfections on one part will be found to have left corresponding marks on the other. This is particularly true of shafts and bearings and even a score on a cylinder wall will show on the piston.

6 Checking end float or rocker clearances by feeler gauge may not always give accurate results because of wear. For instance, the rocker tip which bears on a valve stem may be deeply pitted, in which case the feeler will simply be bridging a depression. Thrust washers may also wear depressions in opposing faces to make accurate measurement difficult. End float is then easier to check by using a dial gauge. It is common practice to adjust end play in bearing assemblies, like front hubs with taper rollers, by doing up the axle nut until the hub becomes stiff to turn and then backing it off a little. Do not use this method with ballbearing hubs as the assembly is often preloaded by tightening the axle nut to its fullest extent. If the splitpin hole will not line up, file the base of the nut a little.

Steering assemblies often wear in the straight-ahead position. If any part is adjusted, make sure that it remains free when moved from lock to lock. Do not be surprised if an assembly like a steering gearbox, which is known to be carefully adjusted outside the car, becomes stiff when it is bolted in place. This will be due to distortion of the case by the pull of the mounting bolts, particularly if the mounting points are not all touching together. This problem may be met in other equipment and is cured by careful attention to the alignment of mounting points.

When a spanner is stamped with a size and A/F it means that the dimension is the width between the jaws and has no connection with ANF, which is the designation for the American National Fine thread. Coarse threads like Whitworth are rarely used on cars to-day except for studs which screw into soft aluminium or cast iron. For this reason it might be found that the top end of a cylinder head stud has a fine thread and the lower end a coarse thread to screw into the cylinder block. If the car has mainly UNF threads then it is likely that any coarse threads will be UNC, which are not the same as Whitworth. Small sizes have the same number of threads in Whitworth and UNC, but in the $\frac{1}{2}$ inch size for example, there are twelve threads to the inch in the former and thirteen in the latter.

7 After a major overhaul, particularly if a great deal of work has been done on the braking, steering and suspension systems, it is advisable to approach the problem of testing with care. If the braking system has been overhauled, apply heavy pressure to the brake pedal and get a second operator to check every possible source of leakage. The brakes may work extremely well, but a leak could cause complete failure after a few miles.

Do not fit the hub caps until every wheel nut has been checked for tightness, and make sure the tyre pressures are correct. Check the levels of coolant, lubricants and hydraulic fluids. Being satisfied that all is well, take the car on the road and test the brakes at once. Check the steering and the action of the handbrake. Do all this at moderate speeds on quiet roads, and make sure there is no other vehicle behind you when you try a rapid stop.

Finally, remember that many parts settle down after a time, so check for tightness of all fixings after the car has been on the road for a hundred miles or so.

8 It is useless to tune an engine which has not reached its normal running temperature. In the same way, the tune of an engine which is stiff after a rebore will be different when the engine is again running free. Remember too, that rocker clearances on pushrod operated valve gear will change when the cylinder head nuts are tightened after an initial period of running with a new head gasket.

Trouble may not always be due to what seems the obvious cause. Ignition, carburation and mechanical condition are interdependent and spitting back through the carburetter, which might be attributed to a weak mixture, can be caused by a sticking inlet valve.

For one final hint on tuning, never adjust more than one thing at a time or it will be impossible to tell which adjustment produced the desired result.

NOTES

GLOSSARY OF TERMS

Allen key Cranked wrench of hexagonal section for use with socket head screws.

Alternator Electrical generator producing alternating current. Rectified to direct current for battery charging.

Ambient temperature Surrounding atmospheric temperature.

Annulus Used in engineering to indicate the outer ring gear of an epicyclic gear train.

Armature The shaft carrying the windings, which rotates in the magnetic field of a generator or starter motor. That part of a solenoid or relay which is activated by the magnetic field.

Axial In line with, or pertaining to, an axis.

Backlash Play in meshing gears.

Balance lever A bar where force applied at the centre is equally divided between connections at the ends.

Banjo axle Axle casing with large diameter housing for the crownwheel and differential.

Bendix pinion A self-engaging and self-disengaging drive on a starter motor shaft.

Bevel pinion A conical shaped gearwheel, designed to mesh with a similar gear with an axis usually at 90 deg. to its own.

bhp Brake horse power, measured on a dynamometer.

bmep Brake mean effective pressure. Average pressure on a piston during the working stroke.

Brake cylinder Cylinder with hydraulically operated piston(s) acting on brake shoes or pad(s).

Brake regulator Control valve fitted in hydraulic braking system which limits brake pressure to rear brakes during heavy braking to prevent rear wheel locking.

Camber Angle at which a wheel is tilted from the vertical.

Capacitor Modern term for an electrical condenser. Part of distributor assembly, connected across contact breaker points, acts as an interference suppressor.

Castellated Top face of a nut, slotted across the flats, to take a locking splitpin.

Castor Angle at which the kingpin or swivel pin is tilted when viewed from the side.

cc Cubic centimetres. Engine capacity is arrived at by multiplying the area of the bore in sq cm by the stroke in cm by the number of cylinders.

Clevis U-shaped forked connector used with a clevis pin, usually at handbrake connections.

Collet A type of collar, usually split and located in a groove in a shaft, and held in place by a retainer. The arrangement used to retain the spring(s) on a valve stem in most cases.

Commutator Rotating segmented current distributor between armature windings and brushes in generator or motor.

Compression ratio The ratio, or quantitative relation, of the total volume (piston at bottom of stroke) to the unswept volume (piston at top of stroke) in an engine cylinder.

Condenser See 'Capacitor'.

Core plug Plug for blanking off a manufacturing hole in a casting.

Crownwheel Large bevel gear in rear axle, driven by a bevel pinion attached to the propeller shaft. Sometimes called a 'ring gear'.

'C'-spanner Like a 'C' with a handle. For use on screwed collars without flats, but with slots or holes.

Damper Modern term for shock absorber, used in vehicle suspension systems to damp out spring oscillations.

Depression The lowering of atmospheric pressure as in the inlet manifold and carburetter.

Dowel Close tolerance pin, peg, tube, or bolt, which accurately locates mating parts.

Drag link Rod connecting steering box drop arm (pitman arm) to nearest front wheel steering arm in certain types of steering systems.

Dry liner Thinwall tube pressed into cylinder bore.

Dry sump Lubrication system where all oil is scavenged from the sump, and returned to a separate tank.

Dynamo See 'Generator'.

Electrode Terminal part of an electrical component, such as the points or 'Electrodes' of a sparking plug.

Electrolyte In lead-acid car batteries a solution of sulphuric acid and distilled water.

End float The axial movement between associated parts, end play.

EP Extreme pressure. In lubricants, special grades for heavily loaded bearing surfaces, such as gear teeth in a gearbox, or crownwheel and pinion in a rear axle.

Fade	Of brakes. Reduced efficiency due to overheating.
Field coils	Windings on the polepieces of motors and generators.
Fillets	Narrow finishing strips usually applied to interior bodywork.
First motion shaft	Input shaft from clutch to gearbox.
Fullflow filter	Filters in which all the oil is pumped to the engine. If the element becomes clogged, a bypass valve operates to pass unfiltered oil to the engine.
FWD	Front wheel drive.
Gear pump	Two meshing gears in a close fitting casing. Oil is carried from the inlet round the outside of both gears in the spaces between the gear teeth and casing to the outlet, the meshing gear teeth prevent oil passing back to the inlet, and the oil is forced through the outlet port.
Generator	Modern term for 'Dynamo'. When rotated produces electrical current.
Grommet	A ring of protective or sealing material. Can be used to protect pipes or leads passing through bulkheads.
Grubscrew	Fully threaded headless screw with screwdriver slot. Used for locking, or alignment purposes.
Gudgeon pin	Shaft which connects a piston to its connecting rod. Sometimes called 'wrist pin', or 'piston pin'.
Halfshaft	One of a pair transmitting drive from the differential.
Helical	In spiral form. The teeth of helical gears are cut at a spiral angle to the side faces of the gearwheel.
Hot pot	Hot area that assists vapourisation of fuel on its way to cylinders. Often provided by close contact between inlet and exhaust manifolds.
HT	High Tension. Applied to electrical current produced by the ignition coil for the sparking plugs.
Hydrometer	A device for checking specific gravity of liquids. Used to check specific gravity of electrolyte.
Hypoid bevel gears	A form of bevel gear used in the rear axle drive gears. The bevel pinion meshes below the centre line of the crownwheel, giving a lower propeller shaft line.
Idler	A device for passing on movement. A free running gear between driving and driven gears. A lever transmitting track rod movement to a side rod in steering gear.
Impeller	A centrifugal pumping element. Used in water pumps to stimulate flow.
Journals	Those parts of a shaft that are in contact with the bearings.
Kingpin	The main vertical pin which carries the front wheel spindle, and permits steering movement. May be called 'steering pin' or 'swivel pin'.
Layshaft	The shaft which carries the laygear in the gearbox. The laygear is driven by the first motion shaft and drives the third motion shaft according to the gear selected. Sometimes called the 'countershaft' or 'second motion shaft'.
lb ft	A measure of twist or torque. A pull of 10 lb at a radius of 1 ft is a torque of 10 lb ft.
lb/sq in	Pounds per square inch.
Little-end	The small, or piston end of a connecting rod. Sometimes called the 'small-end'.
LT	Low Tension. The current output from the battery.
Mandrel	Accurately manufactured bar or rod used for test or centring purposes.
Manifold	A pipe, duct, or chamber, with several branches.
Needle rollers	Bearing rollers with a length many times their diameter.
Oil bath	Reservoir which lubricates parts by immersion. In air filters, a separate oil supply for wetting a wire mesh element to hold the dust.
Oil wetted	In air filters, a wire mesh element lightly oiled to trap and hold airborne dust.
Overlap	Period during which inlet and exhaust valves are open together.
Panhard rod	Bar connected between fixed point on chassis and another on axle to control sideways movement.
Pawl	Pivoted catch which engages in the teeth of a ratchet to permit movement in one direction only.
Peg spanner	Tool with pegs, or pins, to engage in holes or slots in the part to be turned.
Pendant pedals	Pedals with levers that are pivoted at the top end.
Phillips screwdriver	A cross-point screwdriver for use with the cross-slotted heads of Phillips screws.
Pinion	A small gear, usually in relation to another gear.
Piston-type damper	Shock absorber in which damping is controlled by a piston working in a closed oil-filled cylinder.
Preloading	Preset static pressure on ball or roller bearings not due to working loads.
Radial	Radiating from a centre, like the spokes of a wheel.

Radius rod Pivoted arm confining movement of a part to an arc of fixed radius.

Ratchet Toothed wheel or rack which can move in one direction only, movement in the other being prevented by a pawl.

Ring gear A gear tooth ring attached to outer periphery of flywheel. Starter pinion engages with it during starting.

Runout Amount by which rotating part is out of true.

Semi-floating axle Outer end of rear axle halfshaft is carried on bearing inside axle casing. Wheel hub is secured to end of shaft.

Servo A hydraulic or pneumatic system for assisting, or, augmenting a physical effort. See 'Vacuum Servo'.

Setscrew One which is threaded for the full length of the shank.

Shackle A coupling link, used in the form of two parallel pins connected by side plates to secure the end of the master suspension spring and absorb the effects of deflection.

Shell bearing Thinwalled steel shell lined with anti-friction metal. Usually semi-circular and used in pairs for main and big-end bearings.

Shock absorber See 'Damper'.

Silentbloc Rubber bush bonded to inner and outer metal sleeves.

Socket-head screw Screw with hexagonal socket for an Allen key.

Solenoid A coil of wire creating a magnetic field when electric current passes through it. Used with a soft iron core to operate contacts or a mechanical device.

Spur gear A gear with teeth cut axially across the periphery.

Stub axle Short axle fixed at one end only.

Tachometer An instrument for accurate measurement of rotating speed. Usually indicates in revolutions per minute.

TDC Top Dead Centre. The highest point reached by a piston in a cylinder, with the crank and connecting rod in line.

Thermostat Automatic device for regulating temperature. Used in vehicle coolant systems to open a valve which restricts circulation at low temperature.

Third motion shaft Output shaft of gearbox.

Threequarter floating axle Outer end of rear axle halfshaft flanged and bolted to wheel hub, which runs on bearing mounted on outside of axle casing. Vehicle weight is not carried by the axle shaft.

Thrust bearing or washer Used to reduce friction in rotating parts subject to axial loads.

Torque Turning or twisting effort. See 'lb ft'.

Track rod The bar(s) across the vehicle which connect the steering arms and maintain the front wheels in their correct alignment.

UJ Universal joint. A coupling between shafts which permits angular movement.

UNF Unified National Fine screw thread.

Vacuum servo Device used in brake system, using difference between atmospheric pressure and inlet manifold depression to operate a piston which acts to augment brake pressure as required. See 'Servo'.

Venturi A restriction or 'choke' in a tube, as in a carburetter, used to increase velocity to obtain a reduction in pressure.

Vernier A sliding scale for obtaining fractional readings of the graduations of an adjacent scale.

Welch plug A domed thin metal disc which is partially flattened to lock in a recess. Used to plug core holes in castings.

Wet liner Removable cylinder barrel, sealed against coolant leakage, where the coolant is in direct contact with the outer surface.

Wet sump A reservoir attached to the crankcase to hold the lubricating oil.

NOTES

INDEX

NOTES

NOTES

NOTES

NOTES